MznLnx

Missing Links Exam Preps

Exam Prep for

College Algebra

Larson & Hostetler, 6th Edition

The MznLnx Exam Prep is your link from the texbook and lecture to your exams.
The MznLnx Exam Preps are unauthorized and comprehensive reviews of your textbooks.

All material provided by MznLnx and Rico Publications (c) 2010
Textbook publishers and textbook authors do not particpate in or contribute to these reviews.

MznLnx

Rico
Publications

Exam Prep for College Algebra
6th Edition
Larson & Hostetler

Publisher: Raymond Houge
Assistant Editor: Michael Rouger
Text and Cover Designer: Lisa Buckner
Marketing Manager: Sara Swagger
Project Manager, Editorial Production: Jerry Emerson
Art Director: Vernon Lowerui

Product Manager: Dave Mason
Editorial Assitant: Rachel Guzmanji
Pedagogy: Debra Long
Cover Image: Jim Reed/Getty Images
Text and Cover Printer: City Printing, Inc.
Compositor: Media Mix, Inc.

(c) 2010 Rico Publications
ALL RIGHTS RESERVED. No part of this work covered by the copyright may be reproduced or used in any form or by an means--graphic, electronic, or mechanical, including photocopying, recording, taping, Web distribution, information storage, and retrieval systems, or in any other manner--without the written permission of the publisher.

Printed in the United States
ISBN:

For more information about our products, contact us at:
Dave.Mason@RicoPublications.com

For permission to use material from this text or product, submit a request online to:
Dave.Mason@RicoPublications.com

Contents

CHAPTER 1
Prerequisites — 1

CHAPTER 2
Equations and Inequalities — 24

CHAPTER 3
Functions and Their Graphs — 49

CHAPTER 4
Polynomial Functions — 71

CHAPTER 5
Rational Functions and Conics — 92

CHAPTER 6
Exponential and Logarithmic Functions — 109

CHAPTER 7
Systems of Equations and Inequalities — 127

CHAPTER 8
Matrices and Determinants — 146

CHAPTER 9
Sequences, Series, and Probability — 161

ANSWER KEY — 192

TO THE STUDENT

COMPREHENSIVE

The *MznLnx* Exam Prep series is designed to help you pass your exams. Editors at MznLnx review your textbooks and then prepare these practice exams to help you master the textbook material. Unlike study guides, workbooks, and practice tests provided by the texbook publisher and textbook authors, *MznLnx* gives you **all** of the material in each chapter in exam form, not just samples, so you can be sure to nail your exam.

MECHANICAL

The MznLnx Exam Prep series creates exams that will help you learn the subject matter as well as test you on your understanding. Each question is designed to help you master the concept. Just working through the exams, you gain an understanding of the subject--its a simple mechanical process that produces success.

INTEGRATED STUDY GUIDE AND REVIEW

MznLnx is not just a set of exams designed to test you, its also a comprehensive review of the subject content. Each exam question is also a review of the concept, making sure that you will get the answer correct without having to go to other sources of material. You learn as you go! Its the easiest way to pass an exam.

HUMOR

Studying can be tedious and dry. MznLnx's instructional design includes moderate humor within the exam questions on occassion, to break the tedium and revitalize the brain

Chapter 1. Prerequisites

1. In mathematics, a _____ may be described informally as a number that can be given by an infinite decimal representation.
   - a. Thing
   - b. Real number0
   - c. Undefined
   - d. Undefined

2. In sociology and biology a _____ is the collection of people or organisms of a particular species living in a given geographic area or space, usually measured by a census.
   - a. Thing
   - b. Population0
   - c. Undefined
   - d. Undefined

3. A _____ is a unit of length, usually used to measure distance, in a number of different systems, including Imperial units, United States customary units and Norwegian/Swedish mil. Its size can vary from system to system, but in each is between 1 and 10 kilometers. In contemporary English contexts _____ refers to either:
   - a. Thing
   - b. Mile0
   - c. Undefined
   - d. Undefined

4. U.S. liquid _____ is legally defined as 231 cubic inches, and is equal to 3.785411784 litres or abotu 0.13368 cubic feet. This is the most common definition of a _____. The U.S. fluid ounce is defined as 1/128 of a U.S. _____.
   - a. Thing
   - b. Gallon0
   - c. Undefined
   - d. Undefined

5. In mathematics, a _____ can mean either an element of the set {1, 2, 3, ...} (i.e the positive integers or the counting numbers) or an element of the set {0, 1, 2, 3, ...} (i.e. the non-negative integers).
   - a. Thing
   - b. Natural number0
   - c. Undefined
   - d. Undefined

6. In mathematics, a _____ can mean either an element of the set {1, 2, 3, ...} (i.e the positive integers) or an element of the set {0, 1, 2, 3, ...} (i.e. the non-negative integers).
   - a. Concept
   - b. Whole number0
   - c. Undefined
   - d. Undefined

7. A _____ is a quantity that denotes the proportional amount or magnitude of one quantity relative to another.
   - a. Ratio0
   - b. Thing
   - c. Undefined
   - d. Undefined

8. In mathematics, a _____ number is a number which can be expressed as a ratio of two integers. Non-integer _____ numbers (commonly called fractions) are usually written as the vulgar fraction a / b, where b is not zero.
   - a. Rational0
   - b. Thing
   - c. Undefined
   - d. Undefined

9. The _____ are the only integral domain whose positive elements are well-ordered, and in which order is preserved by addition. Like the natural numbers, the _____ form a countably infinite set. The set of all _____ is usually denoted in mathematics by a boldface Z .
   - a. Thing
   - b. Integers0
   - c. Undefined
   - d. Undefined

Chapter 1. Prerequisites

10. In mathematics, a _____ is a number which can be expressed as a ratio of two integers. Non-integer rational numbers (commonly called fractions) are usually written as the vulgar fraction a / b, where b is not zero.
    a. Concept
    b. Rational Number0
    c. Undefined
    d. Undefined

11. In mathematics, an _____ number is any real number that is not a rational number- that is, it is a number which cannot be expressed as a fraction m/n, where m and n are integers.
    a. Thing
    b. Irrational0
    c. Undefined
    d. Undefined

12. _____ is the state of being greater than any finite real or natural number, however large.
    a. Thing
    b. Infinite0
    c. Undefined
    d. Undefined

13. Mathematical _____ are the wide variety of ways to capture an abstract mathematical concept or relationship.
    a. Thing
    b. Representations0
    c. Undefined
    d. Undefined

14. In mathematics, an _____ is any real number that is not a rational number ¡ª that is, it is a number which cannot be expressed as m/n, where m and n are integers.
    a. Thing
    b. Irrational number0
    c. Undefined
    d. Undefined

15. In mathematics, _____ are any real number that is not a rational number ¡ª that is, it is a number which cannot be expressed as m/n, where m and n are integers.
    a. Thing
    b. Irrational numbers0
    c. Undefined
    d. Undefined

16. A _____ is a one-dimensional picture in which the integers are shown as specially-marked points evenly spaced on a line.
    a. Number line0
    b. Thing
    c. Undefined
    d. Undefined

17. In mathematics, the _____ of a coordinate system is the point where the axes of the system intersect.
    a. Origin0
    b. Thing
    c. Undefined
    d. Undefined

18. An _____ is a combination of numbers, operators, grouping symbols and/or free variables and bound variables arranged in a meaningful way which can be evaluated..
    a. Expression0
    b. Thing
    c. Undefined
    d. Undefined

19. In mathematics, an _____ is a statement about the relative size or order of two objects.
    a. Thing
    b. Inequality0
    c. Undefined
    d. Undefined

20. _____ is a branch of mathematics concerning the study of structure, relation and quantity.
   a. Concept
   b. Algebra0
   c. Undefined
   d. Undefined

21. In mathematics, the _____ (or modulus) of a real number is its numerical value without regard to its sign.
   a. Thing
   b. Absolute value0
   c. Undefined
   d. Undefined

22. Order theory is a branch of mathematics that studies various kinds of binary relations that capture the intuitive notion of a mathematical _____.
   a. Ordering0
   b. Thing
   c. Undefined
   d. Undefined

23. In mathematics, an inequality is a statement about the relative size or order of two objects. For example 14 > 10, or 14 is _____ 10.
   a. Thing
   b. Greater than0
   c. Undefined
   d. Undefined

24. The _____, the average in everyday English, which is also called the arithmetic _____ (and is distinguished from the geometric _____ or harmonic _____). The average is also called the sample _____. The expected value of a random variable, which is also called the population _____.
   a. Thing
   b. Mean0
   c. Undefined
   d. Undefined

25. _____ are objects, characters, or other concrete representations of ideas, concepts, or other abstractions.
   a. Thing
   b. Symbols0
   c. Undefined
   d. Undefined

26. A _____ is a set whose members are members of another set or a set contained within another set.
   a. Subset0
   b. Thing
   c. Undefined
   d. Undefined

27. In geometry, an _____ is a point at which a line segment or ray terminates.
   a. Thing
   b. Endpoint0
   c. Undefined
   d. Undefined

28. In mathematical analysis and related areas of mathematics, a set is called _____, if it is, in a certain sense, of finite size.
   a. Bounded0
   b. Thing
   c. Undefined
   d. Undefined

29. In elementary algebra, an _____ is a set that contains every real number between two indicated numbers and may contain the two numbers themselves.
   a. Thing
   b. Interval0
   c. Undefined
   d. Undefined

Chapter 1. Prerequisites

30. _____ is the state of being greater than any finite number, however large.
    a. Infinity0
    b. Thing
    c. Undefined
    d. Undefined

31. In common philosophical language, a proposition or _____, is the content of an assertion, that is, it is true-or-false and defined by the meaning of a particular piece of language.
    a. Statement0
    b. Concept
    c. Undefined
    d. Undefined

32. Generally, a trichotomy is a splitting into three disjoint parts. In mathematics, the _____ is most common the statement that for any real numbers x and y, exactly one of the following relations holds: $x < y$, $x = y$, $x > y$.
    a. Law of Trichotomy0
    b. Thing
    c. Undefined
    d. Undefined

33. _____, either of the curved-bracket punctuation marks that together make a set of _____
    a. Parentheses0
    b. Thing
    c. Undefined
    d. Undefined

34. The _____ of a mathematical object is its size: a property by which it can be larger or smaller than other objects of the same kind; in technical terms, an ordering of the class of objects to which it belongs.
    a. Thing
    b. Magnitude0
    c. Undefined
    d. Undefined

35. The _____ of a ring R is defined to be the smallest positive integer n such that $n\,a = 0$, for all a in R.
    a. Characteristic0
    b. Thing
    c. Undefined
    d. Undefined

36. A _____ is a symbolic representation denoting a quantity or expression. It often represents an "unknown" quantity that has the potential to change.
    a. Thing
    b. Variable0
    c. Undefined
    d. Undefined

37. In combinatorial mathematics, a _____ is an un-ordered collection of unique elements.
    a. Concept
    b. Combination0
    c. Undefined
    d. Undefined

38. In mathematics, _____ is an elementary arithmetic operation. When one of the numbers is a whole number, _____ is the repeated sum of the other number.
    a. Multiplication0
    b. Thing
    c. Undefined
    d. Undefined

39. _____ is a mathematical operation, written a^n, involving two numbers, the base a and the exponent n.
    a. Exponentiation0
    b. Thing
    c. Undefined
    d. Undefined

Chapter 1. Prerequisites

40. In mathematics and the mathematical sciences, a _____ is a fixed, but possibly unspecified, value. This is in contrast to a variable, which is not fixed.
    a. Constant0
    b. Thing
    c. Undefined
    d. Undefined

41. In mathematics, a _____ is a constant multiplicative factor of a certain object. The object can be such things as a variable, a vector, a function, etc. For example, the _____ of $9x^2$ is 9.
    a. Thing
    b. Coefficient0
    c. Undefined
    d. Undefined

42. A _____ signifies a point or points of probability on a subject e.g., the _____ of creativity, which allows for the formation of rule or norm or law by interpretation of the phenomena events that can be created.
    a. Thing
    b. Principle0
    c. Undefined
    d. Undefined

43. The _____ is focused on the substitution of a product, service or process to another that is more efficient or beneficial in some way while retaining the same functionality.
    a. Thing
    b. Substitution Principle0
    c. Undefined
    d. Undefined

44. _____ or arithmetics is the oldest and most elementary branch of mathematics, used by almost everyone, for tasks ranging from simple daily counting to advanced science and business calculations.
    a. Arithmetic0
    b. Thing
    c. Undefined
    d. Undefined

45. The traditional _____ are addition, subtraction, multiplication and division, although more advanced operations (such as manipulations of percentages, square root, exponentiation, and logarithmic functions) are also sometimes included in this subject.
    a. Concept
    b. Arithmetic operations0
    c. Undefined
    d. Undefined

46. _____ element of an element x with respect to a binary operation * with identity element e is an element y such that x * y = y * x = e. In particular,
    a. Inverse0
    b. Thing
    c. Undefined
    d. Undefined

47. In mathematics, the multiplicative inverse of a number x, denoted 1/x or x^{-1}, is the number which, when multiplied by x, yields 1. The multiplicative inverse of x is also called the _____ of x.
    a. Reciprocal0
    b. Thing
    c. Undefined
    d. Undefined

48. In mathematics, the additive inverse, or _____ of a number n is the number that, when added to n, yields zero. The additive inverse of n is denoted −n. For example, 7 is −7, because 7 + (−7) = 0, and the additive inverse of −0.3 is 0.3, because −0.3 + 0.3 = 0.

Chapter 1. Prerequisites

a. Thing
b. Opposite0
c. Undefined
d. Undefined

49. In mathematics, the _____ inverse, or opposite, of a number n is the number that, when added to n, yields zero. The _____ inverse of n is denoted −n.
    a. Additive0
    b. Thing
    c. Undefined
    d. Undefined

50. In mathematics, the _____ of a number n is the number that, when added to n, yields zero. The _____ of n is denoted −n. For example, 7 is −7, because 7 + (−7) = 0, and the _____ of −0.3 is 0.3, because −0.3 + 0.3 = 0.
    a. Thing
    b. Additive inverse0
    c. Undefined
    d. Undefined

51. A _____ is the part of a fraction that tells how many equal parts make up a whole, and which is used in the name of the fraction: "halves", "thirds", "fourths" or "quarters", "fifths" and so on.
    a. Denominator0
    b. Concept
    c. Undefined
    d. Undefined

52. In mathematics, the _____ inverse of a number x, denoted 1/x or x^{-1}, is the number which, when multiplied by x, yields 1. The _____ inverse of x is also called the reciprocal of x.
    a. Thing
    b. Multiplicative0
    c. Undefined
    d. Undefined

53. A _____ is a number that is less than zero.
    a. Thing
    b. Negative number0
    c. Undefined
    d. Undefined

54. The _____ is a property of multiplication or addition where the product or sum remains the same, regardless of whether or not the order of the addends or factors are changed.
    a. Thing
    b. Commutative property0
    c. Undefined
    d. Undefined

55. In mathematics, _____ is a property that a binary operation can have. Within an expression containing two or more of the same associative operators in a row, the order of operations does not matter as long as the sequence of the operands is not changed.
    a. Associativity0
    b. Thing
    c. Undefined
    d. Undefined

56. An _____ is an equality that remains true regardless of the values of any variables that appear within it, to distinguish it from an equality which is true under more particular conditions.
    a. Thing
    b. Identity0
    c. Undefined
    d. Undefined

57. In mathematics the _____ of a set which is equipped with the operation of addition is an element which, when added to any other element x in the set, yields x.

a. Additive identity0
b. Concept
c. Undefined
d. Undefined

58. The _____ states that - a number and its additive inverse have a sum of zero (0).
   a. Additive inverse property0
   b. Concept
   c. Undefined
   d. Undefined

59. In mathematics, and in particular in abstract algebra, the _____ is a property of binary operations that generalises the distributive law from elementary algebra.
   a. Distributive property0
   b. Thing
   c. Undefined
   d. Undefined

60. In logic and mathematics, _____ is an operation on logical values, for example, the logical value of a proposition, that sends true to false and false to true.
   a. Negation0
   b. Person
   c. Undefined
   d. Undefined

61. Two mathematical objects are equal if and only if they are precisely the same in every way. This defines a binary relation, _____, denoted by the sign of _____ "=" in such a way that the statement "x = y" means that x and y are equal.
   a. Equality0
   b. Thing
   c. Undefined
   d. Undefined

62. In mathematics, factorization (British English: factorisation) or factoring is the decomposition of an object (for example, a number, a polynomial, or a matrix) into a product of other objects, or _____, which when multiplied together give the original.
   a. Factors0
   b. Thing
   c. Undefined
   d. Undefined

63. In mathematics, defined and _____ are used to explain whether or not expressions have meaningful, sensible, and unambiguous values.
   a. Undefined0
   b. Thing
   c. Undefined
   d. Undefined

64. Equivalence is the condition of being _____ or essentially equal.
   a. Equivalent0
   b. Thing
   c. Undefined
   d. Undefined

65. In mathematics, a _____ of an integer n, also called a factor of n, is an integer which evenly divides n without leaving a remainder.
   a. Thing
   b. Divisor0
   c. Undefined
   d. Undefined

66. _____ is a natural number that has exactly two distinct natural number divisors, which are 1 and the _____ itself.

Chapter 1. Prerequisites

a. Thing
b. Prime number0
c. Undefined
d. Undefined

67. In mathematics, a _____ is the result of multiplying, or an expression that identifies factors to be multiplied.
    a. Product0
    b. Thing
    c. Undefined
    d. Undefined

68. In mathematics, a _____ number (or a _____) is a natural number that has exactly two (distinct) natural number divisors, which are 1 and the _____ number itself.
    a. Thing
    b. Prime0
    c. Undefined
    d. Undefined

69. A _____ number is a positive integer which has a positive divisor other than one or itself.
    a. Composite0
    b. Thing
    c. Undefined
    d. Undefined

70. A _____ decimal is a decimal for which there is no digit to the right of the decimal point, as all digits farther from the right are zero.
    a. Nonterminating0
    b. Thing
    c. Undefined
    d. Undefined

71. A _____ decimal is a number whose decimal representation eventually becomes periodic (i.e. the same number sequence _____ indefinitely).
    a. Repeating0
    b. Thing
    c. Undefined
    d. Undefined

72. Mathematical _____ is used to represent ideas.
    a. Thing
    b. Notation0
    c. Undefined
    d. Undefined

73. The _____ integers are all the integers from zero on upwards.
    a. Nonnegative0
    b. Thing
    c. Undefined
    d. Undefined

74. A _____ is a special kind of ratio, indicating a relationship between two measurements with different units, such as miles to gallons or cents to pounds.
    a. Rate0
    b. Thing
    c. Undefined
    d. Undefined

75. In mainstream economics, the word _____ refers to a general rise in prices measured against a standard level of purchasing power.
    a. Inflation0
    b. Thing
    c. Undefined
    d. Undefined

76. _____ is a state in both the Midwestern and Western regions of the United States of America. It is the northernmost of the Great Plains states and is the northern half of The Dakotas.

Chapter 1. Prerequisites

a. North Dakota0
b. Thing
c. Undefined
d. Undefined

77. _____ is a physical property of a system that underlies the common notions of hot and cold; something that is hotter has the greater _____.
   a. Temperature0
   b. Thing
   c. Undefined
   d. Undefined

78. The _____ of measurement are a globally standardized and modernized form of the metric system.
   a. Thing
   b. Units0
   c. Undefined
   d. Undefined

79. In mathematics, a _____ is a mathematical statement which appears likely to be true, but has not been formally proven to be true under the rules of mathematical logic.
   a. Conjecture0
   b. Concept
   c. Undefined
   d. Undefined

80. In mathematics, _____ growth occurs when the growth rate of a function is always proportional to the function's current size.
   a. Exponential0
   b. Thing
   c. Undefined
   d. Undefined

81. _____ is a mathematical operation, written a^n, involving two numbers, the base a and the exponent n.
   a. Thing
   b. Exponentiating0
   c. Undefined
   d. Undefined

82. A _____ is a numeral used to indicate a count. The most common use of the word today is to name the part of a fraction that tells the number or count of equal parts.
   a. Numerator0
   b. Thing
   c. Undefined
   d. Undefined

83. _____ is the symbol used to indicate the nth root of a number
   a. Radical0
   b. Thing
   c. Undefined
   d. Undefined

84. In mathematics, _____ are used to indicate the square root of a number.
   a. Thing
   b. Radicals0
   c. Undefined
   d. Undefined

85. _____ is a notation for writing numbers that is often used by scientists and mathematicians to make it easier to write large and small numbers.
   a. Thing
   b. Scientific notation0
   c. Undefined
   d. Undefined

86. _____ is the property of a physical object that quantifies the amount of matter and energy it is equivalent to.

a. Thing
b. Mass0
c. Undefined
d. Undefined

87. _____ is the writing of numbers in the base-ten numeral system, which uses various symbols called digits for ten distinct values 0, 1, 2, 3, 4, 5, 6, 7, 8 and 9 to represent numbers
   a. Decimal notation0
   b. Thing
   c. Undefined
   d. Undefined

88. In mathematics, the _____ of a function is the set of all "output" values produced by that function. Given a function $f: A \to B$, the _____ of f, is defined to be the set $\{x \in B : x = f(a) \text{ for some } a \in A\}$.
   a. Thing
   b. Range0
   c. Undefined
   d. Undefined

89. In plane geometry, a _____ is a polygon with four equal sides, four right angles, and parallel opposite sides. In algebra, the _____ of a number is that number multiplied by itself.
   a. Square0
   b. Thing
   c. Undefined
   d. Undefined

90. In mathematics, a _____ of a number x is a number r such that $r^2 = x$, or in words, a number r whose square (the result of multiplying the number by itself) is x.
   a. Thing
   b. Square root0
   c. Undefined
   d. Undefined

91. In mathematics, a _____ of a complex-valued function f is a member x of the domain of f such that f(x) vanishes at x, that is, $x : f(x) = 0$.
   a. Root0
   b. Thing
   c. Undefined
   d. Undefined

92. An _____ of a number a is a number b such that $b^n = a$.
   a. Nth root0
   b. Thing
   c. Undefined
   d. Undefined

93. The _____ is the number or expression underneath the radical sign.
   a. Thing
   b. Radicand0
   c. Undefined
   d. Undefined

94. The word _____ is used in a variety of ways in mathematics.
   a. Thing
   b. Index0
   c. Undefined
   d. Undefined

95. The term _____ can refer to an integer which is the square of some other integer, or an algebraic expression that can be factored as the square of some other expression.
   a. Thing
   b. Perfect square0
   c. Undefined
   d. Undefined

Chapter 1. Prerequisites

96. _____, or Rationalisation in mathematics is the process of removing a square root or imaginary number from the denominator of a fraction.
   a. Thing
   b. Rationalizing0
   c. Undefined
   d. Undefined

97. A _____ of a number is the product of that number with any integer.
   a. Thing
   b. Multiple0
   c. Undefined
   d. Undefined

98. In mathematics, _____ expressions is used to reduce the expression into the lowest possible term.
   a. Thing
   b. Simplifying0
   c. Undefined
   d. Undefined

99. A _____ is a three-dimensional solid object bounded by six square faces, facets, or sides, with three meeting at each vertex.
   a. Thing
   b. Cube0
   c. Undefined
   d. Undefined

100. A _____ is a number which is the cube of an integer.
   a. Perfect cube0
   b. Thing
   c. Undefined
   d. Undefined

101. In algebra, a _____ is a binomial formed by taking the opposite of the second term of a binomial.
   a. Thing
   b. Conjugate0
   c. Undefined
   d. Undefined

102. A _____ of a number is a number a such that $a^3 = x$.
   a. Cube root0
   b. Thing
   c. Undefined
   d. Undefined

103. _____ is a mathematical subject that includes the study of limits, derivatives, integrals, and power series and constitutes a major part of modern university curriculum.
   a. Calculus0
   b. Thing
   c. Undefined
   d. Undefined

104. _____ has many meanings, most of which simply .
   a. Power0
   b. Thing
   c. Undefined
   d. Undefined

105. A _____ is a unit of length in the metric system, equal to one thousand metres, the current SI base unit of length
   a. Kilometer0
   b. Thing
   c. Undefined
   d. Undefined

106. _____ is electromagnetic radiation with a wavelength that is visible to the eye (visible _____) or, in a technical or scientific context, electromagnetic radiation of any wavelength.

Chapter 1. Prerequisites

    a. Thing
    b. Light0
    c. Undefined
    d. Undefined

107. A _____ or lightyear is a unit of measurement of length, specifically the distance light travels in a vacuum in one year.
    a. Light year0
    b. Thing
    c. Undefined
    d. Undefined

108. _____ is mass m per unit volume V.
    a. Thing
    b. Density0
    c. Undefined
    d. Undefined

109. The metre (or _____, see spelling differences) is a measure of length. It is the basic unit of length in the metric system and in the International System of Units (SI), used around the world for general and scientific purposes.
    a. Meter0
    b. Concept
    c. Undefined
    d. Undefined

110. _____ is, or relates to, the _____ temperature scale .
    a. Thing
    b. Celsius0
    c. Undefined
    d. Undefined

111. In mathematics, there are several meanings of _____ depending on the subject.
    a. Degree0
    b. Thing
    c. Undefined
    d. Undefined

112. In mathematics and more specifically set theory, the _____ set is the unique set which contains no elements.
    a. Empty0
    b. Thing
    c. Undefined
    d. Undefined

113. A _____ is an object that is attached to a pivot point so that it can swing freely.
    a. Pendulum0
    b. Thing
    c. Undefined
    d. Undefined

114. In business, particularly accounting, a _____ is the time intervals that the accounts, statement, payments, or other calculations cover.
    a. Period0
    b. Thing
    c. Undefined
    d. Undefined

115. The _____ in a vacuum is an important physical constant denoted by the letter c for constant or the Latin word celeritas meaning "swiftness
    a. Speed of light0
    b. Thing
    c. Undefined
    d. Undefined

116. In mathematics, a _____ is an expression that is constructed from one or more variables and constants, using only the operations of addition, subtraction, multiplication, and constant positive whole number exponents. is a _____. Note in particular that division by an expression containing a variable is not in general allowed in polynomials. [1]

Chapter 1. Prerequisites

a. Polynomial0   b. Thing
c. Undefined   d. Undefined

117. _____ is a fixed, but possibly unspecified, value. This is in contrast to a variable, which is not fixed.
   a. Constant term0
   b. Thing
   c. Undefined
   d. Undefined

118. A _____ is a polynomial consisting of three terms; in other words, it is the sum of three monomials.
   a. Thing
   b. Trinomial0
   c. Undefined
   d. Undefined

119. In mathematics, a _____ is a particular kind of polynomial, having just one term.
   a. Monomial0
   b. Thing
   c. Undefined
   d. Undefined

120. In elementary algebra, a _____ is a polynomial with two terms: the sum of two monomials. It is the simplest kind of polynomial except for a monomial.
   a. Thing
   b. Binomial0
   c. Undefined
   d. Undefined

121. _____ also sometimes known as the double distributive property or more colloquially as foiling, is commonly taught to US high school students learning algebra as a mnemonic for remembering how to multiply two binomials polynomials with two terms.
   a. Thing
   b. FOIL method0
   c. Undefined
   d. Undefined

122. The _____ is commonly taught to US high school students learning algebra as a mnemonic for remembering how to multiply two binomials.
   a. FOIL rule0
   b. Thing
   c. Undefined
   d. Undefined

123. A _____ is the result of the addition of a set of numbers. The numbers may be natural numbers, complex numbers, matrices, or still more complicated objects. An infinite _____ is a subtle procedure known as a series.
   a. Thing
   b. Sum0
   c. Undefined
   d. Undefined

124. In abstract algebra, _____ consists of sets with binary operations that satisfy certain axioms.
   a. Grouping0
   b. Thing
   c. Undefined
   d. Undefined

125. The _____ of a solid object is the three-dimensional concept of how much space it occupies, often quantified numerically.
   a. Volume0
   b. Thing
   c. Undefined
   d. Undefined

126. _____, from Latin meaning "to make progress", is defined in two different ways. Pure economic _____ is the increase in wealth that an investor has from making an investment, taking into consideration all costs associated with that investment including the opportunity cost of capital.
   a. Profit0
   b. Thing
   c. Undefined
   d. Undefined

127. _____ is a business term for the amount of money that a company receives from its activities in a given period, mostly from sales of products and/or services to customers
   a. Thing
   b. Revenue0
   c. Undefined
   d. Undefined

128. _____ is a kind of property which exists as magnitude or multitude. It is among the basic classes of things along with quality, substance, change, and relation.
   a. Thing
   b. Amount0
   c. Undefined
   d. Undefined

129. _____ is the fee paid on borrowed money.
   a. Thing
   b. Interest0
   c. Undefined
   d. Undefined

130. _____ interest refers to the fact that whenever interest is calculated, it is based not only on the original principal, but also on any unpaid interest that has been added to the principal.
   a. Compound0
   b. Thing
   c. Undefined
   d. Undefined

131. _____ refers to the fact that whenever interest is calculated, it is based not only on the original principal, but also on any unpaid interest that has been added to the principal. The more frequently interest is compounded, the faster the balance grows.
   a. Compound interest0
   b. Concept
   c. Undefined
   d. Undefined

132. An _____ is the fee paid on borrow money.
   a. Concept
   b. Interest rate0
   c. Undefined
   d. Undefined

133. _____ or investing is a term with several closely-related meanings in business management, finance and economics, related to saving or deferring consumption.
   a. Thing
   b. Investment0
   c. Undefined
   d. Undefined

134. In geometry, a _____ is defined as a quadrilateral where all four of its angles are right angles.
   a. Rectangle0
   b. Thing
   c. Undefined
   d. Undefined

135. _____ is the design, analysis, and/or construction of works for practical purposes.

Chapter 1. Prerequisites

   a. Thing
   b. Engineering0
   c. Undefined
   d. Undefined

136. The _____ (symbol _____) and the millibar (symbol mbar, also mb) are units of pressure.
   a. Thing
   b. Bar0
   c. Undefined
   d. Undefined

137. A bar chart, also known as a _____, is a chart with rectangular bars of lengths usually proportional to the magnitudes or frequencies of what they represent.
   a. Bar graph0
   b. Thing
   c. Undefined
   d. Undefined

138. _____ is a unit of speed, expressing the number of international miles covered per hour.
   a. Miles per hour0
   b. Thing
   c. Undefined
   d. Undefined

139. Deductive _____ is the kind of _____ in which the conclusion is necessitated by, or reached from, previously known facts (the premises).
   a. Reasoning0
   b. Thing
   c. Undefined
   d. Undefined

140. _____ is the largest positive integer that divides both numbers without remainder.
   a. Common Factor0
   b. Thing
   c. Undefined
   d. Undefined

141. In mathematics, _____ is the decomposition of an object into a product of other objects, or factors, which when multiplied together give the original.
   a. Thing
   b. Factoring0
   c. Undefined
   d. Undefined

142. _____ are of a number n in its third power-the result of multiplying it by itself three times.
   a. Thing
   b. Cubes0
   c. Undefined
   d. Undefined

143. In mathematics the _____ refers to the identity: $a^2 - b^2 = (a+b)(a-b)$
   a. Thing
   b. Difference of two squares0
   c. Undefined
   d. Undefined

144. A _____ is a negotiable instrument instructing a financial institution to pay a specific amount of a specific currency from a specific demand account held in the maker/depositor's name with that institution. Both the maker and payee may be natural persons or legal entities.
   a. Thing
   b. Check0
   c. Undefined
   d. Undefined

145. _____ are any documents that aim to streamline particular processes according to a set routine.

a. Thing
b. Guidelines0
c. Undefined
d. Undefined

146. In mathematics, the _____ divisor of two non-zero integers, is the largest positive integer that divides both numbers without remainder.
   a. Greatest common0
   b. Thing
   c. Undefined
   d. Undefined

147. In Math the greates common divisor sometimes known as the _____ of two non- zero integers.
   a. Greatest common factor0
   b. Thing
   c. Undefined
   d. Undefined

148. _____ is the study of error, particularly in the fields of applied mathematics, applied linguistics, statistics, and numerical analysis.
   a. Error analysis0
   b. Thing
   c. Undefined
   d. Undefined

149. _____ is a special mathematical relationship between two quantities. Two quantities are called proportional if they vary in such a way that one of the quantities is a constant multiple of the other, or equivalently if they have a constant ratio.
   a. Proportionality0
   b. Thing
   c. Undefined
   d. Undefined

150. In classical geometry, a _____ of a circle or sphere is any line segment from its center to its boundary. By extension, the _____ of a circle or sphere is the length of any such segment. The _____ is half the diameter. In science and engineering the term _____ of curvature is commonly used as a synonym for _____.
   a. Thing
   b. Radius0
   c. Undefined
   d. Undefined

151. In mathematics, an _____, mean, or central tendency of a data set refers to a measure of the "middle" or "expected" value of the data set.
   a. Concept
   b. Average0
   c. Undefined
   d. Undefined

152. In mathematics, the conjugate _____ or adjoint matrix of an m-by-n matrix A with complex entries is the n-by-m matrix A* obtained from A by taking the transpose and then taking the complex conjugate of each entry.
   a. Pairs0
   b. Thing
   c. Undefined
   d. Undefined

153. In mathematics, a _____ of a k-place relation $L \subseteq X_1 \times \ldots \times X_k$ is one of the sets X_j, $1 \leq j \leq k$. In the special case where k = 2 and $L \subseteq X_1 \times X_2$ is a function $L : X_1 \to X_2$, it is conventional to refer to X_1 as the _____ of the function and to refer to X_2 as the codomain of the function.
   a. Domain0
   b. Thing
   c. Undefined
   d. Undefined

Chapter 1. Prerequisites

154. In mathematics, a _____ is the end result of a division problem. It can also be expressed as the number of times the divisor divides into the dividend.
   a. Thing
   b. Quotient0
   c. Undefined
   d. Undefined

155. The _____ of a positive integer are the prime numbers that divide into that integer exactly, without leaving a remainder. The process of finding these numbers is called integer factorization, or prime factorization.
   a. Thing
   b. Prime factor0
   c. Undefined
   d. Undefined

156. The function difference divided by the point difference is known as the _____
   a. Difference quotient0
   b. Thing
   c. Undefined
   d. Undefined

157. _____ is the chance that something is likely to happen or be the case.
   a. Probability0
   b. Thing
   c. Undefined
   d. Undefined

158. A _____ is a type of debt. All material things can be lent but this article focuses exclusively on monetary loans. Like all debt instruments, a _____ entails the redistribution of financial assets over time, between the lender and the borrower.
   a. Thing
   b. Loan0
   c. Undefined
   d. Undefined

159. _____ studies and addresses the ways in which individuals, businesses, and organizations raise, allocate, and use monetary resources over time, taking into account the risks entailed in their projects
   a. Thing
   b. Finance0
   c. Undefined
   d. Undefined

160. In physics, a _____ may refer to the scalar _____ or to the vector _____.
   a. Potential0
   b. Thing
   c. Undefined
   d. Undefined

161. The plus and _____ signs are mathematical symbols used to represent the notions of positive and negative as well as the operations of addition and subtraction.
   a. Thing
   b. Minus0
   c. Undefined
   d. Undefined

162. In algebra, the _____ decomposition or _____ expansion is used to reduce the degree of either the numerator or the denominator of a rational function.
   a. Thing
   b. Partial fraction0
   c. Undefined
   d. Undefined

163. In botany, _____ are above-ground plant organs specialized for photosynthesis. Their characteristics are typically analyzed by using Fiobonacci's sequences.

Chapter 1. Prerequisites

    a. Thing
    b. Leaves0
    c. Undefined
    d. Undefined

164. In geometry, a line _____ is a part of a line that is bounded by two end points, and contains every point on the line between its end points.
    a. Segment0
    b. Concept
    c. Undefined
    d. Undefined

165. A _____ is a set of numbers that designate location in a given reference system, such as x,y in a planar _____ system or an x,y,z in a three-dimensional _____ system.
    a. Thing
    b. Coordinate0
    c. Undefined
    d. Undefined

166. A _____ is a part of a line that is bounded by two end points, and contains every point on the line between its end points.
    a. Line segment0
    b. Thing
    c. Undefined
    d. Undefined

167. In mathematics, a _____ is a two-dimensional manifold or surface that is perfectly flat.
    a. Plane0
    b. Thing
    c. Undefined
    d. Undefined

168. _____ means of or relating to the French philosopher and mathematician René Descartes.
    a. Cartesian0
    b. Thing
    c. Undefined
    d. Undefined

169. _____ is the middle point of a line segment.
    a. Thing
    b. Midpoint0
    c. Undefined
    d. Undefined

170. A _____ consists of one quarter of the coordinate plane.
    a. Quadrant0
    b. Thing
    c. Undefined
    d. Undefined

171. An _____ is when two lines intersect somewhere on a plane creating a right angle at intersection
    a. Thing
    b. Axes0
    c. Undefined
    d. Undefined

172. In mathematics, the _____ of two sets A and B is the set that contains all elements of A that also belong to B (or equivalently, all elements of B that also belong to A), but no other elements.
    a. Thing
    b. Intersection0
    c. Undefined
    d. Undefined

173. An _____ is a collection of two not necessarily distinct objects, one of which is distinguished as the first coordinate and the other as the second coordinate.

a. Ordered pair0
b. Thing
c. Undefined
d. Undefined

174. In astronomy, geography, geometry and related sciences and contexts, a plane is said to be _____ at a given point if it is locally perpendicular to the gradient of the gravity field, i.e., with the direction of the gravitational force at that point.
   a. Thing
   b. Horizontal0
   c. Undefined
   d. Undefined

175. _____ was a highly influential French philosopher, mathematician, scientist, and writer. Dubbed the "Founder of Modern Philosophy", and the "Father of Modern Mathematics". His theories provided the basis for the calculus of Newton and Leibniz, by applying infinitesimal calculus to the tangent line problem, thus permitting the evolution of that branch of modern mathematics
   a. Person
   b. Descartes0
   c. Undefined
   d. Undefined

176. _____ is a synonym for information.
   a. Data0
   b. Thing
   c. Undefined
   d. Undefined

177. A _____, scatter diagram or scatter graph is a chart that uses Cartesian coordinates to display values for two variables.
   a. Thing
   b. Scatter plot0
   c. Undefined
   d. Undefined

178. In mathematics, a _____ is a statement that can be proved on the basis of explicitly stated or previously agreed assumptions.
   a. Theorem0
   b. Thing
   c. Undefined
   d. Undefined

179. A _____ is one of the basic shapes of geometry: a polygon with three vertices and three sides which are straight line segments.
   a. Thing
   b. Triangle0
   c. Undefined
   d. Undefined

180. In geometry, a _____ is a special kind of point, usually a corner of a polygon, polyhedron, or higher dimensional polytope. In the geometry of curves a _____ is a point of where the first derivative of curvature is zero. In graph theory, a _____ is the fundamental unit out of which graphs are formed
   a. Thing
   b. Vertex0
   c. Undefined
   d. Undefined

181. _____ has one 90° internal angle a right angle.
   a. Thing
   b. Right triangle0
   c. Undefined
   d. Undefined

182. In Euclidean geometry, a uniform _____ is a linear transformation that enlargers or diminishes objects, and whose _____ factor is the same in all directions. This is also called homothethy.

Chapter 1. Prerequisites

    a. Thing
    b. Scale0
    c. Undefined
    d. Undefined

183. The word _____ comes from the Latin word linearis, which means created by lines.
    a. Linear0
    b. Thing
    c. Undefined
    d. Undefined

184. In mathematics, a _____ in elementary terms is any of a variety of different functions from geometry, such as rotations, reflections and translations.
    a. Transformation0
    b. Thing
    c. Undefined
    d. Undefined

185. In Euclidean geometry, a _____ is moving every point a constant distance in a specified direction.
    a. Translation0
    b. Concept
    c. Undefined
    d. Undefined

186. In mathematics, a _____ (also spelled reflexion) is a map that transforms an object into its mirror image.
    a. Reflection0
    b. Concept
    c. Undefined
    d. Undefined

187. A _____ is a movement of an object in a circular motion. A two-dimensional object rotates around a center (or point) of _____. A three-dimensional object rotates around a line called an axis. If the axis of _____ is within the body, the body is said to rotate upon itself, or spinâ€"which implies relative speed and perhaps free-movement with angular momentum. A circular motion about an external point, e.g. the Earth about the Sun, is called an orbit or more properly an orbital revolution.
    a. Rotation0
    b. Thing
    c. Undefined
    d. Undefined

188. In geometry a _____ is a plane figure that is bounded by a closed path or circuit, composed of a finite number of sequential line segments.
    a. Polygon0
    b. Thing
    c. Undefined
    d. Undefined

189. _____ is a mathematical science pertaining to the collection, analysis, interpretation or explanation, and presentation of data. It is applicable to a wide variety of academic disciplines, from the physical and social sciences to the humanities.
    a. Thing
    b. Statistics0
    c. Undefined
    d. Undefined

190. _____ is a way of expressing a number as a fraction of 100 per cent meaning "per hundred".
    a. Percent0
    b. Thing
    c. Undefined
    d. Undefined

191. _____ is a relation in Euclidean geometry among the three sides of a right triangle.

Chapter 1. Prerequisites

a. Pythagorean Theorem0
b. Thing
c. Undefined
d. Undefined

192. An _____ triange is a triangle with at least two sides of equal length.
 a. Isosceles0
 b. Thing
 c. Undefined
 d. Undefined

193. In mathematics and its applications, a _____ is a system for assigning an n-tuple of numbers or scalars to each point in an n-dimensional space.
 a. Concept
 b. Coordinate system0
 c. Undefined
 d. Undefined

194. Multiple Signal Classification, also known as _____, is an algorithm used for frequency estimation and emitter location.
 a. Music0
 b. Thing
 c. Undefined
 d. Undefined

195. In mathematics, a _____ is a demonstration that, assuming certain axioms, some statement is necessarily true.
 a. Proof0
 b. Thing
 c. Undefined
 d. Undefined

196. A _____ is a four-sided plane figure that has two sets of opposite parallel sides.
 a. Concept
 b. Parallelogram0
 c. Undefined
 d. Undefined

197. A _____ can refer to a line joining two nonadjacent vertices of a polygon or polyhedron, or in some contexts any upward or downward sloping line. .
 a. Thing
 b. Diagonal0
 c. Undefined
 d. Undefined

198. In geometry, a _____ is the intersection of a body in 2-dimensional space with a line, or of a body in 3-dimensional space with a plane
 a. Cross section0
 b. Thing
 c. Undefined
 d. Undefined

199. In geometry, a _____ (Greek words diairo = divide and metro = measure) of a circle is any straight line segment that passes through the centre and whose endpoints are on the circular boundary, or, in more modern usage, the length of such a line segment. When using the word in the more modern sense, one speaks of the _____ rather than a _____, because all diameters of a circle have the same length. This length is twice the radius. The _____ of a circle is also the longest chord that the circle has.
 a. Diameter0
 b. Thing
 c. Undefined
 d. Undefined

200. In mathematics, a _____ is a quadric surface, with the following equation in Cartesian coordinates: $(x/a)^2 + (y/b)^2 = 1$.

a. Cylinder0   b. Thing
c. Undefined   d. Undefined

201. A _____ is a function that assigns a number to subsets of a given set.
a. Thing   b. Measure0
c. Undefined   d. Undefined

202. _____ is the interdisciplinary scientific study of the atmosphere that focuses on weather processes and forecasting.
a. Thing   b. Meteorology0
c. Undefined   d. Undefined

203. Acid _____ ratio measures the ability of a company to use its near cash or quick assets to immediately extinguish its current liabilities.
a. Thing   b. Test0
c. Undefined   d. Undefined

204. In statistics, a _____ measure is one which is measuring what is supposed to measure.
a. Valid0   b. Thing
c. Undefined   d. Undefined

205. _____ is a set of statements, one of which is the conclusion and the rest of which are premises.
a. Thing   b. Valid argument0
c. Undefined   d. Undefined

206. In mathematics, science including computer science, linguistics and engineering, an _____ is, generally speaking, an independent variable or input to a function.
a. Thing   b. Argument0
c. Undefined   d. Undefined

207. In geometry, the _____ of an object is a point in some sense in the middle of the object.
a. Thing   b. Center0
c. Undefined   d. Undefined

208. In geographic information systems, a _____ comprises an entity with a geographic location, typically determined by points, arcs, or polygons. Carriageways and cadastres exemplify _____ data.
a. Feature0   b. Thing
c. Undefined   d. Undefined

209. In mathematics, a _____ is the set of all points in three-dimensional space (R^3) which are at distance r from a fixed point of that space, where r is a positive real number called the radius of the _____. The fixed point is called the center or centre, and is not part of the _____ itself.
a. Sphere0   b. Thing
c. Undefined   d. Undefined

210. _____ is a statistical measure of the average length of survival of a living thing.

Chapter 1. Prerequisites

a. Thing
c. Undefined
b. Life expectancy0
d. Undefined

211. _____ is the level of functional and/or metabolic efficiency of an organism at both the micro level.
a. Thing
c. Undefined
b. Health0
d. Undefined

212. _____ is a term used in accounting, economics and finance with reference to the fact that assets with finite lives lose value over time.
a. Depreciation0
c. Undefined
b. Thing
d. Undefined

213. _____ was a German Lutheran mathematician, astronomer and astrologer, and a key figure in the 17th century astronomical revolution.
a. Johannes Kepler0
c. Undefined
b. Person
d. Undefined

214. In physics, an _____ is the path that an object makes around another object while under the influence of a source of centripetal force, such as gravity.
a. Orbit0
c. Undefined
b. Thing
d. Undefined

215. A _____, as defined by the International Astronomical Union , is a celestial body orbiting a star or stellar remnant that is massive enough to be rounded by its own gravity, not massive enough to cause thermonuclear fusion in its core, and has cleared its neighboring region of planetesimals.
a. Thing
c. Undefined
b. Planet0
d. Undefined

216. In banking and accountancy, the outstanding _____ is the amount of money owned, or due, that remains in a deposit account or a loan account at a given date, after all past remittances, payments and withdrawal have been accounted for.
a. Thing
c. Undefined
b. Balance0
d. Undefined

217. _____ is the distance around a given two-dimensional object. As a general rule, the _____ of a polygon can always be calculated by adding all the length of the sides together. So, the formula for triangles is P = a + b + c, where a, b and c stand for each side of it. For quadrilaterals the equation is P = a + b + c + d. For equilateral polygons, P = na, where n is the number of sides and a is the side length.
a. Thing
c. Undefined
b. Perimeter0
d. Undefined

218. _____ are the basic objects of study in graph theory. Informally speaking, a graph is a set of objects called points, nodes, or vertices connected by links called lines or edges.
a. Thing
c. Undefined
b. Graphs0
d. Undefined

Chapter 2. Equations and Inequalities

1. A _____ is a set of numbers that designate location in a given reference system, such as x,y in a planar _____ system or an x,y,z in a three-dimensional _____ system.
   - a. Thing
   - b. Coordinate0
   - c. Undefined
   - d. Undefined

2. In mathematics and its applications, a _____ is a system for assigning an n-tuple of numbers or scalars to each point in an n-dimensional space.
   - a. Concept
   - b. Coordinate system0
   - c. Undefined
   - d. Undefined

3. In mathematics, a _____ is a two-dimensional manifold or surface that is perfectly flat.
   - a. Thing
   - b. Plane0
   - c. Undefined
   - d. Undefined

4. A _____ is a symbolic representation denoting a quantity or expression. It often represents an "unknown" quantity that has the potential to change.
   - a. Variable0
   - b. Thing
   - c. Undefined
   - d. Undefined

5. An _____ is a collection of two not necessarily distinct objects, one of which is distinguished as the first coordinate and the other as the second coordinate.
   - a. Thing
   - b. Ordered pair0
   - c. Undefined
   - d. Undefined

6. In Euclidean geometry, a _____ is the set of all points in a plane at a fixed distance, called the radius, from a given point, the center.
   - a. Thing
   - b. Circle0
   - c. Undefined
   - d. Undefined

7. _____ are the basic objects of study in graph theory. Informally speaking, a graph is a set of objects called points, nodes, or vertices connected by links called lines or edges.
   - a. Thing
   - b. Graphs0
   - c. Undefined
   - d. Undefined

8. _____ means "constancy", i.e. if something retains a certain feature even after we change a way of looking at it, then it is symmetric.
   - a. Thing
   - b. Symmetry0
   - c. Undefined
   - d. Undefined

9. Acid _____ ratio measures the ability of a company to use its near cash or quick assets to immediately extinguish its current liabilities.
   - a. Test0
   - b. Thing
   - c. Undefined
   - d. Undefined

10. In mathematics, the _____ of a coordinate system is the point where the axes of the system intersect.

a. Origin0
b. Thing
c. Undefined
d. Undefined

11. Equivalence is the condition of being _____ or essentially equal.
   a. Equivalent0
   b. Thing
   c. Undefined
   d. Undefined

12. The _____ integers are all the integers from zero on upwards.
   a. Nonnegative0
   b. Thing
   c. Undefined
   d. Undefined

13. In mathematics, the _____ (or modulus) of a real number is its numerical value without regard to its sign.
   a. Absolute value0
   b. Thing
   c. Undefined
   d. Undefined

14. A _____ is a negotiable instrument instructing a financial institution to pay a specific amount of a specific currency from a specific demand account held in the maker/depositor's name with that institution. Both the maker and payee may be natural persons or legal entities.
   a. Thing
   b. Check0
   c. Undefined
   d. Undefined

15. _____ is a branch of mathematics concerning the study of structure, relation and quantity.
   a. Concept
   b. Algebra0
   c. Undefined
   d. Undefined

16. An _____ is when two lines intersect somewhere on a plane creating a right angle at intersection
   a. Axes0
   b. Thing
   c. Undefined
   d. Undefined

17. In geometry, the _____ of an object is a point in some sense in the middle of the object.
   a. Center0
   b. Thing
   c. Undefined
   d. Undefined

18. In classical geometry, a _____ of a circle or sphere is any line segment from its center to its boundary. By extension, the _____ of a circle or sphere is the length of any such segment. The _____ is half the diameter. In science and engineering the term _____ of curvature is commonly used as a synonym for _____.
   a. Thing
   b. Radius0
   c. Undefined
   d. Undefined

19. In mathematics, an _____ is a statement about the relative size or order of two objects.
   a. Thing
   b. Inequality0
   c. Undefined
   d. Undefined

20. _____ is a notation for writing numbers that is often used by scientists and mathematicians to make it easier to write large and small numbers.

Chapter 2. Equations and Inequalities

a. Scientific notation0
c. Undefined
b. Thing
d. Undefined

21. In geometry, a _____ is defined as a quadrilateral where all four of its angles are right angles.
    a. Thing
    b. Rectangle0
    c. Undefined
    d. Undefined

22. _____ is the distance around a given two-dimensional object. As a general rule, the _____ of a polygon can always be calculated by adding all the length of the sides together. So, the formula for triangles is P = a + b + c, where a, b and c stand for each side of it. For quadrilaterals the equation is P = a + b + c + d. For equilateral polygons, P = na, where n is the number of sides and a is the side length.
    a. Thing
    b. Perimeter0
    c. Undefined
    d. Undefined

23. The metre (or _____, see spelling differences) is a measure of length. It is the basic unit of length in the metric system and in the International System of Units (SI), used around the world for general and scientific purposes.
    a. Meter0
    b. Concept
    c. Undefined
    d. Undefined

24. In common philosophical language, a proposition or _____, is the content of an assertion, that is, it is true-or-false and defined by the meaning of a particular piece of language.
    a. Concept
    b. Statement0
    c. Undefined
    d. Undefined

25. The word _____ comes from the Latin word linearis, which means created by lines.
    a. Linear0
    b. Thing
    c. Undefined
    d. Undefined

26. A _____ is an equation in which each term is either a constant or the product of a constant times the first power of a variable.
    a. Thing
    b. Linear equation0
    c. Undefined
    d. Undefined

27. The deductive-nomological model is a formalized view of scientific _____ in natural language.
    a. Thing
    b. Explanation0
    c. Undefined
    d. Undefined

28. An _____ is a combination of numbers, operators, grouping symbols and/or free variables and bound variables arranged in a meaningful way which can be evaluated..
    a. Expression0
    b. Thing
    c. Undefined
    d. Undefined

29. _____ is a synonym for information.
    a. Thing
    b. Data0
    c. Undefined
    d. Undefined

Chapter 2. Equations and Inequalities

30. _____ is a statistical measure of the average length of survival of a living thing.
    a. Thing
    b. Life expectancy0
    c. Undefined
    d. Undefined

31. In business, particularly accounting, a _____ is the time intervals that the accounts, statement, payments, or other calculations cover.
    a. Period0
    b. Thing
    c. Undefined
    d. Undefined

32. A _____, scatter diagram or scatter graph is a chart that uses Cartesian coordinates to display values for two variables.
    a. Scatter plot0
    b. Thing
    c. Undefined
    d. Undefined

33. The _____, the average in everyday English, which is also called the arithmetic _____ (and is distinguished from the geometric _____ or harmonic _____). The average is also called the sample _____. The expected value of a random variable, which is also called the population _____.
    a. Mean0
    b. Thing
    c. Undefined
    d. Undefined

34. In mathematics, a _____ may be described informally as a number that can be given by an infinite decimal representation.
    a. Real number0
    b. Thing
    c. Undefined
    d. Undefined

35. The material _____, also known as the material implication or truth functional _____, expresses a property of certain conditionals in logic.
    a. Conditional0
    b. Thing
    c. Undefined
    d. Undefined

36. In mathematics, a _____ of a k-place relation $L \subseteq X_1 \times ... \times X_k$ is one of the sets X_j, $1 \leq j \leq k$. In the special case where k = 2 and $L \subseteq X_1 \times X_2$ is a function $L : X_1 \to X_2$, it is conventional to refer to X_1 as the _____ of the function and to refer to X_2 as the codomain of the function.
    a. Domain0
    b. Thing
    c. Undefined
    d. Undefined

37. _____ over a given field is a polynomial with coefficients in that field.
    a. Algebraic equation0
    b. Thing
    c. Undefined
    d. Undefined

38. _____ of Alexandria, sometimes called the father of algebra was a Hellenistic mathematician.
    a. Person
    b. Diophantus0
    c. Undefined
    d. Undefined

Chapter 2. Equations and Inequalities

39. In mathematics, a _____ is an ordered list of objects. Like a set, it contains members, also called elements or terms, and the number of terms is called the length of the _____. Unlike a set, order matters, and the exact same elements can appear multiple times at different positions in the _____.
   a. Thing
   b. Sequence0
   c. Undefined
   d. Undefined

40. A _____ is the result of the addition of a set of numbers. The numbers may be natural numbers, complex numbers, matrices, or still more complicated objects. An infinite _____ is a subtle procedure known as a series.
   a. Sum0
   b. Thing
   c. Undefined
   d. Undefined

41. In mathematics, the _____ of two sets A and B is the set that contains all elements of A that also belong to B (or equivalently, all elements of B that also belong to A), but no other elements.
   a. Intersection0
   b. Thing
   c. Undefined
   d. Undefined

42. A _____ is the part of a fraction that tells how many equal parts make up a whole, and which is used in the name of the fraction: "halves", "thirds", "fourths" or "quarters", "fifths" and so on.
   a. Concept
   b. Denominator0
   c. Undefined
   d. Undefined

43. _____ variables are variables other than the independent variable that may bear any effect on the behavior of the subject being studied.
   a. Thing
   b. Extraneous0
   c. Undefined
   d. Undefined

44. _____ is the largest positive integer that divides both numbers without remainder.
   a. Thing
   b. Common Factor0
   c. Undefined
   d. Undefined

45. In mathematics, factorization (British English: factorisation) or factoring is the decomposition of an object (for example, a number, a polynomial, or a matrix) into a product of other objects, or _____, which when multiplied together give the original.
   a. Factors0
   b. Thing
   c. Undefined
   d. Undefined

46. A _____ is a numeral used to indicate a count. The most common use of the word today is to name the part of a fraction that tells the number or count of equal parts.
   a. Thing
   b. Numerator0
   c. Undefined
   d. Undefined

47. Any point where a graph makes contact with an coordinate axis is called an _____ of the graph
   a. Intercept0
   b. Thing
   c. Undefined
   d. Undefined

Chapter 2. Equations and Inequalities

48. An _____ is an equality that remains true regardless of the values of any variables that appear within it, to distinguish it from an equality which is true under more particular conditions.
    a. Thing
    b. Identity0
    c. Undefined
    d. Undefined

49. In plane geometry, a _____ is a polygon with four equal sides, four right angles, and parallel opposite sides. In algebra, the _____ of a number is that number multiplied by itself.
    a. Square0
    b. Thing
    c. Undefined
    d. Undefined

50. In mathematics, a _____ is a quadric surface, with the following equation in Cartesian coordinates: $(x/_a)^2 + (y/_b)^2 = 1$.
    a. Thing
    b. Cylinder0
    c. Undefined
    d. Undefined

51. In mathematics, _____ geometry was the traditional name for the geometry of three-dimensional Euclidean space — for practical purposes the kind of space we live in.
    a. Solid0
    b. Thing
    c. Undefined
    d. Undefined

52. _____ are the recurring expenses which are related to the operation of a business, or to the operation of a device, component, piece of equipment or facility.
    a. Thing
    b. Operating cost0
    c. Undefined
    d. Undefined

53. A _____ is a unit of length, usually used to measure distance, in a number of different systems, including Imperial units, United States customary units and Norwegian/Swedish mil. Its size can vary from system to system, but in each is between 1 and 10 kilometers. In contemporary English contexts _____ refers to either:
    a. Mile0
    b. Thing
    c. Undefined
    d. Undefined

54. A _____ is a special kind of ratio, indicating a relationship between two measurements with different units, such as miles to gallons or cents to pounds.
    a. Rate0
    b. Thing
    c. Undefined
    d. Undefined

55. Two mathematical objects are equal if and only if they are precisely the same in every way. This defines a binary relation, _____, denoted by the sign of _____ "=" in such a way that the statement "x = y" means that x and y are equal.
    a. Equality0
    b. Thing
    c. Undefined
    d. Undefined

56. _____ is a kind of property which exists as magnitude or multitude. It is among the basic classes of things along with quality, substance, change, and relation.

30 **Chapter 2. Equations and Inequalities**

    a. Amount0   b. Thing
    c. Undefined   d. Undefined

57. In mathematics, _____ is an elementary arithmetic operation. When one of the numbers is a whole number, _____ is the repeated sum of the other number.
    a. Thing   b. Multiplication0
    c. Undefined   d. Undefined

58. In mathematics, a _____ is the result of multiplying, or an expression that identifies factors to be multiplied.
    a. Thing   b. Product0
    c. Undefined   d. Undefined

59. In mathematics, an inequality is a statement about the relative size or order of two objects. For example 14 > 10, or 14 is _____ 10.
    a. Thing   b. Greater than0
    c. Undefined   d. Undefined

60. In mathematics, a _____ is the end result of a division problem. It can also be expressed as the number of times the divisor divides into the dividend.
    a. Quotient0   b. Thing
    c. Undefined   d. Undefined

61. A _____ is a quantity that denotes the proportional amount or magnitude of one quantity relative to another.
    a. Thing   b. Ratio0
    c. Undefined   d. Undefined

62. _____ of a product is the price the manufacturer recommends that the retailer sell it for.
    a. List price0   b. Thing
    c. Undefined   d. Undefined

63. A _____ is an abstract model that uses mathematical language to describe the behavior of a system. Eykhoff defined a _____ as 'a representation of the essential aspects of an existing system which presents knowledge of that system in usable form'.
    a. Thing   b. Mathematical model0
    c. Undefined   d. Undefined

64. _____ is a way of expressing a number as a fraction of 100 per cent meaning "per hundred".
    a. Thing   b. Percent0
    c. Undefined   d. Undefined

65. The plus and _____ signs are mathematical symbols used to represent the notions of positive and negative as well as the operations of addition and subtraction.
    a. Thing   b. Minus0
    c. Undefined   d. Undefined

66. A _____ is a compensation which workers receive in exchange for their labor.

Chapter 2. Equations and Inequalities

    a. Thing
    b. Wage0
    c. Undefined
    d. Undefined

67. A _____ is a function that assigns a number to subsets of a given set.
    a. Thing
    b. Measure0
    c. Undefined
    d. Undefined

68. _____ is a unit of speed, expressing the number of international miles covered per hour.
    a. Thing
    b. Miles per hour0
    c. Undefined
    d. Undefined

69. _____ are a measure of time.
    a. Minutes0
    b. Thing
    c. Undefined
    d. Undefined

70. A _____ is one of the basic shapes of geometry: a polygon with three vertices and three sides which are straight line segments.
    a. Thing
    b. Triangle0
    c. Undefined
    d. Undefined

71. In Euclidean geometry, a uniform _____ is a linear transformation that enlargers or diminishes objects, and whose _____ factor is the same in all directions. This is also called homothethy.
    a. Thing
    b. Scale0
    c. Undefined
    d. Undefined

72. In chemistry, a _____ is substance made by combining two or more different materials in such a way that no chemical reaction occurs.
    a. Thing
    b. Mixture0
    c. Undefined
    d. Undefined

73. _____ is the fee paid on borrowed money.
    a. Thing
    b. Interest0
    c. Undefined
    d. Undefined

74. _____ is a list of goods and materials, or those goods and materials themselves, held available in stock by a business
    a. Thing
    b. Inventory0
    c. Undefined
    d. Undefined

75. _____, from Latin meaning "to make progress", is defined in two different ways. Pure economic _____ is the increase in wealth that an investor has from making an investment, taking into consideration all costs associated with that investment including the opportunity cost of capital.
    a. Profit0
    b. Thing
    c. Undefined
    d. Undefined

32   *Chapter 2. Equations and Inequalities*

76. _____ or investing is a term with several closely-related meanings in business management, finance and economics, related to saving or deferring consumption.
    a. Investment0
    b. Thing
    c. Undefined
    d. Undefined

77. The _____ of a solid object is the three-dimensional concept of how much space it occupies, often quantified numerically.
    a. Volume0
    b. Thing
    c. Undefined
    d. Undefined

78. The _____ is the distance around a closed curve. _____ is a kind of perimeter.
    a. Circumference0
    b. Thing
    c. Undefined
    d. Undefined

79. _____ is a temperature scale named after the German physicist Daniel Gabriel _____ , who proposed it in 1724.
    a. Fahrenheit0
    b. Thing
    c. Undefined
    d. Undefined

80. _____ is, or relates to, the _____ temperature scale .
    a. Thing
    b. Celsius0
    c. Undefined
    d. Undefined

81. In mathematics, there are several meanings of _____ depending on the subject.
    a. Degree0
    b. Thing
    c. Undefined
    d. Undefined

82. _____ is a physical property of a system that underlies the common notions of hot and cold; something that is hotter has the greater _____.
    a. Thing
    b. Temperature0
    c. Undefined
    d. Undefined

83. In banking and accountancy, the outstanding _____ is the amount of money owned, or due, that remains in a deposit account or a loan account at a given date, after all past remittances, payments and withdrawal have been accounted for.
    a. Thing
    b. Balance0
    c. Undefined
    d. Undefined

84. _____ interest refers to the fact that whenever interest is calculated, it is based not only on the original principal, but also on any unpaid interest that has been added to the principal.
    a. Compound0
    b. Thing
    c. Undefined
    d. Undefined

85. _____ refers to the fact that whenever interest is calculated, it is based not only on the original principal, but also on any unpaid interest that has been added to the principal. The more frequently interest is compounded, the faster the balance grows.

Chapter 2. Equations and Inequalities

a. Compound interest0
b. Concept
c. Undefined
d. Undefined

86. An _____ is the fee paid on borrow money.
a. Concept
b. Interest rate0
c. Undefined
d. Undefined

87. _____ mathematical functions take numeric arguments and produce numeric results.
a. Thing
b. Miscellaneous0
c. Undefined
d. Undefined

88. A _____ is a deliberate process for transforming one or more inputs into one or more results.
a. Calculation0
b. Thing
c. Undefined
d. Undefined

89. _____ is the transport of people on a trip/journey or the process or time involved in a person or object moving from one location to another.
a. Travel0
b. Thing
c. Undefined
d. Undefined

90. In mathematics, a _____ can mean either an element of the set {1, 2, 3, ...} (i.e the positive integers or the counting numbers) or an element of the set {0, 1, 2, 3, ...} (i.e. the non-negative integers).
a. Thing
b. Natural number0
c. Undefined
d. Undefined

91. The _____ of measurement are a globally standardized and modernized form of the metric system.
a. Thing
b. Units0
c. Undefined
d. Undefined

92. A _____ is a unit of length in the metric system, equal to one thousand metres, the current SI base unit of length
a. Kilometer0
b. Thing
c. Undefined
d. Undefined

93. The _____ are the only integral domain whose positive elements are well-ordered, and in which order is preserved by addition. Like the natural numbers, the _____ form a countably infinite set. The set of all _____ is usually denoted in mathematics by a boldface Z .
a. Integers0
b. Thing
c. Undefined
d. Undefined

94. _____ is a business term for the amount of money that a company receives from its activities in a given period, mostly from sales of products and/or services to customers
a. Revenue0
b. Thing
c. Undefined
d. Undefined

95. _____ means in succession or back-to-back

Chapter 2. Equations and Inequalities

a. Consecutive0
b. Thing
c. Undefined
d. Undefined

96. Fixed costs are expenses whose total does not change in proportion to the activity of a business. Unit fixed costs decline with volume following a retangular hyperbola as the volume of production. Variable costs by contrast change in relation to the activity of a business such as sales or production volume. Along with variable costs, fixed costs make up one of the two components of total cost. In the most simple production function total cost is equal to fixed costs plus variable costs. In accounting terminology, fixed costs will broadly include all costs which are not included in cost of goods sold, and variable costs are those captured in costs of goods sold. The implicit assumption required to make the equivalence between the accounting and economics terminology is that the accounting period is equal to the period in which fixed costs do not vary in relation to production. In practice, this equivalence does not always hold and depending on the period under consideration by management, some overhead expenses can be adjusted by management, and the specific allocation of each expense to each category will be decided under cost accounting. In business planning and management accounting, usage of the terms fixed costs, variable costs and others will often differ from usage in economics, and may depend on the intended use. For example, costs may be segregated into per unit costs fixed costs per period, and variable costs as a proportion of revenue. Capital expenditures will usually be allocated separately, and depending on the purpose, a portion may be regularly allocated to expenses as depreciation and amortization and seen as a _____ per period, or the entire amount may be considered upfront fixed costs.

a. Thing
b. Fixed cost0
c. Undefined
d. Undefined

97. _____ are expenses whose total does not change in proportion to the activity of a business, within the relevant time period or scale of production

a. Fixed costs0
b. Thing
c. Undefined
d. Undefined

98. In mathematics, the multiplicative inverse of a number x, denoted $1/x$ or x^{-1}, is the number which, when multiplied by x, yields 1. The multiplicative inverse of x is also called the _____ of x.

a. Thing
b. Reciprocal0
c. Undefined
d. Undefined

99. A _____ is a type of debt. All material things can be lent but this article focuses exclusively on monetary loans. Like all debt instruments, a _____ entails the redistribution of financial assets over time, between the lender and the borrower.

a. Thing
b. Loan0
c. Undefined
d. Undefined

100. _____ studies and addresses the ways in which individuals, businesses, and organizations raise, allocate, and use monetary resources over time, taking into account the risks entailed in their projects

a. Thing
b. Finance0
c. Undefined
d. Undefined

101. In finance and economics, _____ is the process of finding the present value of an amount of cash at some future date, and along with compounding cash forms the basis of time value of money calculations.

Chapter 2. Equations and Inequalities

  a. Thing
  b. Discount0
  c. Undefined
  d. Undefined

102. U.S. liquid _____ is legally defined as 231 cubic inches, and is equal to 3.785411784 litres or abotu 0.13368 cubic feet. This is the most common definition of a _____. The U.S. fluid ounce is defined as 1/128 of a U.S. _____.
  a. Gallon0
  b. Thing
  c. Undefined
  d. Undefined

103. A _____ is a simplified and structured visual representation of concepts, ideas, constructions, relations, statistical data, anatomy etc used in all aspects of human activities to visualize and clarify the topic.
  a. Thing
  b. Diagram0
  c. Undefined
  d. Undefined

104. In mathematics, an _____, mean, or central tendency of a data set refers to a measure of the "middle" or "expected" value of the data set.
  a. Average0
  b. Concept
  c. Undefined
  d. Undefined

105. _____ is the level of functional and/or metabolic efficiency of an organism at both the micro level.
  a. Thing
  b. Health0
  c. Undefined
  d. Undefined

106. In mathematics, a subset of Euclidean space R^n is called _____ if it is closed and bounded.
  a. Thing
  b. Compact0
  c. Undefined
  d. Undefined

107. In mathematics, the additive inverse, or _____ of a number n is the number that, when added to n, yields zero. The additive inverse of n is denoted −n. For example, 7 is −7, because 7 + (−7) = 0, and the additive inverse of −0.3 is 0.3, because −0.3 + 0.3 = 0.
  a. Opposite0
  b. Thing
  c. Undefined
  d. Undefined

108. _____, Greek for "knowledge of nature," is the branch of science concerned with the discovery and characterization of universal laws which govern matter, energy, space, and time.
  a. Physics0
  b. Thing
  c. Undefined
  d. Undefined

109. In mathematics, the _____ of a number n is the number that, when added to n, yields zero. The _____ of n is denoted −n. For example, 7 is −7, because 7 + (−7) = 0, and the _____ of −0.3 is 0.3, because −0.3 + 0.3 = 0.
  a. Additive inverse0
  b. Thing
  c. Undefined
  d. Undefined

110. The _____ (symbol _____) and the millibar (symbol mbar, also mb) are units of pressure.

a. Bar0
b. Thing
c. Undefined
d. Undefined

111. In geometry, a line _____ is a part of a line that is bounded by two end points, and contains every point on the line between its end points.
   a. Segment0
   b. Concept
   c. Undefined
   d. Undefined

112. A _____ is the sum of the elements of a sequence.
   a. Thing
   b. Series0
   c. Undefined
   d. Undefined

113. _____ or arithmetics is the oldest and most elementary branch of mathematics, used by almost everyone, for tasks ranging from simple daily counting to advanced science and business calculations.
   a. Thing
   b. Arithmetic0
   c. Undefined
   d. Undefined

114. _____ is a term used in marketing to indicate how much the price of a product is above the cost of producing and distributing the product.
   a. Markup0
   b. Thing
   c. Undefined
   d. Undefined

115. A _____ is a sequence of numbers where each term after the first is found by multiplying the previous one by a fixed non-zero number called the common ratio.
   a. Thing
   b. Geometric sequence0
   c. Undefined
   d. Undefined

116. In geometry, a _____ (Greek words diairo = divide and metro = measure) of a circle is any straight line segment that passes through the centre and whose endpoints are on the circular boundary, or, in more modern usage, the length of such a line segment. When using the word in the more modern sense, one speaks of the _____ rather than a _____, because all diameters of a circle have the same length. This length is twice the radius. The _____ of a circle is also the longest chord that the circle has.
   a. Diameter0
   b. Thing
   c. Undefined
   d. Undefined

117. A _____ is a three-dimensional solid object bounded by six square faces, facets, or sides, with three meeting at each vertex.
   a. Thing
   b. Cube0
   c. Undefined
   d. Undefined

118. In mathematics, a _____ is the set of all points in three-dimensional space (R^3) which are at distance r from a fixed point of that space, where r is a positive real number called the radius of the _____. The fixed point is called the center or centre, and is not part of the _____ itself.
   a. Thing
   b. Sphere0
   c. Undefined
   d. Undefined

Chapter 2. Equations and Inequalities

119. In mathematics, a _____ is a polynomial equation of the second degree. The general form is $ax^2 + bx + c = 0$.
- a. Thing
- b. Quadratic equation0
- c. Undefined
- d. Undefined

120. In mathematics, _____ is the decomposition of an object into a product of other objects, or factors, which when multiplied together give the original.
- a. Thing
- b. Factoring0
- c. Undefined
- d. Undefined

121. In mathematics, a _____ is an expression that is constructed from one or more variables and constants, using only the operations of addition, subtraction, multiplication, and constant positive whole number exponents. is a _____. Note in particular that division by an expression containing a variable is not in general allowed in polynomials. [1]
- a. Polynomial0
- b. Thing
- c. Undefined
- d. Undefined

122. One of the three formats applicable to a quadratic function is the _____ which is defined as $f = ax^2 + bx + c$.
- a. General form0
- b. Thing
- c. Undefined
- d. Undefined

123. A quadratic equation with real solutions, called roots, which may be real or complex, is given by the _____: $x = \frac{-b \pm \sqrt{b^2 - 4ac}}{2a}$.
- a. Quadratic formula0
- b. Thing
- c. Undefined
- d. Undefined

124. In mathematics, a _____ of a number x is a number r such that $r^2 = x$, or in words, a number r whose square (the result of multiplying the number by itself) is x.
- a. Thing
- b. Square root0
- c. Undefined
- d. Undefined

125. In mathematics, a _____ of a complex-valued function f is a member x of the domain of f such that f(x) vanishes at x, that is, $x : f(x) = 0$.
- a. Root0
- b. Thing
- c. Undefined
- d. Undefined

126. _____ is a technique used in algebra to solve quadratic equations, in analytic geometry for determining the shapes of graphs, and in calculus for computing integrals, including, but hardly limited to, the integrals that define Laplace transforms. The essential objective is to reduce a quadratic polynomial in a variable in an equation or expression to a squared polynomial of linear order. This can reduce an equation or integral to one that is more easily solved or evaluated.
- a. Thing
- b. Completing the square0
- c. Undefined
- d. Undefined

127. In mathematics, a _____ is a constant multiplicative factor of a certain object. The object can be such things as a variable, a vector, a function, etc. For example, the _____ of $9x^2$ is 9.
- a. Thing
- b. Coefficient0
- c. Undefined
- d. Undefined

128. A _____ is a polynomial consisting of three terms; in other words, it is the sum of three monomials.
  a. Thing
  b. Trinomial0
  c. Undefined
  d. Undefined

129. _____ is the symbol used to indicate the nth root of a number
  a. Thing
  b. Radical0
  c. Undefined
  d. Undefined

130. In mathematics and the mathematical sciences, a _____ is a fixed, but possibly unspecified, value. This is in contrast to a variable, which is not fixed.
  a. Thing
  b. Constant0
  c. Undefined
  d. Undefined

131. _____ of a polynomial with real or complex coefficients is a certain expression in the coefficients of the polynomial which is equal to zero if and only if the polynomial has a multiple root i.e. a root with multiplicity greater than one in the complex numbers.
  a. Thing
  b. Discriminant0
  c. Undefined
  d. Undefined

132. In mathematics, an _____ number is a complex number whose square is a negative real number. They were defined in 1572 by Rafael Bombelli.
  a. Thing
  b. Imaginary0
  c. Undefined
  d. Undefined

133. Compass and straightedge or ruler-and-compass _____ is the _____ of lengths or angles using only an idealized ruler and compass.
  a. Thing
  b. Construction0
  c. Undefined
  d. Undefined

134. _____ of an object is its speed in a particular direction.
  a. Velocity0
  b. Thing
  c. Undefined
  d. Undefined

135. Initial objects are also called _____, and terminal objects are also called final.
  a. Thing
  b. Coterminal0
  c. Undefined
  d. Undefined

136. _____ is a mathematical science pertaining to the collection, analysis, interpretation or explanation, and presentation of data. It is applicable to a wide variety of academic disciplines, from the physical and social sciences to the humanities.
  a. Thing
  b. Statistics0
  c. Undefined
  d. Undefined

137. A _____ can refer to a line joining two nonadjacent vertices of a polygon or polyhedron, or in some contexts any upward or downward sloping line. .

Chapter 2. Equations and Inequalities

a. Diagonal0
b. Thing
c. Undefined
d. Undefined

138. _____ is a relation in Euclidean geometry among the three sides of a right triangle.
   a. Thing
   b. Pythagorean Theorem0
   c. Undefined
   d. Undefined

139. In mathematics, a _____ is a statement that can be proved on the basis of explicitly stated or previously agreed assumptions.
   a. Theorem0
   b. Thing
   c. Undefined
   d. Undefined

140. In mathematics the _____ refers to the identity: $a^2 - b^2 = (a+b)(a-b)$
   a. Difference of two squares0
   b. Thing
   c. Undefined
   d. Undefined

141. _____ is a set, with some particular properties and usually some additional structure, such as the operations of addition or multiplication, for instance.
   a. Thing
   b. Space0
   c. Undefined
   d. Undefined

142. In geometry, _____ angles are angles that have a common ray coming out of the vertex going between two other rays.
   a. Adjacent0
   b. Concept
   c. Undefined
   d. Undefined

143. _____ are activities that are governed by a set of rules or customs and often engaged in competitively.
   a. Thing
   b. Sports0
   c. Undefined
   d. Undefined

144. The _____ of a right triangle is the triangle's longest side; the side opposite the right angle.
   a. Thing
   b. Hypotenuse0
   c. Undefined
   d. Undefined

145. _____ has one 90° internal angle a right angle.
   a. Right triangle0
   b. Thing
   c. Undefined
   d. Undefined

146. An _____ triange is a triangle with at least two sides of equal length.
   a. Thing
   b. Isosceles0
   c. Undefined
   d. Undefined

147. In geometry, an _____ polygon is a polygon which has all sides of the same length.
   a. Thing
   b. Equilateral0
   c. Undefined
   d. Undefined

Chapter 2. Equations and Inequalities

148. An _____ is a triangle in which all sides are of equal length.
    a. Thing
    b. Equilateral triangle0
    c. Undefined
    d. Undefined

149. In mathematics, _____ are two-dimensional manifolds or surfaces that are perfectly flat.
    a. Planes0
    b. Thing
    c. Undefined
    d. Undefined

150. In economics, supply and _____ describe market relations between prospective sellers and buyers of a good.
    a. Demand0
    b. Thing
    c. Undefined
    d. Undefined

151. In sociology and biology a _____ is the collection of people or organisms of a particular species living in a given geographic area or space, usually measured by a census.
    a. Population0
    b. Thing
    c. Undefined
    d. Undefined

152. In geometry, a _____ is a special kind of point, usually a corner of a polygon, polyhedron, or higher dimensional polytope. In the geometry of curves a _____ is a point of where the first derivative of curvature is zero. In graph theory, a _____ is the fundamental unit out of which graphs are formed
    a. Thing
    b. Vertex0
    c. Undefined
    d. Undefined

153. A _____ is a one-dimensional picture in which the integers are shown as specially-marked points evenly spaced on a line.
    a. Number line0
    b. Thing
    c. Undefined
    d. Undefined

154. In mathematics, the _____ i (or sometimes the Latin j or the Greek iota, see below) allows the real number system R to be extended to the complex number system C. Its precise definition is dependent upon the particular method of extension.
    a. Imaginary unit0
    b. Thing
    c. Undefined
    d. Undefined

155. In mathematics, a _____ is a number in the form of a + bi where a and b are real numbers, and i is the imaginary unit, with the property i 2 = −1. The real number a is called the real part of the _____, and the real number b is the imaginary part.
    a. Complex number0
    b. Thing
    c. Undefined
    d. Undefined

156. In mathematics, the _____ of a complex number z, is the first element of the ordered pair of real numbers representing z, i.e. if z = (x,y), or equivalently, z = x + iy, then the _____ of z is x. It is denoted by Re{z} . The complex function which maps z to the _____ of z is not holomorphic.
    a. Thing
    b. Real part0
    c. Undefined
    d. Undefined

Chapter 2. Equations and Inequalities

157. In mathematics, the _____ of a complex number z, is the second element of the ordered pair of real numbers representing z, i.e. if z = (x,y), or equivalently, z = x + iy, then the _____ of z is y.
   a. Thing
   b. Imaginary part0
   c. Undefined
   d. Undefined

158. In mathematics, an _____ is a complex number whose square is a negative real number. They were defined in 1572 by Rafael Bombelli.
   a. Imaginary number0
   b. Thing
   c. Undefined
   d. Undefined

159. In algebra, a _____ is a binomial formed by taking the opposite of the second term of a binomial.
   a. Conjugate0
   b. Thing
   c. Undefined
   d. Undefined

160. _____ is a set of numbers, in the broadest sense of the word, together with one or more operations, such as addition or multiplication.
   a. Thing
   b. Number system0
   c. Undefined
   d. Undefined

161. _____ element of an element x with respect to a binary operation * with identity element e is an element y such that x * y = y * x = e. In particular,
   a. Thing
   b. Inverse0
   c. Undefined
   d. Undefined

162. In mathematics, the _____ inverse, or opposite, of a number n is the number that, when added to n, yields zero. The _____ inverse of n is denoted −n.
   a. Thing
   b. Additive0
   c. Undefined
   d. Undefined

163. In mathematics the _____ of a set which is equipped with the operation of addition is an element which, when added to any other element x in the set, yields x.
   a. Concept
   b. Additive identity0
   c. Undefined
   d. Undefined

164. _____, either of the curved-bracket punctuation marks that together make a set of _____
   a. Parentheses0
   b. Thing
   c. Undefined
   d. Undefined

165. In statistics, a _____ measure is one which is measuring what is supposed to measure.
   a. Thing
   b. Valid0
   c. Undefined
   d. Undefined

166. In mathematics, and in particular in abstract algebra, the _____ is a property of binary operations that generalises the distributive law from elementary algebra.

Chapter 2. Equations and Inequalities

a. Distributive property0
b. Thing
c. Undefined
d. Undefined

167. A _____ is a number that is less than zero.
a. Negative number0
b. Thing
c. Undefined
d. Undefined

168. Electrical _____, or simply _____, is a term coined by Oliver Heaviside in July of 1886 to describe a measure of opposition to a sinusoidal alternating current.
a. Impedance0
b. Thing
c. Undefined
d. Undefined

169. _____ has many meanings, most of which simply .
a. Thing
b. Power0
c. Undefined
d. Undefined

170. In mathematics, in the field of group theory, a _____ of a group is a quasisimple subnormal subgroup.
a. Concept
b. Component0
c. Undefined
d. Undefined

171. _____ is the study of error, particularly in the fields of applied mathematics, applied linguistics, statistics, and numerical analysis.
a. Thing
b. Error analysis0
c. Undefined
d. Undefined

172. In mathematics, a _____ is a demonstration that, assuming certain axioms, some statement is necessarily true.
a. Proof0
b. Thing
c. Undefined
d. Undefined

173. In mathematics, _____ are used to indicate the square root of a number.
a. Thing
b. Radicals0
c. Undefined
d. Undefined

174. In abstract algebra, _____ consists of sets with binary operations that satisfy certain axioms.
a. Grouping0
b. Thing
c. Undefined
d. Undefined

175. In mathematics, a _____ number is a number which can be expressed as a ratio of two integers. Non-integer _____ numbers (commonly called fractions) are usually written as the vulgar fraction a / b, where b is not zero.
a. Thing
b. Rational0
c. Undefined
d. Undefined

176. _____ systems represent systems whose behavior is not expressible as a sum of the behaviors of its descriptors.

Chapter 2. Equations and Inequalities 43

    a. Thing
    c. Undefined
    b. Nonlinear0
    d. Undefined

177. _____ is the speed of an aircraft relative to the air.
    a. Airspeed0
    c. Undefined
    b. Thing
    d. Undefined

178. _____ is mass m per unit volume V.
    a. Density0
    c. Undefined
    b. Thing
    d. Undefined

179. A _____ is a form of collective investment that pools money from many investors and invests their money in stocks, bonds, short-term money market instruments, and/or other securities.
    a. Thing
    c. Undefined
    b. Mutual fund0
    d. Undefined

180. _____ is steam at the temperature at which evaporation occurs.
    a. Saturated steam0
    c. Undefined
    b. Thing
    d. Undefined

181. _____ is the interdisciplinary scientific study of the atmosphere that focuses on weather processes and forecasting.
    a. Meteorology0
    c. Undefined
    b. Thing
    d. Undefined

182. A _____ is a three-dimensional geometric shape formed by straight lines through a fixed point (vertex) to the points of a fixed curve (directrix)
    a. Concept
    c. Undefined
    b. Cone0
    d. Undefined

183. In linear algebra, the _____ of an n-by-n square matrix A is defined to be the sum of the elements on the main diagonal of A,
    a. Thing
    c. Undefined
    b. Trace0
    d. Undefined

184. In geographic information systems, a _____ comprises an entity with a geographic location, typically determined by points, arcs, or polygons. Carriageways and cadastres exemplify _____ data.
    a. Feature0
    c. Undefined
    b. Thing
    d. Undefined

185. The mathematical concept of a _____ expresses the intuitive idea of deterministic dependence between two quantities, one of which is viewed as primary and the other as secondary. A _____ then is a way to associate a unique output for each input of a specified type, for example, a real number or an element of a given set.
    a. Thing
    c. Undefined
    b. Function0
    d. Undefined

Chapter 2. Equations and Inequalities

186. A _____ is a set whose members are members of another set or a set contained within another set.
   a. Thing
   b. Subset0
   c. Undefined
   d. Undefined

187. _____ are groups whose members are members of another set or a set contained within another set.
   a. Subsets0
   b. Thing
   c. Undefined
   d. Undefined

188. A _____ is a set of possible values that a variable can take on in order to satisfy a given set of conditions, which may include equations and inequalities.
   a. Solution set0
   b. Thing
   c. Undefined
   d. Undefined

189. In elementary algebra, an _____ is a set that contains every real number between two indicated numbers and may contain the two numbers themselves.
   a. Interval0
   b. Thing
   c. Undefined
   d. Undefined

190. In mathematical analysis and related areas of mathematics, a set is called _____, if it is, in a certain sense, of finite size.
   a. Bounded0
   b. Thing
   c. Undefined
   d. Undefined

191. Mathematical _____ is used to represent ideas.
   a. Notation0
   b. Thing
   c. Undefined
   d. Undefined

192. The _____ is the number or expression underneath the radical sign.
   a. Thing
   b. Radicand0
   c. Undefined
   d. Undefined

193. _____ is the act of transforming data with the aim of extracting useful information and facilitating conclusions.
   a. Data analysis0
   b. Concept
   c. Undefined
   d. Undefined

194. _____ are determined by the level of intelligence performed by an individual.
   a. IQ scores0
   b. Thing
   c. Undefined
   d. Undefined

195. _____ is the production of food, feed, fiber, fuel and other goods by the systematic raizing of plants and animals.
   a. Thing
   b. Agriculture0
   c. Undefined
   d. Undefined

196. _____ is the estimation of a physical quantity such as distance, energy, temperature, or time.

a. Thing
b. Measurement0
c. Undefined
d. Undefined

197. _____ is the application of tools and a processing medium to the transformation of raw materials into finished goods for sale.
   a. Manufacturing0
   b. Thing
   c. Undefined
   d. Undefined

198. Multiple Signal Classification, also known as _____, is an algorithm used for frequency estimation and emitter location.
   a. Thing
   b. Music0
   c. Undefined
   d. Undefined

199. In statistics the _____ of an event i is the number n_i of times the event occurred in the experiment or the study. These frequencies are often graphically represented in histograms.
   a. Concept
   b. Frequency0
   c. Undefined
   d. Undefined

200. A _____ consists of one quarter of the coordinate plane.
   a. Thing
   b. Quadrant0
   c. Undefined
   d. Undefined

201. In mathematics, defined and _____ are used to explain whether or not expressions have meaningful, sensible, and unambiguous values.
   a. Undefined0
   b. Thing
   c. Undefined
   d. Undefined

202. _____ is the notation in which permitted values for a variable are expressed as ranging over a certain interval; "5 < x < 9" is an example of the application of _____.
   a. Interval notation0
   b. Thing
   c. Undefined
   d. Undefined

203. A _____ is any object propelled through space by the applicationp of a force.
   a. Thing
   b. Projectile0
   c. Undefined
   d. Undefined

204. Deductive _____ is the kind of _____ in which the conclusion is necessitated by, or reached from, previously known facts (the premises).
   a. Thing
   b. Reasoning0
   c. Undefined
   d. Undefined

205. In mathematics, a _____ is a mathematical statement which appears likely to be true, but has not been formally proven to be true under the rules of mathematical logic.
   a. Conjecture0
   b. Concept
   c. Undefined
   d. Undefined

206. In geometry, an _____ is a point at which a line segment or ray terminates.
   a. Thing
   b. Endpoint0
   c. Undefined
   d. Undefined

207. In physics, _____ is an influence that may cause an object to accelerate. It may be experienced as a lift, a push, or a pull. The actual acceleration of the body is determined by the vector sum of all forces acting on it, known as net _____ or resultant _____.
   a. Force0
   b. Thing
   c. Undefined
   d. Undefined

208. A _____, lamp post, street lamp, light standard or lamp standard, is a raised source of light on the edge of a road, turned on or lit at a certain time every night.
   a. Thing
   b. Streetlight0
   c. Undefined
   d. Undefined

209. The _____ of an object is the extra energy which it possesses due to its motion.
   a. Kinetic energy0
   b. Thing
   c. Undefined
   d. Undefined

210. _____, in economics and political economy, are the distributions or payments awarded to the various suppliers of the factors of production.
   a. Returns0
   b. Thing
   c. Undefined
   d. Undefined

211. In mathematics, an _____ .
   a. Ellipse0
   b. Thing
   c. Undefined
   d. Undefined

212. In mathematics, a _____ is a condition that a solution to an optimization problem must satisfy in order to be acceptable.
   a. Thing
   b. Constraint0
   c. Undefined
   d. Undefined

213. Mathematical _____ are demonstrations that, assuming certain axioms, some statement is necessarily true.
   a. Thing
   b. Proofs0
   c. Undefined
   d. Undefined

214. A _____ consists either of a suggested explanation for a phenomenon or of a reasoned proposal suggesting a possible correlation between multiple phenomena.
   a. Hypothesis0
   b. Thing
   c. Undefined
   d. Undefined

215. In a mathematical proof or a syllogism, a _____ is a statement that is the logical consequence of preceding statements.

Chapter 2. Equations and Inequalities   47

a. Concept
b. Conclusion0
c. Undefined
d. Undefined

216. In logic, and especially in its applications to mathematics and philosophy, a _____ is an exception to a proposed general rule, i.e., a specific instance of the falsity of a universal quantification (a "for all" statement).
a. Thing
b. Counterexample0
c. Undefined
d. Undefined

217. In logic and mathematics, _____ is an operation on logical values, for example, the logical value of a proposition, that sends true to false and false to true.
a. Person
b. Negation0
c. Undefined
d. Undefined

218. Contraposition is the concept of how two qualities or statements relate to each other. In mathematics, in a statement "if P then Q" for any two propositions P and Q, then the converse is "if Q then P", the inverse is "if not P then not Q", and the _____ is "if not Q then not P".
a. Thing
b. Contrapositive0
c. Undefined
d. Undefined

219. _____ Logic is a concept in traditional logic referring to a "type of immediate inference in which from a given proposition another proposition is inferred which has as its subject the predicate of the original proposition and as its predicate the subject of the original proposition (the quality of the proposition being retained)."
a. Concept
b. Converse0
c. Undefined
d. Undefined

220. In mathematical logic, a Gödel numbering (or Gödel _____) is a function that assigns to each symbol and well-formed formula of some formal language a unique natural number called its Gödel number.
a. Thing
b. Code0
c. Undefined
d. Undefined

221. _____ is a term applied when talking about the movement of air from one place to the next.
a. Thing
b. Wind speed0
c. Undefined
d. Undefined

222. In mathematics, a _____ is an n-tuple with n being 3.
a. Triple0
b. Thing
c. Undefined
d. Undefined

223. In mathematics, the _____ of an integer n, also called a factor of n, is an integer which evenly divides n without leaving a remainder.
a. Divisibility0
b. Thing
c. Undefined
d. Undefined

224. A _____ of a number is a number a such that $a^3 = x$.

a. Thing
c. Undefined
b. Cube root0
d. Undefined

225. In mathematics, the _____ inverse of a number x, denoted 1/x or x^{-1}, is the number which, when multiplied by x, yields 1. The _____ inverse of x is also called the reciprocal of x.
a. Thing
c. Undefined
b. Multiplicative0
d. Undefined

226. In colloquial usage, a _____ is "a rough or fragmented geometric shape that can be subdivided in parts, each of which is, at least approximately, a reduced-size copy of the whole."
a. Fractal0
c. Undefined
b. Concept
d. Undefined

227. _____, is a Franco-American mathematician, best known as the "father of fractal geometry".
a. Benoit Mandelbrot0
c. Undefined
b. Person
d. Undefined

Chapter 3. Functions and Their Graphs

1. A _____ is a symbolic representation denoting a quantity or expression. It often represents an "unknown" quantity that has the potential to change.
   - a. Variable0
   - b. Thing
   - c. Undefined
   - d. Undefined

2. _____ are the basic objects of study in graph theory. Informally speaking, a graph is a set of objects called points, nodes, or vertices connected by links called lines or edges.
   - a. Graphs0
   - b. Thing
   - c. Undefined
   - d. Undefined

3. _____ is often used to describe the measurement of the steepness, incline, gradient, or grade of a straight line. The _____ is defined as the ratio of the "rise" divided by the "run" between two points on a line, or in other words, the ratio of the altitude change to the horizontal distance between any two points on the line.
   - a. Thing
   - b. Slope0
   - c. Undefined
   - d. Undefined

4. The word _____ comes from the Latin word linearis, which means created by lines.
   - a. Linear0
   - b. Thing
   - c. Undefined
   - d. Undefined

5. A _____ is an equation in which each term is either a constant or the product of a constant times the first power of a variable.
   - a. Thing
   - b. Linear equation0
   - c. Undefined
   - d. Undefined

6. A _____ is an abstract model that uses mathematical language to describe the behavior of a system. Eykhoff defined a _____ as 'a representation of the essential aspects of an existing system which presents knowledge of that system in usable form'.
   - a. Thing
   - b. Mathematical model0
   - c. Undefined
   - d. Undefined

7. The mathematical concept of a _____ expresses the intuitive idea of deterministic dependence between two quantities, one of which is viewed as primary and the other as secondary. A _____ then is a way to associate a unique output for each input of a specified type, for example, a real number or an element of a given set.
   - a. Thing
   - b. Function0
   - c. Undefined
   - d. Undefined

8. In plane geometry, a _____ is a polygon with four equal sides, four right angles, and parallel opposite sides. In algebra, the _____ of a number is that number multiplied by itself.
   - a. Thing
   - b. Square0
   - c. Undefined
   - d. Undefined

9. In geometry, two lines or planes if one falls on the other in such a way as to create congruent adjacent angles. The term may be used as a noun or adjective. Thus, referring to Figure 1, the line AB is the _____ to CD through the point B.
   - a. Perpendicular0
   - b. Thing
   - c. Undefined
   - d. Undefined

Chapter 3. Functions and Their Graphs

10. In mathematics, defined and _____ are used to explain whether or not expressions have meaningful, sensible, and unambiguous values.
    a. Undefined0
    b. Thing
    c. Undefined
    d. Undefined

11. The _____ of measurement are a globally standardized and modernized form of the metric system.
    a. Units0
    b. Thing
    c. Undefined
    d. Undefined

12. A _____ is a quantity that denotes the proportional amount or magnitude of one quantity relative to another.
    a. Ratio0
    b. Thing
    c. Undefined
    d. Undefined

13. A _____ is a function that assigns a number to subsets of a given set.
    a. Measure0
    b. Thing
    c. Undefined
    d. Undefined

14. A _____ is a special kind of ratio, indicating a relationship between two measurements with different units, such as miles to gallons or cents to pounds.
    a. Thing
    b. Rate0
    c. Undefined
    d. Undefined

15. _____ is the application of tools and a processing medium to the transformation of raw materials into finished goods for sale.
    a. Thing
    b. Manufacturing0
    c. Undefined
    d. Undefined

16. Fixed costs are expenses whose total does not change in proportion to the activity of a business.Unit fixed costs decline with volume following a retangular hyperbola as the volume of production.Variable costs by contrast change in relation to the activity of a business such as sales or production volume.Along with variable costs,fixed costs make up one of the two components of total cost. In the most simple production function total cost is equal to fixed costs plus variable costs.In accounting terminology, fixed costs will broadly include all costs which are not included in cost of goods sold, and variable costs are those captured in costs of goods sold. The implicit assumption required to make the equivalence between the accounting and economics terminology is that the accounting period is equal to the period in which fixed costs do not vary in relation to production. In practice, this equivalence does not always hold and depending on the period under consideration by management, some overhead expenses can be adjusted by management, and the specific allocation of each expense to each category will be decided under cost accounting.In business planning and management accounting, usage of the terms fixed costs, variable costs and others will often differ from usage in economics, and may depend on the intended use. For example, costs may be segregated into per unit costs fixed costs per period, and variable costs as a proportion of revenue. Capital expenditures will usually be allocated separately, and depending on the purpose, a portion may be regularly allocated to expenses as depreciation and amortization and seen as a _____ per period, or the entire amount may be considered upfront fixed costs.
    a. Thing
    b. Fixed cost0
    c. Undefined
    d. Undefined

Chapter 3. Functions and Their Graphs

17. In finance, a _____ is collateral that the holder of a position in securities, options, or futures contracts has to deposit to cover the credit risk of his counterparty.
   a. Margin0
   b. Thing
   c. Undefined
   d. Undefined

18. _____ is a kind of property which exists as magnitude or multitude. It is among the basic classes of things along with quality, substance, change, and relation.
   a. Thing
   b. Amount0
   c. Undefined
   d. Undefined

19. A _____ is a numeral used to indicate a count. The most common use of the word today is to name the part of a fraction that tells the number or count of equal parts.
   a. Thing
   b. Numerator0
   c. Undefined
   d. Undefined

20. A _____ is the part of a fraction that tells how many equal parts make up a whole, and which is used in the name of the fraction: "halves", "thirds", "fourths" or "quarters", "fifths" and so on.
   a. Denominator0
   b. Concept
   c. Undefined
   d. Undefined

21. In mathematics, an _____ on a real vector space is a choice of which ordered bases are "positively" oriented, or right-handed, and which are "negatively" oriented, or left-handed.
   a. Thing
   b. Orientation0
   c. Undefined
   d. Undefined

22. _____ is a business term for the amount of money that a company receives from its activities in a given period, mostly from sales of products and/or services to customers
   a. Thing
   b. Revenue0
   c. Undefined
   d. Undefined

23. _____ is a synonym for information.
   a. Thing
   b. Data0
   c. Undefined
   d. Undefined

24. One of the three formats applicable to a quadratic function is the _____ which is defined as $f = ax^2 + bx + c$.
   a. General form0
   b. Thing
   c. Undefined
   d. Undefined

25. _____ is a term used in accounting, economics and finance with reference to the fact that assets with finite lives lose value over time.
   a. Depreciation0
   b. Thing
   c. Undefined
   d. Undefined

26. _____ is a term that has several possible meanings all closely related to a firm's financial statements.

a. Thing
b. Book value0
c. Undefined
d. Undefined

27. A _____ is a set of numbers that designate location in a given reference system, such as x,y in a planar _____ system or an x,y,z in a three-dimensional _____ system.
   a. Coordinate0
   b. Thing
   c. Undefined
   d. Undefined

28. An _____ is when two lines intersect somewhere on a plane creating a right angle at intersection
   a. Axes0
   b. Thing
   c. Undefined
   d. Undefined

29. In mathematics, the conjugate _____ or adjoint matrix of an m-by-n matrix A with complex entries is the n-by-m matrix A* obtained from A by taking the transpose and then taking the complex conjugate of each entry.
   a. Pairs0
   b. Thing
   c. Undefined
   d. Undefined

30. _____, or EPS are the earnings returned on the initial investment amount.
   a. Thing
   b. Earnings per share0
   c. Undefined
   d. Undefined

31. In geometry, a line _____ is a part of a line that is bounded by two end points, and contains every point on the line between its end points.
   a. Segment0
   b. Concept
   c. Undefined
   d. Undefined

32. A _____ is a part of a line that is bounded by two end points, and contains every point on the line between its end points.
   a. Line segment0
   b. Thing
   c. Undefined
   d. Undefined

33. In topology and related areas of mathematics a _____ or Moore-Smith sequence is a generalization of a sequence, intended to unify the various notions of limit and generalize them to arbitrary topological spaces.
   a. Net0
   b. Thing
   c. Undefined
   d. Undefined

34. _____ is an accounting term which is commonly used in business.
   a. Thing
   b. Net profit0
   c. Undefined
   d. Undefined

35. _____, from Latin meaning "to make progress", is defined in two different ways. Pure economic _____ is the increase in wealth that an investor has from making an investment, taking into consideration all costs associated with that investment including the opportunity cost of capital.
   a. Profit0
   b. Thing
   c. Undefined
   d. Undefined

Chapter 3. Functions and Their Graphs

36. A _____ is a tool similar to a ruler, but without markings.
    a. Straightedge0
    b. Thing
    c. Undefined
    d. Undefined

37. In mathematics, a _____ is the result of multiplying, or an expression that identifies factors to be multiplied.
    a. Thing
    b. Product0
    c. Undefined
    d. Undefined

38. A _____ is a type of debt. All material things can be lent but this article focuses exclusively on monetary loans. Like all debt instruments, a _____ entails the redistribution of financial assets over time, between the lender and the borrower.
    a. Thing
    b. Loan0
    c. Undefined
    d. Undefined

39. A _____ is a unit of length, usually used to measure distance, in a number of different systems, including Imperial units, United States customary units and Norwegian/Swedish mil. Its size can vary from system to system, but in each is between 1 and 10 kilometers. In contemporary English contexts _____ refers to either:
    a. Thing
    b. Mile0
    c. Undefined
    d. Undefined

40. Any point where a graph makes contact with an coordinate axis is called an _____ of the graph
    a. Intercept0
    b. Thing
    c. Undefined
    d. Undefined

41. The existence and properties of _____ are the basis of Euclid's parallel postulate. _____ are two lines on the same plane that do not intersect even assuming that lines extend to infinity in either direction.
    a. Parallel lines0
    b. Thing
    c. Undefined
    d. Undefined

42. In geometry and trigonometry, a _____ is defined as an angle between two straight intersecting lines of ninety degrees, or one-quarter of a circle.
    a. Thing
    b. Right angle0
    c. Undefined
    d. Undefined

43. _____ usually refers to money in the form of liquid currency, such as banknotes or coins.
    a. Cash0
    b. Thing
    c. Undefined
    d. Undefined

44. _____ is a form of periodic payment from an employer to an employee, which is specified in an employment contract.
    a. Gross pay0
    b. Thing
    c. Undefined
    d. Undefined

45. A _____ is a craftsman who creates jewelry using jewels, precious metals, or other substances.

Chapter 3. Functions and Their Graphs

    a. Thing   b. Jeweler0
    c. Undefined   d. Undefined

46. A _____ is a form of periodic payment from an employer to an employee, which is specified in an employment contract.
    a. Thing   b. Salary0
    c. Undefined   d. Undefined

47. In finance and economics, _____ is the process of finding the present value of an amount of cash at some future date, and along with compounding cash forms the basis of time value of money calculations.
    a. Thing   b. Discount0
    c. Undefined   d. Undefined

48. In mathematics, an _____, mean, or central tendency of a data set refers to a measure of the "middle" or "expected" value of the data set.
    a. Average0   b. Concept
    c. Undefined   d. Undefined

49. In economics, supply and _____ describe market relations between prospective sellers and buyers of a good.
    a. Thing   b. Demand0
    c. Undefined   d. Undefined

50. The metre (or _____, see spelling differences) is a measure of length. It is the basic unit of length in the metric system and in the International System of Units (SI), used around the world for general and scientific purposes.
    a. Concept   b. Meter0
    c. Undefined   d. Undefined

51. A _____ is a simplified and structured visual representation of concepts, ideas, constructions, relations, statistical data, anatomy etc used in all aspects of human activities to visualize and clarify the topic.
    a. Thing   b. Diagram0
    c. Undefined   d. Undefined

52. _____ is the distance around a given two-dimensional object. As a general rule, the _____ of a polygon can always be calculated by adding all the length of the sides together. So, the formula for triangles is P = a + b + c, where a, b and c stand for each side of it. For quadrilaterals the equation is P = a + b + c + d. For equilateral polygons, P = na, where n is the number of sides and a is the side length.
    a. Perimeter0   b. Thing
    c. Undefined   d. Undefined

53. The payment of _____ as remuneration for services rendered or products sold is a common way to reward sales people.
    a. Thing   b. Commission0
    c. Undefined   d. Undefined

54. _____ are activities that are governed by a set of rules or customs and often engaged in competitively.

Chapter 3. Functions and Their Graphs

a. Sports0
b. Thing
c. Undefined
d. Undefined

55. A _____, scatter diagram or scatter graph is a chart that uses Cartesian coordinates to display values for two variables.
   a. Scatter plot0
   b. Thing
   c. Undefined
   d. Undefined

56. _____ is the act of transforming data with the aim of extracting useful information and facilitating conclusions.
   a. Concept
   b. Data analysis0
   c. Undefined
   d. Undefined

57. In mathematics, a _____ function in the sense of algebraic geometry is an everywhere-defined, polynomial function on an algebraic variety V with values in the field K over which V is defined.
   a. Thing
   b. Regular0
   c. Undefined
   d. Undefined

58. _____ is a branch of mathematics concerning the study of structure, relation and quantity.
   a. Concept
   b. Algebra0
   c. Undefined
   d. Undefined

59. Acid _____ ratio measures the ability of a company to use its near cash or quick assets to immediately extinguish its current liabilities.
   a. Thing
   b. Test0
   c. Undefined
   d. Undefined

60. In common philosophical language, a proposition or _____, is the content of an assertion, that is, it is true-or-false and defined by the meaning of a particular piece of language.
   a. Concept
   b. Statement0
   c. Undefined
   d. Undefined

61. Mathematical _____ is used to represent ideas.
   a. Thing
   b. Notation0
   c. Undefined
   d. Undefined

62. An _____ or member of a set is an object that when collected together make up the set.
   a. Element0
   b. Thing
   c. Undefined
   d. Undefined

63. In mathematics, the _____ of a function is the set of all "output" values produced by that function. Given a function $f : A \to B$, the _____ of f, is defined to be the set $\{x \in B : x = f(a) \text{ for some } a \in A\}$.
   a. Thing
   b. Range0
   c. Undefined
   d. Undefined

64. In mathematics, there are several meanings of _____ depending on the subject.

Chapter 3. Functions and Their Graphs

    a. Thing
    c. Undefined
    b. Degree0
    d. Undefined

65. _____ is a physical property of a system that underlies the common notions of hot and cold; something that is hotter has the greater _____.
    a. Temperature0
    b. Thing
    c. Undefined
    d. Undefined

66. In mathematics, a _____ of a k-place relation $L \subseteq X_1 \times \ldots \times X_k$ is one of the sets X_j, $1 \leq j \leq k$. In the special case where k = 2 and $L \subseteq X_1 \times X_2$ is a function $L : X_1 \to X_2$, it is conventional to refer to X_1 as the _____ of the function and to refer to X_2 as the codomain of the function.
    a. Thing
    b. Domain0
    c. Undefined
    d. Undefined

67. In mathematics and the mathematical sciences, a _____ is a fixed, but possibly unspecified, value. This is in contrast to a variable, which is not fixed.
    a. Constant0
    b. Thing
    c. Undefined
    d. Undefined

68. _____ is a function whose values do not vary and thus are constant.
    a. Constant function0
    b. Thing
    c. Undefined
    d. Undefined

69. An _____ is a collection of two not necessarily distinct objects, one of which is distinguished as the first coordinate and the other as the second coordinate.
    a. Ordered pair0
    b. Thing
    c. Undefined
    d. Undefined

70. The word _____ comes from the 15th Century Latin word discretus which means separate.
    a. Thing
    b. Discrete0
    c. Undefined
    d. Undefined

71. _____ are objects, characters, or other concrete representations of ideas, concepts, or other abstractions.
    a. Thing
    b. Symbols0
    c. Undefined
    d. Undefined

72. Leonhard _____ was a pioneering Swiss mathematician and physicist, who spent most of his life in Russia and Germany.
    a. Euler0
    b. Person
    c. Undefined
    d. Undefined

73. In mathematics, an _____ is any of the arguments, i.e. "inputs", to a function. Thus if we have a function f(x), then x is a _____.
    a. Thing
    b. Independent variable0
    c. Undefined
    d. Undefined

Chapter 3. Functions and Their Graphs

74. In a function the _____, is the variable which is the value, i.e. the "output", of the function.
    a. Thing
    b. Dependent variable0
    c. Undefined
    d. Undefined

75. An _____ is a combination of numbers, operators, grouping symbols and/or free variables and bound variables arranged in a meaningful way which can be evaluated..
    a. Thing
    b. Expression0
    c. Undefined
    d. Undefined

76. In financial mathematics, the _____ volatility of an option contract is the volatility _____ by the market price of the option based on an option pricing model.
    a. Thing
    b. Implied0
    c. Undefined
    d. Undefined

77. In mathematics, a _____ may be described informally as a number that can be given by an infinite decimal representation.
    a. Real number0
    b. Thing
    c. Undefined
    d. Undefined

78. A _____ is a number that is less than zero.
    a. Negative number0
    b. Thing
    c. Undefined
    d. Undefined

79. In mathematics, a _____ of a complex-valued function f is a member x of the domain of f such that f(x) vanishes at x, that is, x : f (x) = 0.
    a. Thing
    b. Root0
    c. Undefined
    d. Undefined

80. In elementary algebra, an _____ is a set that contains every real number between two indicated numbers and may contain the two numbers themselves.
    a. Interval0
    b. Thing
    c. Undefined
    d. Undefined

81. The _____ of a solid object is the three-dimensional concept of how much space it occupies, often quantified numerically.
    a. Thing
    b. Volume0
    c. Undefined
    d. Undefined

82. In classical geometry, a _____ of a circle or sphere is any line segment from its center to its boundary. By extension, the _____ of a circle or sphere is the length of any such segment. The _____ is half the diameter. In science and engineering the term _____ of curvature is commonly used as a synonym for _____.
    a. Thing
    b. Radius0
    c. Undefined
    d. Undefined

Chapter 3. Functions and Their Graphs

83. In mathematics, a _____ is the set of all points in three-dimensional space (R^3) which are at distance r from a fixed point of that space, where r is a positive real number called the radius of the _____. The fixed point is called the center or centre, and is not part of the _____ itself.
   a. Sphere0
   b. Thing
   c. Undefined
   d. Undefined

84. _____ of an object is its speed in a particular direction.
   a. Thing
   b. Velocity0
   c. Undefined
   d. Undefined

85. In economics _____ means before deductions brutto, e.g. _____ domestic or national product, or _____ profit or income
   a. Gross0
   b. Thing
   c. Undefined
   d. Undefined

86. _____ is a United States tax term for an amount used in the calculation of an individual's income tax liability
   a. Thing
   b. Adjusted gross income0
   c. Undefined
   d. Undefined

87. In mathematics, a _____ is the end result of a division problem. It can also be expressed as the number of times the divisor divides into the dividend.
   a. Thing
   b. Quotient0
   c. Undefined
   d. Undefined

88. The function difference divided by the point difference is known as the _____
   a. Difference quotient0
   b. Thing
   c. Undefined
   d. Undefined

89. _____ is a mathematical subject that includes the study of limits, derivatives, integrals, and power series and constitutes a major part of modern university curriculum.
   a. Thing
   b. Calculus0
   c. Undefined
   d. Undefined

90. A _____ is one of the basic shapes of geometry: a polygon with three vertices and three sides which are straight line segments.
   a. Triangle0
   b. Thing
   c. Undefined
   d. Undefined

91. A _____ consists of one quarter of the coordinate plane.
   a. Quadrant0
   b. Thing
   c. Undefined
   d. Undefined

92. _____ has one 90° internal angle a right angle.
   a. Right triangle0
   b. Thing
   c. Undefined
   d. Undefined

Chapter 3. Functions and Their Graphs 59

93. In geometry, a _____ is defined as a quadrilateral where all four of its angles are right angles.
   a. Rectangle0
   b. Thing
   c. Undefined
   d. Undefined

94. In mathematical analysis and related areas of mathematics, a set is called _____, if it is, in a certain sense, of finite size.
   a. Bounded0
   b. Thing
   c. Undefined
   d. Undefined

95. In geometry, a _____ is the intersection of a body in 2-dimensional space with a line, or of a body in 3-dimensional space with a plane
   a. Thing
   b. Cross section0
   c. Undefined
   d. Undefined

96. _____ are expenses whose total does not change in proportion to the activity of a business, within the relevant time period or scale of production
   a. Thing
   b. Fixed costs0
   c. Undefined
   d. Undefined

97. A _____ is the result of the addition of a set of numbers. The numbers may be natural numbers, complex numbers, matrices, or still more complicated objects. An infinite _____ is a subtle procedure known as a series.
   a. Sum0
   b. Thing
   c. Undefined
   d. Undefined

98. Transport or _____ is the movement of people and goods from one place to another.
   a. Transportation0
   b. Thing
   c. Undefined
   d. Undefined

99. _____, Greek for "knowledge of nature," is the branch of science concerned with the discovery and characterization of universal laws which govern matter, energy, space, and time.
   a. Thing
   b. Physics0
   c. Undefined
   d. Undefined

100. In physics, _____ is an influence that may cause an object to accelerate. It may be experienced as a lift, a push, or a pull. The actual acceleration of the body is determined by the vector sum of all forces acting on it, known as net _____ or resultant _____.
   a. Force0
   b. Thing
   c. Undefined
   d. Undefined

101. In astronomy, geography, geometry and related sciences and contexts, a plane is said to be _____ at a given point if it is locally perpendicular to the gradient of the gravity field, i.e., with the direction of the gravitational force at that point.
   a. Thing
   b. Horizontal0
   c. Undefined
   d. Undefined

102. _____ refers to all non-domesticated plants, animals, and other organisms.

Chapter 3. Functions and Their Graphs

a. Thing
b. Wildlife0
c. Undefined
d. Undefined

103. _____ is a test to determine if a relation or its graph is a function or not
   a. Thing
   b. Vertical line test0
   c. Undefined
   d. Undefined

104. In mathematics, the _____ f is the collection of all ordered pairs . In particular, graph means the graphical representation of this collection, in the form of a curve or surface, together with axes, etc. Graphing on a Cartesian plane is sometimes referred to as curve sketching.
   a. Graph of a function0
   b. Thing
   c. Undefined
   d. Undefined

105. In mathematics, a _____ is a two-dimensional manifold or surface that is perfectly flat.
   a. Thing
   b. Plane0
   c. Undefined
   d. Undefined

106. The _____ is the highest point in a certain portion of a graph.
   a. Relative maximum0
   b. Thing
   c. Undefined
   d. Undefined

107. The _____ is the lowest point in a certain portion of a graph.
   a. Relative minimum0
   b. Thing
   c. Undefined
   d. Undefined

108. In mathematics, a _____ is an expression that is constructed from one or more variables and constants, using only the operations of addition, subtraction, multiplication, and constant positive whole number exponents. is a _____. Note in particular that division by an expression containing a variable is not in general allowed in polynomials. [1]
   a. Polynomial0
   b. Thing
   c. Undefined
   d. Undefined

109. _____ means "constancy", i.e. if something retains a certain feature even after we change a way of looking at it, then it is symmetric.
   a. Thing
   b. Symmetry0
   c. Undefined
   d. Undefined

110. In mathematics, the _____ of a coordinate system is the point where the axes of the system intersect.
   a. Thing
   b. Origin0
   c. Undefined
   d. Undefined

111. _____ is the study of terms and their use — of words and compound words that are used in specific contexts.
   a. Terminology0
   b. Thing
   c. Undefined
   d. Undefined

112. In mathematics, and in particular in abstract algebra, the _____ is a property of binary operations that generalises the distributive law from elementary algebra.

Chapter 3. Functions and Their Graphs

a. Distributive property0
b. Thing
c. Undefined
d. Undefined

113. _____ are functions which satisfy particular symmetry relations, with respect to taking additive inverses.
   a. Even function0
   b. Thing
   c. Undefined
   d. Undefined

114. _____ is electric power as defined as the amount of work done by an electric current, or the rate at which electrical energy is transferred.
   a. Wattage0
   b. Thing
   c. Undefined
   d. Undefined

115. _____ is electromagnetic radiation with a wavelength that is visible to the eye (visible _____) or, in a technical or scientific context, electromagnetic radiation of any wavelength.
   a. Light0
   b. Thing
   c. Undefined
   d. Undefined

116. In geographic information systems, a _____ comprises an entity with a geographic location, typically determined by points, arcs, or polygons. Carriageways and cadastres exemplify _____ data.
   a. Feature0
   b. Thing
   c. Undefined
   d. Undefined

117. _____ is the difference between the monetary value of exports and imports in an economy over a certain period of time.
   a. Thing
   b. Trade balance0
   c. Undefined
   d. Undefined

118. In banking and accountancy, the outstanding _____ is the amount of money owned, or due, that remains in a deposit account or a loan account at a given date, after all past remittances, payments and withdrawal have been accounted for.
   a. Balance0
   b. Thing
   c. Undefined
   d. Undefined

119. In sociology and biology a _____ is the collection of people or organisms of a particular species living in a given geographic area or space, usually measured by a census.
   a. Thing
   b. Population0
   c. Undefined
   d. Undefined

120. _____ is a way of expressing a number as a fraction of 100 per cent meaning "per hundred".
   a. Percent0
   b. Thing
   c. Undefined
   d. Undefined

121. In mathematics, a _____ is a mathematical statement which appears likely to be true, but has not been formally proven to be true under the rules of mathematical logic.

Chapter 3. Functions and Their Graphs

    a. Conjecture0
    b. Concept
    c. Undefined
    d. Undefined

122. In mathematics, a _____ of a number x is a number r such that $r^2 = x$, or in words, a number r whose square (the result of multiplying the number by itself) is x.
    a. Square root0
    b. Thing
    c. Undefined
    d. Undefined

123. A _____ is a first degree polynomial mathematical function of the form: $f(x) = mx + b$ where m and b are real constants and x is a real variable.
    a. Thing
    b. Linear function0
    c. Undefined
    d. Undefined

124. An _____ is an equality that remains true regardless of the values of any variables that appear within it, to distinguish it from an equality which is true under more particular conditions.
    a. Identity0
    b. Thing
    c. Undefined
    d. Undefined

125. An _____ is a function that does not have any effect: it always returns the same value that was used as its argument.
    a. Identity function0
    b. Thing
    c. Undefined
    d. Undefined

126. The _____ integers are all the integers from zero on upwards.
    a. Nonnegative0
    b. Thing
    c. Undefined
    d. Undefined

127. In mathematics, the multiplicative inverse of a number x, denoted $1/x$ or x^{-1}, is the number which, when multiplied by x, yields 1. The multiplicative inverse of x is also called the _____ of x.
    a. Thing
    b. Reciprocal0
    c. Undefined
    d. Undefined

128. A function on the real numbers is called a _____ if it can be written as a finite linear combination of indicator functions of half-open intervals.
    a. Thing
    b. Step function0
    c. Undefined
    d. Undefined

129. The _____ are the only integral domain whose positive elements are well-ordered, and in which order is preserved by addition. Like the natural numbers, the _____ form a countably infinite set. The set of all _____ is usually denoted in mathematics by a boldface Z .
    a. Thing
    b. Integers0
    c. Undefined
    d. Undefined

130. _____ means in succession or back-to-back

Chapter 3. Functions and Their Graphs 63

    a. Thing
    c. Undefined
    b. Consecutive0
    d. Undefined

131. A _____ defined function $f(x)$ of a real variable x is a function whose definition is given differently on disjoint subsets of its domain.
    a. Piecewise0
    c. Undefined
    b. Thing
    d. Undefined

132. _____ are procedures that allow people to exchange information by one of several methods.
    a. Thing
    c. Undefined
    b. Communications0
    d. Undefined

133. _____ are a measure of time.
    a. Thing
    c. Undefined
    b. Minutes0
    d. Undefined

134. A _____ is a compensation which workers receive in exchange for their labor.
    a. Wage0
    c. Undefined
    b. Thing
    d. Undefined

135. _____ is the amount of time someone works beyond normal working hours.
    a. Compensatory time0
    c. Undefined
    b. Thing
    d. Undefined

136. _____ is the sub-discipline of fluid mechanics dealing with fluids liquids and gases in motion.
    a. Thing
    c. Undefined
    b. Fluid flow0
    d. Undefined

137. U.S. liquid _____ is legally defined as 231 cubic inches, and is equal to 3.785411784 litres or abotu 0.13368 cubic feet. This is the most common definition of a _____. The U.S. fluid ounce is defined as 1/128 of a U.S. _____.
    a. Thing
    c. Undefined
    b. Gallon0
    d. Undefined

138. In combinatorial mathematics, a _____ is an un-ordered collection of unique elements.
    a. Concept
    c. Undefined
    b. Combination0
    d. Undefined

139. A _____ is a one-dimensional picture in which the integers are shown as specially-marked points evenly spaced on a line.
    a. Number line0
    c. Undefined
    b. Thing
    d. Undefined

140. In mathematics, an _____ is a statement about the relative size or order of two objects.

64 **Chapter 3. Functions and Their Graphs**

a. Thing
b. Inequality0
c. Undefined
d. Undefined

141. In mathematics, a _____ in elementary terms is any of a variety of different functions from geometry, such as rotations, reflections and translations.
a. Transformation0
b. Thing
c. Undefined
d. Undefined

142. In mathematics, a _____ (also spelled reflexion) is a map that transforms an object into its mirror image.
a. Reflection0
b. Concept
c. Undefined
d. Undefined

143. In Euclidean geometry, a _____ is moving every point a constant distance in a specified direction.
a. Concept
b. Translation0
c. Undefined
d. Undefined

144. _____ is the symbold used to indicate the nth root of a number
a. Thing
b. Radical0
c. Undefined
d. Undefined

145. The _____ of a ring R is defined to be the smallest positive integer n such that n a = 0, for all a in R.
a. Characteristic0
b. Thing
c. Undefined
d. Undefined

146. Deductive _____ is the kind of _____ in which the conclusion is necessitated by, or reached from, previously known facts (the premises).
a. Thing
b. Reasoning0
c. Undefined
d. Undefined

147. In mathematics, a _____ of a positive integer n is a way of writing n as a sum of positive integers.
a. Composition0
b. Thing
c. Undefined
d. Undefined

148. A _____ number is a positive integer which has a positive divisor other than one or itself.
a. Composite0
b. Thing
c. Undefined
d. Undefined

149. A _____, formed by the composition of one function on another, represents the application of the former to the result of the application of the latter to the argument of the composite.
a. Thing
b. Composite function0
c. Undefined
d. Undefined

150. In linear algebra, the _____ of an n-by-n square matrix A is defined to be the sum of the elements on the main diagonal of A,

Chapter 3. Functions and Their Graphs

a. Trace0
b. Thing
c. Undefined
d. Undefined

151. _____ is, or relates to, the _____ temperature scale .
a. Celsius0
b. Thing
c. Undefined
d. Undefined

152. In Euclidean geometry, an _____ is a closed segment of a differentiable curve in the two-dimensional plane; for example, a circular _____ is a segment of a circle.
a. Concept
b. Arc0
c. Undefined
d. Undefined

153. _____ is the transport of people on a trip/journey or the process or time involved in a person or object moving from one location to another.
a. Thing
b. Travel0
c. Undefined
d. Undefined

154. In mathematics, a _____ is a countable collection of open covers of a topological space that satisfies certain separation axioms.
a. Thing
b. Development0
c. Undefined
d. Undefined

155. _____ is a unit of speed, expressing the number of international miles covered per hour.
a. Miles per hour0
b. Thing
c. Undefined
d. Undefined

156. In business, particularly accounting, a _____ is the time intervals that the accounts, statement, payments, or other calculations cover.
a. Period0
b. Thing
c. Undefined
d. Undefined

157. _____ is the level of functional and/or metabolic efficiency of an organism at both the micro level.
a. Thing
b. Health0
c. Undefined
d. Undefined

158. _____ is a temperature scale named after the German physicist Daniel Gabriel _____ , who proposed it in 1724.
a. Thing
b. Fahrenheit0
c. Undefined
d. Undefined

159. In Euclidean geometry, a _____ is the set of all points in a plane at a fixed distance, called the radius, from a given point, the center.
a. Circle0
b. Thing
c. Undefined
d. Undefined

Chapter 3. Functions and Their Graphs

160. In physics, _____ are surface waves on a liquid with wavelengths so short that the liquid's motion is governed almost entirely by surface tension forces.
- a. Ripples0
- b. Thing
- c. Undefined
- d. Undefined

161. A _____ is a set whose members are members of another set or a set contained within another set.
- a. Thing
- b. Subset0
- c. Undefined
- d. Undefined

162. In mathematics, a _____ is a demonstration that, assuming certain axioms, some statement is necessarily true.
- a. Proof0
- b. Thing
- c. Undefined
- d. Undefined

163. In mathematics, _____ and odd functions are functions which satisfy particular symmetry relations, with respect to taking additive inverses.
- a. Thing
- b. Even functions0
- c. Undefined
- d. Undefined

164. _____ is a test used to determine if a function is injective, surjective or bijective.
- a. Horizontal line test0
- b. Thing
- c. Undefined
- d. Undefined

165. _____ element of an element x with respect to a binary operation * with identity element e is an element y such that x * y = y * x = e. In particular,
- a. Inverse0
- b. Thing
- c. Undefined
- d. Undefined

166. An _____ is a function which does the reverse of a given function.
- a. Inverse function0
- b. Thing
- c. Undefined
- d. Undefined

167. In mathematics and its applications, a _____ is a system for assigning an n-tuple of numbers or scalars to each point in an n-dimensional space.
- a. Concept
- b. Coordinate system0
- c. Undefined
- d. Undefined

168. _____ the expected value of a random variable displays the average or central value of the variable. It is a summary value of the distribution of the variable.
- a. Thing
- b. Determining0
- c. Undefined
- d. Undefined

169. _____ are any documents that aim to streamline particular processes according to a set routine.
- a. Thing
- b. Guidelines0
- c. Undefined
- d. Undefined

Chapter 3. Functions and Their Graphs

170. A _____ is a negotiable instrument instructing a financial institution to pay a specific amount of a specific currency from a specific demand account held in the maker/depositor's name with that institution. Both the maker and payee may be natural persons or legal entities.
   a. Thing
   b. Check0
   c. Undefined
   d. Undefined

171. A _____ is a consumption tax charged at the point of purchase for certain goods and services.
   a. Sales tax0
   b. Thing
   c. Undefined
   d. Undefined

172. In mainstream economics, the word _____ refers to a general rise in prices measured against a standard level of purchasing power.
   a. Thing
   b. Inflation0
   c. Undefined
   d. Undefined

173. In chemistry, a _____ is substance made by combining two or more different materials in such a way that no chemical reaction occurs.
   a. Thing
   b. Mixture0
   c. Undefined
   d. Undefined

174. Mathematical _____ are demonstrations that,assuming certain axioms, some statement is necessarily true.
   a. Thing
   b. Proofs0
   c. Undefined
   d. Undefined

175. In logic and mathematics, logical _____ (sometimes also known as the material _____) is a logical operator connecting two statements to assert, p if and only if q where p is a hypothesis (or antecedent) and q is a conclusion (or consequent). The operator is denoted using a doubleheaded arrow "â†"" or EQV. It is logically equivalent to (p â†' q) â˘§ (q â†' p), or the XNOR boolean operator. It is equivalent to (not p or q) and (not q or p). It is also logically equivalent to (not p and not q) or (p and q).
   a. Biconditional0
   b. Thing
   c. Undefined
   d. Undefined

176. A _____ states that the presence of one property is necessary for the application of another related property to determine absolute truth.
   a. Biconditional statement0
   b. Concept
   c. Undefined
   d. Undefined

177. The material _____, also known as the material implication or truth functional _____, expresses a property of certain conditionals in logic.
   a. Thing
   b. Conditional0
   c. Undefined
   d. Undefined

178. _____ Logic is a concept in traditional logic referring to a "type of immediate inference in which from a given proposition another proposition is inferred which has as its subject the predicate of the original proposition and as its predicate the subject of the original proposition (the quality of the proposition being retained)."

a. Converse0
b. Concept
c. Undefined
d. Undefined

179. In logic and mathematics, logical _____ (usual symbol and) is a two-place logical operation that results in a value of true if both of its operands are true, otherwise a value of false.
   a. Conjunction0
   b. Concept
   c. Undefined
   d. Undefined

180. In mathematics, a _____ of an integer n, also called a factor of n, is an integer which evenly divides n without leaving a remainder.
   a. Thing
   b. Divisor0
   c. Undefined
   d. Undefined

181. _____ is the design, analysis, and/or construction of works for practical purposes.
   a. Engineering0
   b. Thing
   c. Undefined
   d. Undefined

182. The _____ of a member of a multiset is how many memberships in the multiset it has.
   a. Multiplicity0
   b. Thing
   c. Undefined
   d. Undefined

183. In mathematics, two quantities are called _____ if they vary in such a way that one of the quantities is a constant multiple of the other, or equivalently if they have a constant ratio.
   a. Proportional0
   b. Thing
   c. Undefined
   d. Undefined

184. A _____ is a polynomial function of the form f(x) = ax^2 + bx +c , where a, b, c are real numbers and a , 0.
   a. Quadratic function0
   b. Event
   c. Undefined
   d. Undefined

185. In mathematics, especially in order theory, an _____ of a subset S of some partially ordered set is an element of P which is greater than or equal to every element of S.
   a. Upper bound0
   b. Thing
   c. Undefined
   d. Undefined

186. In geometry, a _____ is a special kind of point, usually a corner of a polygon, polyhedron, or higher dimensional polytope. In the geometry of curves a _____ is a point of where the first derivative of curvature is zero. In graph theory, a _____ is the fundamental unit out of which graphs are formed
   a. Vertex0
   b. Thing
   c. Undefined
   d. Undefined

187. A _____ function is a function for which, intuitively, small changes in the input result in small changes in the output.
   a. Event
   b. Continuous0
   c. Undefined
   d. Undefined

Chapter 3. Functions and Their Graphs

188. In mathematics, a _____ number is a number which can be expressed as a ratio of two integers. Non-integer _____ numbers (commonly called fractions) are usually written as the vulgar fraction a / b, where b is not zero.
   a. Thing
   b. Rational0
   c. Undefined
   d. Undefined

189. In mathematics, a _____ is a constant multiplicative factor of a certain object. The object can be such things as a variable, a vector, a function, etc. For example, the _____ of $9x^2$ is 9.
   a. Thing
   b. Coefficient0
   c. Undefined
   d. Undefined

190. An _____ is a straight line around which a geometric figure can be rotated.
   a. Thing
   b. Axis0
   c. Undefined
   d. Undefined

191. In mathematics, the _____ is a conic section generated by the intersection of a right circular conical surface and a plane parallel to a generating straight line of that surface. It can also be defined as locus of points in a plane which are equidistant from a given point.
   a. Thing
   b. Parabola0
   c. Undefined
   d. Undefined

192. The term _____ is defined dually as an element of P which is lesser than or equal to every element of S.
   a. Lower bound0
   b. Thing
   c. Undefined
   d. Undefined

193. In mathematics, computing, linguistics, and related disciplines, an _____ is a finite list of well-defined instructions for accomplishing some task which, given an initial state, will terminate in a defined end-state.
   a. Concept
   b. Algorithm0
   c. Undefined
   d. Undefined

194. In mathematics, a _____ is a statement that can be proved on the basis of explicitly stated or previously agreed assumptions.
   a. Thing
   b. Theorem0
   c. Undefined
   d. Undefined

195. _____ is a notation for writing numbers that is often used by scientists and mathematicians to make it easier to write large and small numbers.
   a. Scientific notation0
   b. Thing
   c. Undefined
   d. Undefined

196. In algebra, a _____ is a binomial formed by taking the opposite of the second term of a binomial.
   a. Conjugate0
   b. Thing
   c. Undefined
   d. Undefined

Chapter 3. Functions and Their Graphs

197. _____ was a highly influential French philosopher, mathematician, scientist, and writer. Dubbed the "Founder of Modern Philosophy", and the "Father of Modern Mathematics". His theories provided the basis for the calculus of Newton and Leibniz, by applying infinitesimal calculus to the tangent line problem, thus permitting the evolution of that branch of modern mathematics
   a. Person
   b. Descartes0
   c. Undefined
   d. Undefined

198. The _____ implies that on any great circle around the world, the temperature, pressure, elevation, carbon dioxide concentration, or anything else that varies continuously, there will always exist two antipodal points that share the same value for that variable.
   a. Intermediate Value Theorem0
   b. Thing
   c. Undefined
   d. Undefined

199. The _____ is a theorem in mathematics which precisely expresses the outcome of the usual process of division of integers. The name is something of a misnomer, as it is a theorem, not an algorithm, i.e. a well-defined procedure for achieving a specific task — although the _____ can be used to find the greatest common divisor of two integers.
   a. Thing
   b. Division Algorithm0
   c. Undefined
   d. Undefined

Chapter 4. Polynomial Functions

1. The _____ integers are all the integers from zero on upwards.
   a. Thing
   b. Nonnegative0
   c. Undefined
   d. Undefined

2. In mathematics, a _____ may be described informally as a number that can be given by an infinite decimal representation.
   a. Real number0
   b. Thing
   c. Undefined
   d. Undefined

3. In mathematics, there are several meanings of _____ depending on the subject.
   a. Thing
   b. Degree0
   c. Undefined
   d. Undefined

4. In mathematics, a _____ is an expression that is constructed from one or more variables and constants, using only the operations of addition, subtraction, multiplication, and constant positive whole number exponents. is a _____. Note in particular that division by an expression containing a variable is not in general allowed in polynomials. [1]
   a. Thing
   b. Polynomial0
   c. Undefined
   d. Undefined

5. The mathematical concept of a _____ expresses the intuitive idea of deterministic dependence between two quantities, one of which is viewed as primary and the other as secondary. A _____ then is a way to associate a unique output for each input of a specified type, for example, a real number or an element of a given set.
   a. Thing
   b. Function0
   c. Undefined
   d. Undefined

6. A _____ is a polynomial function of the form $f(x) = ax^2 + bx + c$, where a, b, c are real numbers and a , 0.
   a. Event
   b. Quadratic function0
   c. Undefined
   d. Undefined

7. In mathematics, the concept of a _____ tries to capture the intuitive idea of a geometrical one-dimensional and continuous object. A simple example is the circle.
   a. Thing
   b. Curve0
   c. Undefined
   d. Undefined

8. In mathematics, the _____ is a conic section generated by the intersection of a right circular conical surface and a plane parallel to a generating straight line of that surface. It can also be defined as locus of points in a plane which are equidistant from a given point.
   a. Thing
   b. Parabola0
   c. Undefined
   d. Undefined

9. The Yakovlev Yak-25, NATO designation _____-A / Mandrake, was a swept wing, turbojet-powered interceptor aircraft and reconnaissance aircraft used by the Soviet Union.
   a. Thing
   b. Flashlight0
   c. Undefined
   d. Undefined

10. _____ means "constancy", i.e. if something retains a certain feature even after we change a way of looking at it, then it is symmetric.

Chapter 4. Polynomial Functions

    a. Thing
    b. Symmetry0
    c. Undefined
    d. Undefined

11. An _____ is a straight line around which a geometric figure can be rotated.
    a. Thing
    b. Axis0
    c. Undefined
    d. Undefined

12. _____ of a two-dimensional figure is a line such that, if a perpendicular is constructed, any two points lying on the perpendicular at equal distances from the _____ are identical.
    a. Thing
    b. Axis of symmetry0
    c. Undefined
    d. Undefined

13. In mathematics, a _____ is a constant multiplicative factor of a certain object. The object can be such things as a variable, a vector, a function, etc. For example, the _____ of $9x^2$ is 9.
    a. Coefficient0
    b. Thing
    c. Undefined
    d. Undefined

14. In geometry, a _____ is a special kind of point, usually a corner of a polygon, polyhedron, or higher dimensional polytope. In the geometry of curves a _____ is a point of where the first derivative of curvature is zero. In graph theory, a _____ is the fundamental unit out of which graphs are formed
    a. Vertex0
    b. Thing
    c. Undefined
    d. Undefined

15. _____ are the basic objects of study in graph theory. Informally speaking, a graph is a set of objects called points, nodes, or vertices connected by links called lines or edges.
    a. Graphs0
    b. Thing
    c. Undefined
    d. Undefined

16. _____ is a notation for writing numbers that is often used by scientists and mathematicians to make it easier to write large and small numbers.
    a. Thing
    b. Scientific notation0
    c. Undefined
    d. Undefined

17. In plane geometry, a _____ is a polygon with four equal sides, four right angles, and parallel opposite sides. In algebra, the _____ of a number is that number multiplied by itself.
    a. Square0
    b. Thing
    c. Undefined
    d. Undefined

18. _____ is a technique used in algebra to solve quadratic equations, in analytic geometry for determining the shapes of graphs, and in calculus for computing integrals, including, but hardly limited to, the integrals that define Laplace transforms. The essential objective is to reduce a quadratic polynomial in a variable in an equation or expression to a squared polynomial of linear order. This can reduce an equation or integral to one that is more easily solved or evaluated.
    a. Completing the square0
    b. Thing
    c. Undefined
    d. Undefined

Chapter 4. Polynomial Functions   73

19. A quadratic equation with real solutions, called roots, which may be real or complex, is given by the _____: $x = \frac{-b \pm \sqrt{b^2 - 4ac}}{2a}$.
    a. Quadratic formula0   b. Thing
    c. Undefined   d. Undefined

20. _____, either of the curved-bracket punctuation marks that together make a set of _____
    a. Thing   b. Parentheses0
    c. Undefined   d. Undefined

21. _____ of an object is its speed in a particular direction.
    a. Velocity0   b. Thing
    c. Undefined   d. Undefined

22. Deductive _____ is the kind of _____ in which the conclusion is necessitated by, or reached from, previously known facts (the premises).
    a. Thing   b. Reasoning0
    c. Undefined   d. Undefined

23. In mathematics, a _____ is the result of multiplying, or an expression that identifies factors to be multiplied.
    a. Product0   b. Thing
    c. Undefined   d. Undefined

24. A _____ is the result of the addition of a set of numbers. The numbers may be natural numbers, complex numbers, matrices, or still more complicated objects. An infinite _____ is a subtle procedure known as a series.
    a. Thing   b. Sum0
    c. Undefined   d. Undefined

25. In geometry, _____ angles are angles that have a common ray coming out of the vertex going between two other rays.
    a. Concept   b. Adjacent0
    c. Undefined   d. Undefined

26. _____ is the distance around a given two-dimensional object. As a general rule, the _____ of a polygon can always be calculated by adding all the length of the sides together. So, the formula for triangles is P = a + b + c, where a, b and c stand for each side of it. For quadrilaterals the equation is P = a + b + c + d. For equilateral polygons, P = na, where n is the number of sides and a is the side length.
    a. Perimeter0   b. Thing
    c. Undefined   d. Undefined

27. In classical geometry, a _____ of a circle or sphere is any line segment from its center to its boundary. By extension, the _____ of a circle or sphere is the length of any such segment. The _____ is half the diameter. In science and engineering the term _____ of curvature is commonly used as a synonym for _____.
    a. Radius0   b. Thing
    c. Undefined   d. Undefined

28. The _____ of measurement are a globally standardized and modernized form of the metric system.

a. Units0
b. Thing
c. Undefined
d. Undefined

29. _____ is the level of functional and/or metabolic efficiency of an organism at both the micro level.
    a. Health0
    b. Thing
    c. Undefined
    d. Undefined

30. _____ is a business term for the amount of money that a company receives from its activities in a given period, mostly from sales of products and/or services to customers
    a. Thing
    b. Revenue0
    c. Undefined
    d. Undefined

31. _____, from Latin meaning "to make progress", is defined in two different ways. Pure economic _____ is the increase in wealth that an investor has from making an investment, taking into consideration all costs associated with that investment including the opportunity cost of capital.
    a. Thing
    b. Profit0
    c. Undefined
    d. Undefined

32. _____ is a synonym for information.
    a. Data0
    b. Thing
    c. Undefined
    d. Undefined

33. In geographic information systems, a _____ comprises an entity with a geographic location, typically determined by points, arcs, or polygons. Carriageways and cadastres exemplify _____ data.
    a. Feature0
    b. Thing
    c. Undefined
    d. Undefined

34. A _____, scatter diagram or scatter graph is a chart that uses Cartesian coordinates to display values for two variables.
    a. Scatter plot0
    b. Thing
    c. Undefined
    d. Undefined

35. In linear algebra, the _____ of an n-by-n square matrix A is defined to be the sum of the elements on the main diagonal of A,
    a. Thing
    b. Trace0
    c. Undefined
    d. Undefined

36. In mathematics, an _____, mean, or central tendency of a data set refers to a measure of the "middle" or "expected" value of the data set.
    a. Average0
    b. Concept
    c. Undefined
    d. Undefined

37. In sociology and biology a _____ is the collection of people or organisms of a particular species living in a given geographic area or space, usually measured by a census.

Chapter 4. Polynomial Functions

a. Population0
b. Thing
c. Undefined
d. Undefined

38. _____ has many meanings, most of which simply .
a. Power0
b. Thing
c. Undefined
d. Undefined

39. A _____ is a unit of length, usually used to measure distance, in a number of different systems, including Imperial units, United States customary units and Norwegian/Swedish mil. Its size can vary from system to system, but in each is between 1 and 10 kilometers. In contemporary English contexts _____ refers to either:
a. Mile0
b. Thing
c. Undefined
d. Undefined

40. _____ is a unit of speed, expressing the number of international miles covered per hour.
a. Miles per hour0
b. Thing
c. Undefined
d. Undefined

41. U.S. liquid _____ is legally defined as 231 cubic inches, and is equal to 3.785411784 litres or abotu 0.13368 cubic feet. This is the most common definition of a _____. The U.S. fluid ounce is defined as 1/128 of a U.S. _____.
a. Gallon0
b. Thing
c. Undefined
d. Undefined

42. In common philosophical language, a proposition or _____, is the content of an assertion, that is, it is true-or-false and defined by the meaning of a particular piece of language.
a. Concept
b. Statement0
c. Undefined
d. Undefined

43. In mathematics, a _____ is a polynomial equation of the second degree. The general form is $ax^2 + bx + c = 0$.
a. Quadratic equation0
b. Thing
c. Undefined
d. Undefined

44. The _____ of a ring R is defined to be the smallest positive integer n such that n a = 0, for all a in R.
a. Characteristic0
b. Thing
c. Undefined
d. Undefined

45. _____ is often used to describe the measurement of the steepness, incline, gradient, or grade of a straight line. The _____ is defined as the ratio of the "rise" divided by the "run" between two points on a line, or in other words, the ratio of the altitude change to the horizontal distance between any two points on the line.
a. Slope0
b. Thing
c. Undefined
d. Undefined

46. In geometry, two lines or planes if one falls on the other in such a way as to create congruent adjacent angles. The term may be used as a noun or adjective. Thus, referring to Figure 1, the line AB is the _____ to CD through the point B.

a. Perpendicular0
b. Thing
c. Undefined
d. Undefined

47. A _____ is 360° or 2δ radians.
   a. Thing
   b. Turn0
   c. Undefined
   d. Undefined

48. In mathematics, the _____ of a coordinate system is the point where the axes of the system intersect.
   a. Thing
   b. Origin0
   c. Undefined
   d. Undefined

49. In mathematics, a _____ in elementary terms is any of a variety of different functions from geometry, such as rotations, reflections and translations.
   a. Thing
   b. Transformation0
   c. Undefined
   d. Undefined

50. In mathematics, a _____ is a particular kind of polynomial, having just one term.
   a. Thing
   b. Monomial0
   c. Undefined
   d. Undefined

51. Acid _____ ratio measures the ability of a company to use its near cash or quick assets to immediately extinguish its current liabilities.
   a. Thing
   b. Test0
   c. Undefined
   d. Undefined

52. Mathematical _____ is used to represent ideas.
   a. Notation0
   b. Thing
   c. Undefined
   d. Undefined

53. _____ is a branch of mathematics concerning the study of structure, relation and quantity.
   a. Concept
   b. Algebra0
   c. Undefined
   d. Undefined

54. In mathematics, the _____ f is the collection of all ordered pairs . In particular, graph means the graphical representation of this collection, in the form of a curve or surface, together with axes, etc. Graphing on a Cartesian plane is sometimes referred to as curve sketching.
   a. Graph of a function0
   b. Thing
   c. Undefined
   d. Undefined

55. In mathematics, factorization (British English: factorisation) or factoring is the decomposition of an object (for example, a number, a polynomial, or a matrix) into a product of other objects, or _____, which when multiplied together give the original.
   a. Factors0
   b. Thing
   c. Undefined
   d. Undefined

56. The _____ of a member of a multiset is how many memberships in the multiset it has.

Chapter 4. Polynomial Functions 77

a. Thing
c. Undefined
b. Multiplicity0
d. Undefined

57. _____ is the largest positive integer that divides both numbers without remainder.
a. Common Factor0
c. Undefined
b. Thing
d. Undefined

58. In mathematics, _____ is the decomposition of an object into a product of other objects, or factors, which when multiplied together give the original.
a. Factoring0
c. Undefined
b. Thing
d. Undefined

59. A _____ is a negotiable instrument instructing a financial institution to pay a specific amount of a specific currency from a specific demand account held in the maker/depositor's name with that institution. Both the maker and payee may be natural persons or legal entities.
a. Thing
c. Undefined
b. Check0
d. Undefined

60. In set theory and other branches of mathematics, two kinds of complements are defined, the relative _____ and the absolute _____.
a. Thing
c. Undefined
b. Complement0
d. Undefined

61. In mathematics, a _____ is a statement that can be proved on the basis of explicitly stated or previously agreed assumptions.
a. Theorem0
c. Undefined
b. Thing
d. Undefined

62. The _____ implies that on any great circle around the world, the temperature, pressure, elevation, carbon dioxide concentration, or anything else that varies continuously, there will always exist two antipodal points that share the same value for that variable.
a. Thing
c. Undefined
b. Intermediate Value Theorem0
d. Undefined

63. In elementary algebra, an _____ is a set that contains every real number between two indicated numbers and may contain the two numbers themselves.
a. Thing
c. Undefined
b. Interval0
d. Undefined

64. In mathematics, a _____ of a complex-valued function f is a member x of the domain of f such that f(x) vanishes at x, that is, x : f (x) = 0.
a. Root0
c. Undefined
b. Thing
d. Undefined

65. A _____ function is a function for which, intuitively, small changes in the input result in small changes in the output.

78 Chapter 4. Polynomial Functions

a. Continuous0
b. Event
c. Undefined
d. Undefined

66. The _____ of a solid object is the three-dimensional concept of how much space it occupies, often quantified numerically.
   a. Volume0
   b. Thing
   c. Undefined
   d. Undefined

67. In mathematics, a _____ of a k-place relation $L \subseteq X_1 \times ... \times X_k$ is one of the sets X_j, $1 \leq j \leq k$. In the special case where k = 2 and $L \subseteq X_1 \times X_2$ is a function $L : X_1 \to X_2$, it is conventional to refer to X_1 as the _____ of the function and to refer to X_2 as the codomain of the function.
   a. Domain0
   b. Thing
   c. Undefined
   d. Undefined

68. _____, in economics and political economy, are the distributions or payments awarded to the various suppliers of the factors of production.
   a. Thing
   b. Returns0
   c. Undefined
   d. Undefined

69. _____ is a mathematical subject that includes the study of limits, derivatives, integrals, and power series and constitutes a major part of modern university curriculum.
   a. Calculus0
   b. Thing
   c. Undefined
   d. Undefined

70. According to _____ relationship, in a production system with fixed and variable inputs , beyond some point, each additional unit of variable input yields less and less additional output.
   a. Thing
   b. Diminishing returns0
   c. Undefined
   d. Undefined

71. _____ is a kind of property which exists as magnitude or multitude. It is among the basic classes of things along with quality, substance, change, and relation.
   a. Amount0
   b. Thing
   c. Undefined
   d. Undefined

72. An _____ is a combination of numbers, operators, grouping symbols and/or free variables and bound variables arranged in a meaningful way which can be evaluated..
   a. Expression0
   b. Thing
   c. Undefined
   d. Undefined

73. The _____ is a theorem for finding out the factors of a polynomial.
   a. Factor theorem0
   b. Thing
   c. Undefined
   d. Undefined

74. In arithmetic, _____ is a procedure for calculating the division of one integer, called the dividend, by another integer called the divisor, to produce a result called the quotient.

Chapter 4. Polynomial Functions

a. Thing
b. Long division0
c. Undefined
d. Undefined

75. A _____ is the part of the dividend that is left over when the dividend is not evenly divisible by the divisor.
a. Remainder0
b. Thing
c. Undefined
d. Undefined

76. _____ in algebra is an application of polynomial long division.
a. Remainder theorem0
b. Thing
c. Undefined
d. Undefined

77. In mathematics, _____ allows the rapid division of any polynomial by a binomial of the form x − r. It was described by Paolo Ruffini in 1809. _____ is a special case of long division when the divisor is a linear factor.
a. Ruffini's rule0
b. Thing
c. Undefined
d. Undefined

78. In elementary algebra, a _____ is a polynomial with two terms: the sum of two monomials. It is the simplest kind of polynomial except for a monomial.
a. Thing
b. Binomial0
c. Undefined
d. Undefined

79. A _____ fraction is a fraction in which the absolute value of the numerator is less than the denominator--hence, the absolute value of the fraction is less than 1.
a. Thing
b. Proper0
c. Undefined
d. Undefined

80. In mathematics, an inequality is a statement about the relative size or order of two objects. For example 14 > 10, or 14 is _____ 10.
a. Thing
b. Greater than0
c. Undefined
d. Undefined

81. In mathematics, a _____ is the end result of a division problem. It can also be expressed as the number of times the divisor divides into the dividend.
a. Thing
b. Quotient0
c. Undefined
d. Undefined

82. In mathematics, a _____ number is a number which can be expressed as a ratio of two integers. Non-integer _____ numbers (commonly called fractions) are usually written as the vulgar fraction a / b, where b is not zero.
a. Thing
b. Rational0
c. Undefined
d. Undefined

83. In mathematics, computing, linguistics, and related disciplines, an _____ is a finite list of well-defined instructions for accomplishing some task which, given an initial state, will terminate in a defined end-state.
a. Algorithm0
b. Concept
c. Undefined
d. Undefined

Chapter 4. Polynomial Functions

84. _____ is a payment made by a company to its shareholders
    a. Thing
    b. Dividend0
    c. Undefined
    d. Undefined

85. The _____ is a theorem in mathematics which precisely expresses the outcome of the usual process of division of integers. The name is something of a misnomer, as it is a theorem, not an algorithm, i.e. a well-defined procedure for achieving a specific task — although the _____ can be used to find the greatest common divisor of two integers.
    a. Division Algorithm0
    b. Thing
    c. Undefined
    d. Undefined

86. A _____ is a symbolic representation denoting a quantity or expression. It often represents an "unknown" quantity that has the potential to change.
    a. Variable0
    b. Thing
    c. Undefined
    d. Undefined

87. In mathematics, a _____ of an integer n, also called a factor of n, is an integer which evenly divides n without leaving a remainder.
    a. Divisor0
    b. Thing
    c. Undefined
    d. Undefined

88. _____ is a set, with some particular properties and usually some additional structure, such as the operations of addition or multiplication, for instance.
    a. Thing
    b. Space0
    c. Undefined
    d. Undefined

89. In computer science an _____ is a data structure that consists of a group of elements having a single name that are accessed by indexing. In most programming languages each element has the same data type and the _____ occupies a continuous area of storage.
    a. Array0
    b. Thing
    c. Undefined
    d. Undefined

90. The _____, the average in everyday English, which is also called the arithmetic _____ (and is distinguished from the geometric _____ or harmonic _____). The average is also called the sample _____. The expected value of a random variable, which is also called the population _____.
    a. Thing
    b. Mean0
    c. Undefined
    d. Undefined

91. Equivalence is the condition of being _____ or essentially equal.
    a. Equivalent0
    b. Thing
    c. Undefined
    d. Undefined

92. A _____ is a numeral used to indicate a count. The most common use of the word today is to name the part of a fraction that tells the number or count of equal parts.
    a. Numerator0
    b. Thing
    c. Undefined
    d. Undefined

Chapter 4. Polynomial Functions

93. In mathematics and the mathematical sciences, a _____ is a fixed, but possibly unspecified, value. This is in contrast to a variable, which is not fixed.
    a. Constant0
    b. Thing
    c. Undefined
    d. Undefined

94. A _____ is the part of a fraction that tells how many equal parts make up a whole, and which is used in the name of the fraction: "halves", "thirds", "fourths" or "quarters", "fifths" and so on.
    a. Denominator0
    b. Concept
    c. Undefined
    d. Undefined

95. In number theory, the _____ of arithmetic (or unique factorization theorem) states that every natural number greater than 1 can be written as a unique product of prime numbers.
    a. Concept
    b. Fundamental theorem0
    c. Undefined
    d. Undefined

96. _____ states that every non-zero single-variable polynomial, with complex coefficients, has exactly as many complex roots as its degree, if repeated roots are counted up to their multiplicity.
    a. Thing
    b. Fundamental theorem of algebra0
    c. Undefined
    d. Undefined

97. _____ is a set of numbers, in the broadest sense of the word, together with one or more operations, such as addition or multiplication.
    a. Number system0
    b. Thing
    c. Undefined
    d. Undefined

98. In mathematics, a _____ is a number in the form of a + bi where a and b are real numbers, and i is the imaginary unit, with the property i 2 = −1. The real number a is called the real part of the _____, and the real number b is the imaginary part.
    a. Thing
    b. Complex number0
    c. Undefined
    d. Undefined

99. The word _____ comes from the Latin word linearis, which means created by lines.
    a. Linear0
    b. Thing
    c. Undefined
    d. Undefined

100. _____ is the mathematical action of repeatedly adding or subtracting one, usually to find out how many objects there are or to set aside a desired number of objects.
    a. Thing
    b. Counting0
    c. Undefined
    d. Undefined

101. The term _____ is defined dually as an element of P which is lesser than or equal to every element of S.
    a. Thing
    b. Lower bound0
    c. Undefined
    d. Undefined

Chapter 4. Polynomial Functions

102. _____ was a highly influential French philosopher, mathematician, scientist, and writer. Dubbed the "Founder of Modern Philosophy", and the "Father of Modern Mathematics". His theories provided the basis for the calculus of Newton and Leibniz, by applying infinitesimal calculus to the tangent line problem, thus permitting the evolution of that branch of modern mathematics
   a. Descartes0
   b. Person
   c. Undefined
   d. Undefined

103. _____ is a fixed, but possibly unspecified, value. This is in contrast to a variable, which is not fixed.
   a. Thing
   b. Constant term0
   c. Undefined
   d. Undefined

104. In mathematics, a _____ is a number which can be expressed as a ratio of two integers. Non-integer rational numbers (commonly called fractions) are usually written as the vulgar fraction a / b, where b is not zero.
   a. Concept
   b. Rational Number0
   c. Undefined
   d. Undefined

105. Johann Carl Friedrich Gauss or _____ was a German mathematician and scientist of profound genius who contributed significantly to many fields, including number theory, analysis, differential geometry, geodesy, magnetism, astronomy, and optics.
   a. Carl Gauss0
   b. Person
   c. Undefined
   d. Undefined

106. In mathematics, the conjugate _____ or adjoint matrix of an m-by-n matrix A with complex entries is the n-by-m matrix A* obtained from A by taking the transpose and then taking the complex conjugate of each entry.
   a. Pairs0
   b. Thing
   c. Undefined
   d. Undefined

107. In algebra, a _____ is a binomial formed by taking the opposite of the second term of a binomial.
   a. Thing
   b. Conjugate0
   c. Undefined
   d. Undefined

108. In mathematics, a _____ number (or a _____) is a natural number that has exactly two (distinct) natural number divisors, which are 1 and the _____ number itself.
   a. Prime0
   b. Thing
   c. Undefined
   d. Undefined

109. In mathematics, the additive inverse, or _____ of a number n is the number that, when added to n, yields zero. The additive inverse of n is denoted −n. For example, 7 is −7, because 7 + (−7) = 0, and the additive inverse of −0.3 is 0.3, because −0.3 + 0.3 = 0.
   a. Opposite0
   b. Thing
   c. Undefined
   d. Undefined

110. _____ means in succession or back-to-back
   a. Consecutive0
   b. Thing
   c. Undefined
   d. Undefined

Chapter 4. Polynomial Functions 83

111. In mathematics, the _____ of a number n is the number that, when added to n, yields zero. The _____ of n is denoted −n. For example, 7 is −7, because 7 + (−7) = 0, and the _____ of −0.3 is 0.3, because −0.3 + 0.3 = 0.
   a. Thing
   b. Additive inverse0
   c. Undefined
   d. Undefined

112. In mathematics, especially in order theory, an _____ of a subset S of some partially ordered set is an element of P which is greater than or equal to every element of S.
   a. Upper bound0
   b. Thing
   c. Undefined
   d. Undefined

113. An n-sided _____ is a polyhedron formed by connecting an n-sided polygonal base and a point, called the apex, by n triangular faces. In other words, it is a conic solid with polygonal base.
   a. Thing
   b. Pyramid0
   c. Undefined
   d. Undefined

114. One of the three formats applicable to a quadratic function is the _____ which is defined as f = ax^2 + bx + c.
   a. General form0
   b. Thing
   c. Undefined
   d. Undefined

115. In mathematics, an _____ number is a complex number whose square is a negative real number. They were defined in 1572 by Rafael Bombelli.
   a. Imaginary0
   b. Thing
   c. Undefined
   d. Undefined

116. _____ is a function of the form
   a. Thing
   b. Cubic function0
   c. Undefined
   d. Undefined

117. In mathematics, an _____ number is any real number that is not a rational number- that is, it is a number which cannot be expressed as a fraction m/n, where m and n are integers.
   a. Irrational0
   b. Thing
   c. Undefined
   d. Undefined

118. A _____ is a simplified and structured visual representation of concepts, ideas, constructions, relations, statistical data, anatomy etc used in all aspects of human activities to visualize and clarify the topic.
   a. Diagram0
   b. Thing
   c. Undefined
   d. Undefined

119. In geometry, a _____ is the intersection of a body in 2-dimensional space with a line, or of a body in 3-dimensional space with a plane
   a. Thing
   b. Cross section0
   c. Undefined
   d. Undefined

120. Initial objects are also called _____, and terminal objects are also called final.

a. Thing
b. Coterminal0
c. Undefined
d. Undefined

121. In economics, supply and _____ describe market relations between prospective sellers and buyers of a good.
a. Thing
b. Demand0
c. Undefined
d. Undefined

122. Transport or _____ is the movement of people and goods from one place to another.
a. Transportation0
b. Thing
c. Undefined
d. Undefined

123. Order theory is a branch of mathematics that studies various kinds of binary relations that capture the intuitive notion of a mathematical _____.
a. Ordering0
b. Thing
c. Undefined
d. Undefined

124. _____ is the application of tools and a processing medium to the transformation of raw materials into finished goods for sale.
a. Manufacturing0
b. Thing
c. Undefined
d. Undefined

125. In mathematics, in the field of group theory, a _____ of a group is a quasisimple subnormal subgroup.
a. Concept
b. Component0
c. Undefined
d. Undefined

126. In mathematics, a _____ is any function which can be written as the ratio of two polynomial functions.
a. Rational function0
b. Thing
c. Undefined
d. Undefined

127. _____, in law and economics, is a form of risk management primarily used to hedge against the risk of a contingent loss.
a. Thing
b. Insurance0
c. Undefined
d. Undefined

128. _____ is a relationship among three or more variables in which each pair of variables varies directly or inversely.
a. Thing
b. Joint variation0
c. Undefined
d. Undefined

129. In regression analysis, _____, also known as ordinary _____ analysis is a method for linear regression that determines the values of unknown quantities in a statistical model by minimizing the sum of the residuals difference between the predicted and observed values squared.
a. Least squares0
b. Thing
c. Undefined
d. Undefined

Chapter 4. Polynomial Functions 85

130. A _____ is an abstract model that uses mathematical language to describe the behavior of a system. Eykhoff defined a _____ as 'a representation of the essential aspects of an existing system which presents knowledge of that system in usable form'.
   a. Mathematical model0
   b. Thing
   c. Undefined
   d. Undefined

131. _____ element of an element x with respect to a binary operation * with identity element e is an element y such that x * y = y * x = e. In particular,
   a. Thing
   b. Inverse0
   c. Undefined
   d. Undefined

132. In mathematics and logic, a _____ proof is a way of showing the truth or falsehood of a given statement by a straightforward combination of established facts, usually existing lemmas and theorems, without making any further assumptions.
   a. Direct0
   b. Thing
   c. Undefined
   d. Undefined

133. _____ is the relationship between two variables, like a ratio in which the two quantities being compared are different units.
   a. Direct variation0
   b. Thing
   c. Undefined
   d. Undefined

134. In mathematics, two quantities are called _____ if they vary in such a way that one of the quantities is a constant multiple of the other, or equivalently if they have a constant ratio.
   a. Thing
   b. Proportional0
   c. Undefined
   d. Undefined

135. In economics _____ means before deductions brutto, e.g. _____ domestic or national product, or _____ profit or income
   a. Gross0
   b. Thing
   c. Undefined
   d. Undefined

136. A _____ is a special kind of ratio, indicating a relationship between two measurements with different units, such as miles to gallons or cents to pounds.
   a. Rate0
   b. Thing
   c. Undefined
   d. Undefined

137. _____ is a way of expressing a number as a fraction of 100 per cent meaning "per hundred".
   a. Percent0
   b. Thing
   c. Undefined
   d. Undefined

138. The _____ is one of the classical simple machines; as the name suggests, it is a flat surface whose endpoints are at different heights. By moving an object up an _____ rather than directly from one height to another, the amount of force required is reduced, at the expense of increasing the distance the object must travel. The mechanical advantage of an _____ is the ratio of the length of the sloped surface to the height it spans; this may also be expressed as the cosecant of the angle between the plane and the horizontal.

a. Thing
b. Inclined plane0
c. Undefined
d. Undefined

139. In mathematics, a _____ is a two-dimensional manifold or surface that is perfectly flat.
a. Thing
b. Plane0
c. Undefined
d. Undefined

140. The _____ or kilogramme is the SI base unit of mass. It is defined as being equal to the mass of the international prototype of the _____.
a. Thing
b. Kilogram0
c. Undefined
d. Undefined

141. _____ is a physical property of a system that underlies the common notions of hot and cold; something that is hotter has the greater _____.
a. Thing
b. Temperature0
c. Undefined
d. Undefined

142. _____ is the fee paid on borrowed money.
a. Thing
b. Interest0
c. Undefined
d. Undefined

143. A _____ are accounts maintained by commercial banks, savings and loan associations, credit unions, and mutual savings banks that pay interest but can not be used directly as money by, for example, writing a cheque.
a. Thing
b. Savings account0
c. Undefined
d. Undefined

144. A _____ is a function that assigns a number to subsets of a given set.
a. Measure0
b. Thing
c. Undefined
d. Undefined

145. _____ is a regression method that models the relationship between a dependent variable Y, independent variables Xp, and a random term å.
a. Linear regression0
b. Thing
c. Undefined
d. Undefined

146. In probability theory and statistics, _____, also called _____ coefficient, indicates the strength and direction of a linear relationship between two random variables.
a. Thing
b. Correlation0
c. Undefined
d. Undefined

147. A _____ is a set of numbers that designate location in a given reference system, such as x,y in a planar _____ system or an x,y,z in a three-dimensional _____ system.
a. Coordinate0
b. Thing
c. Undefined
d. Undefined

148. An _____ is when two lines intersect somewhere on a plane creating a right angle at intersection

Chapter 4. Polynomial Functions

   a. Thing   b. Axes0
   c. Undefined   d. Undefined

149. _____ are a measure of time.
   a. Thing   b. Minutes0
   c. Undefined   d. Undefined

150. _____ or investing is a term with several closely-related meanings in business management, finance and economics, related to saving or deferring consumption.
   a. Thing   b. Investment0
   c. Undefined   d. Undefined

151. _____ finance, in finance, a debt security, issued by Issuer
   a. Thing   b. Bond0
   c. Undefined   d. Undefined

152. _____ is the estimation of a physical quantity such as distance, energy, temperature, or time.
   a. Measurement0   b. Thing
   c. Undefined   d. Undefined

153. A _____ is a consumption tax charged at the point of purchase for certain goods and services.
   a. Thing   b. Sales tax0
   c. Undefined   d. Undefined

154. _____ are flexible, elastic objects used to store mechanical energy.
   a. Thing   b. Springs0
   c. Undefined   d. Undefined

155. In physics, _____ is an influence that may cause an object to accelerate. It may be experienced as a lift, a push, or a pull. The actual acceleration of the body is determined by the vector sum of all forces acting on it, known as net _____ or resultant _____.
   a. Thing   b. Force0
   c. Undefined   d. Undefined

156. Sir Isaac _____, was an English physicist, mathematician, astronomer, natural philosopher, and alchemist, regarded by many as the greatest figure in the history of science
   a. Newton0   b. Person
   c. Undefined   d. Undefined

157. The metre (or _____, see spelling differences) is a measure of length. It is the basic unit of length in the metric system and in the International System of Units (SI), used around the world for general and scientific purposes.
   a. Concept   b. Meter0
   c. Undefined   d. Undefined

158. In business, _____, _____ cost or _____ expense refers to an ongoing expense of operating a business.

88 Chapter 4. Polynomial Functions

a. Thing
b. Overhead0
c. Undefined
d. Undefined

159. _____ is the transport of people on a trip/journey or the process or time involved in a person or object moving from one location to another.
   a. Thing
   b. Travel0
   c. Undefined
   d. Undefined

160. _____ algebra (sometimes called General algebra) is the field of mathematics that studies the ideas common to all algebraic structures.
   a. Thing
   b. Universal0
   c. Undefined
   d. Undefined

161. _____ is the property of a physical object that quantifies the amount of matter and energy it is equivalent to.
   a. Thing
   b. Mass0
   c. Undefined
   d. Undefined

162. A _____ is one of the basic shapes of geometry: a polygon with three vertices and three sides which are straight line segments.
   a. Thing
   b. Triangle0
   c. Undefined
   d. Undefined

163. In mathematics, a _____ is the set of all points in three-dimensional space (R^3) which are at distance r from a fixed point of that space, where r is a positive real number called the radius of the _____. The fixed point is called the center or centre, and is not part of the _____ itself.
   a. Thing
   b. Sphere0
   c. Undefined
   d. Undefined

164. In mathematics, a _____ is a quadric surface, with the following equation in Cartesian coordinates: $(x/_a)^2 + (y/_b)^2 = 1$.
   a. Thing
   b. Cylinder0
   c. Undefined
   d. Undefined

165. In geometry, a _____ (Greek words diairo = divide and metro = measure) of a circle is any straight line segment that passes through the centre and whose endpoints are on the circular boundary, or, in more modern usage, the length of such a line segment. When using the word in the more modern sense, one speaks of the _____ rather than a _____, because all diameters of a circle have the same length. This length is twice the radius. The _____ of a circle is also the longest chord that the circle has.
   a. Diameter0
   b. Thing
   c. Undefined
   d. Undefined

166. _____ is a special mathematical relationship between two quantities.Two quantities are called proportional if they vary in such a way that one of the quantities is a constant multiple of the other, or equivalently if they have a constant ratio.

Chapter 4. Polynomial Functions

a. Proportionality0
c. Undefined
b. Thing
d. Undefined

167. _____ is the sub-discipline of fluid mechanics dealing with fluids liquids and gases in motion.
a. Thing
c. Undefined
b. Fluid flow0
d. Undefined

168. In astronomy, geography, geometry and related sciences and contexts, a plane is said to be _____ at a given point if it is locally perpendicular to the gradient of the gravity field, i.e., with the direction of the gravitational force at that point.
a. Thing
c. Undefined
b. Horizontal0
d. Undefined

169. _____ is the act of transforming data with the aim of extracting useful information and facilitating conclusions.
a. Concept
c. Undefined
b. Data analysis0
d. Undefined

170. In the scientific method, an _____ (Latin: ex-+-periri, "of (or from) trying"), is a set of actions and observations, performed in the context of solving a particular problem or question, in order to support or falsify a hypothesis or research concerning phenomena.
a. Experiment0
c. Undefined
b. Thing
d. Undefined

171. _____, Greek for "knowledge of nature," is the branch of science concerned with the discovery and characterization of universal laws which govern matter, energy, space, and time.
a. Physics0
c. Undefined
b. Thing
d. Undefined

172. _____ is electromagnetic radiation with a wavelength that is visible to the eye (visible _____) or, in a technical or scientific context, electromagnetic radiation of any wavelength.
a. Light0
c. Undefined
b. Thing
d. Undefined

173. The deductive-nomological model is a formalized view of scientific _____ in natural language.
a. Thing
c. Undefined
b. Explanation0
d. Undefined

174. A _____ is a tool similar to a ruler, but without markings.
a. Thing
c. Undefined
b. Straightedge0
d. Undefined

175. The _____ of an object is the extra energy which it possesses due to its motion.
a. Thing
c. Undefined
b. Kinetic energy0
d. Undefined

176. A _____ is a one-dimensional picture in which the integers are shown as specially-marked points evenly spaced on a line.

a. Number line0
b. Thing
c. Undefined
d. Undefined

177. In mathematics, an _____ is a statement about the relative size or order of two objects.
a. Thing
b. Inequality0
c. Undefined
d. Undefined

178. In mathematics, an _____ is any of the arguments, i.e. "inputs", to a function. Thus if we have a function f(x), then x is a _____.
a. Independent variable0
b. Thing
c. Undefined
d. Undefined

179. In geometry, a _____ is defined as a quadrilateral where all four of its angles are right angles.
a. Rectangle0
b. Thing
c. Undefined
d. Undefined

180. A _____ is a unit of length in the metric system, equal to one thousand metres, the current SI base unit of length
a. Thing
b. Kilometer0
c. Undefined
d. Undefined

181. A _____ is a three-dimensional solid object bounded by six square faces, facets, or sides, with three meeting at each vertex.
a. Cube0
b. Thing
c. Undefined
d. Undefined

182. _____ is a term applied when talking about the movement of air from one place to the next.
a. Thing
b. Wind speed0
c. Undefined
d. Undefined

183. In mathematics, a _____ of a number x is a number r such that $r^2 = x$, or in words, a number r whose square (the result of multiplying the number by itself) is x.
a. Thing
b. Square root0
c. Undefined
d. Undefined

184. Any point where a graph makes contact with an coordinate axis is called an _____ of the graph
a. Thing
b. Intercept0
c. Undefined
d. Undefined

185. In mathematics, a _____ is a demonstration that, assuming certain axioms, some statement is necessarily true.
a. Proof0
b. Thing
c. Undefined
d. Undefined

186. Mathematical _____ are demonstrations that, assuming certain axioms, some statement is necessarily true.

Chapter 4. Polynomial Functions

a. Proofs0
b. Thing
c. Undefined
d. Undefined

187. In mathematics, an _____ is a complex number whose square is a negative real number. They were defined in 1572 by Rafael Bombelli.
   a. Thing
   b. Imaginary number0
   c. Undefined
   d. Undefined

188. A _____ was a citizen of Babylonia, named for its capital city, Babylon, which was an ancient state in the south part of Mesopotamia (in modern Iraq), combining the territories of Sumer and Akkad.
   a. Place
   b. Babylonian0
   c. Undefined
   d. Undefined

189. In Euclidean geometry, a _____ is the set of all points in a plane at a fixed distance, called the radius, from a given point, the center.
   a. Circle0
   b. Thing
   c. Undefined
   d. Undefined

190. In algebra, the _____ decomposition or _____ expansion is used to reduce the degree of either the numerator or the denominator of a rational function.
   a. Partial fraction0
   b. Thing
   c. Undefined
   d. Undefined

191. In geometry, the _____ of an object is a point in some sense in the middle of the object.
   a. Thing
   b. Center0
   c. Undefined
   d. Undefined

192. In mathematics, an _____ .
   a. Ellipse0
   b. Thing
   c. Undefined
   d. Undefined

193. In mathematics, a _____ is a type of conic section defined as the intersection between a right circular conical surface and a plane which cuts through both halves of the cone.
   a. Thing
   b. Hyperbola0
   c. Undefined
   d. Undefined

194. In mathematics, a _____ section is a curve that can be formed by intersecting a cone with a plane.
   a. Thing
   b. Conic0
   c. Undefined
   d. Undefined

Chapter 5. Rational Functions and Conics

1. _____ is a straight line or curve A to which another curve B the one being studied approaches closer and closer as one moves along it.
   - a. Thing
   - b. Vertical asymptote0
   - c. Undefined
   - d. Undefined

2. _____ are the basic objects of study in graph theory. Informally speaking, a graph is a set of objects called points, nodes, or vertices connected by links called lines or edges.
   - a. Graphs0
   - b. Thing
   - c. Undefined
   - d. Undefined

3. In mathematics, a _____ number is a number which can be expressed as a ratio of two integers. Non-integer _____ numbers (commonly called fractions) are usually written as the vulgar fraction a / b, where b is not zero.
   - a. Rational0
   - b. Thing
   - c. Undefined
   - d. Undefined

4. In mathematics, a _____ is any function which can be written as the ratio of two polynomial functions.
   - a. Rational function0
   - b. Thing
   - c. Undefined
   - d. Undefined

5. An _____ is a straight line or curve A to which another curve B approaches closer and closer as one moves along it. As one moves along B, the space between it and the _____ A becomes smaller and smaller, and can in fact be made as small as one could wish by going far enough along. A curve may or may not touch or cross its _____. In fact, the curve may intersect the _____ an infinite number of times.
   - a. Thing
   - b. Asymptote0
   - c. Undefined
   - d. Undefined

6. In astronomy, geography, geometry and related sciences and contexts, a plane is said to be _____ at a given point if it is locally perpendicular to the gradient of the gravity field, i.e., with the direction of the gravitational force at that point.
   - a. Horizontal0
   - b. Thing
   - c. Undefined
   - d. Undefined

7. The mathematical concept of a _____ expresses the intuitive idea of deterministic dependence between two quantities, one of which is viewed as primary and the other as secondary. A _____ then is a way to associate a unique output for each input of a specified type, for example, a real number or an element of a given set.
   - a. Function0
   - b. Thing
   - c. Undefined
   - d. Undefined

8. In mathematics, a _____ of a k-place relation $L \subseteq X_1 \times ... \times X_k$ is one of the sets X_j, $1 \leq j \leq k$. In the special case where k = 2 and $L \subseteq X_1 \times X_2$ is a function $L : X_1 \to X_2$, it is conventional to refer to X_1 as the _____ of the function and to refer to X_2 as the codomain of the function.
   - a. Thing
   - b. Domain0
   - c. Undefined
   - d. Undefined

9. In mathematics, a _____ is an expression that is constructed from one or more variables and constants, using only the operations of addition, subtraction, multiplication, and constant positive whole number exponents. is a _____. Note in particular that division by an expression containing a variable is not in general allowed in polynomials. [1]

a. Polynomial0 b. Thing
c. Undefined d. Undefined

10. In mathematics, a _____ may be described informally as a number that can be given by an infinite decimal representation.
   a. Thing b. Real number0
   c. Undefined d. Undefined

11. A _____ is the part of a fraction that tells how many equal parts make up a whole, and which is used in the name of the fraction: "halves", "thirds", "fourths" or "quarters", "fifths" and so on.
   a. Concept b. Denominator0
   c. Undefined d. Undefined

12. In mathematics, a _____ is a type of conic section defined as the intersection between a right circular conical surface and a plane which cuts through both halves of the cone.
   a. Thing b. Hyperbola0
   c. Undefined d. Undefined

13. In mathematics, there are several meanings of _____ depending on the subject.
   a. Degree0 b. Thing
   c. Undefined d. Undefined

14. A _____ is a numeral used to indicate a count. The most common use of the word today is to name the part of a fraction that tells the number or count of equal parts.
   a. Thing b. Numerator0
   c. Undefined d. Undefined

15. In mathematics, a _____ is a constant multiplicative factor of a certain object. The object can be such things as a variable, a vector, a function, etc. For example, the _____ of $9x^2$ is 9.
   a. Coefficient0 b. Thing
   c. Undefined d. Undefined

16. The word _____ comes from the Latin word linearis, which means created by lines.
   a. Thing b. Linear0
   c. Undefined d. Undefined

17. A _____ is a first degree polynomial mathematical function of the form: f(x) = mx + b where m and b are real constants and x is a real variable.
   a. Linear function0 b. Thing
   c. Undefined d. Undefined

18. _____ is a way of expressing a number as a fraction of 100 per cent meaning "per hundred".
   a. Thing b. Percent0
   c. Undefined d. Undefined

Chapter 5. Rational Functions and Conics

19. _____ is a kind of property which exists as magnitude or multitude. It is among the basic classes of things along with quality, substance, change, and relation.
    a. Amount0
    b. Thing
    c. Undefined
    d. Undefined

20. In Euclidean geometry, a uniform _____ is a linear transformation that enlargers or diminishes objects, and whose _____ factor is the same in all directions. This is also called homothethy.
    a. Scale0
    b. Thing
    c. Undefined
    d. Undefined

21. In mathematics, a _____ section is a curve that can be formed by intersecting a cone with a plane.
    a. Conic0
    b. Thing
    c. Undefined
    d. Undefined

22. In geometry and physics, _____ are half-lines that continue forever in one direction.
    a. Thing
    b. Rays0
    c. Undefined
    d. Undefined

23. The _____ of a mathematical object is its size: a property by which it can be larger or smaller than other objects of the same kind; in technical terms, an ordering of the class of objects to which it belongs.
    a. Thing
    b. Magnitude0
    c. Undefined
    d. Undefined

24. _____ is the property of a physical object that quantifies the amount of matter and energy it is equivalent to.
    a. Mass0
    b. Thing
    c. Undefined
    d. Undefined

25. In mathematics, a _____ is the result of multiplying, or an expression that identifies factors to be multiplied.
    a. Thing
    b. Product0
    c. Undefined
    d. Undefined

26. In sociology and biology a _____ is the collection of people or organisms of a particular species living in a given geographic area or space, usually measured by a census.
    a. Thing
    b. Population0
    c. Undefined
    d. Undefined

27. The payment of _____ as remuneration for services rendered or products sold is a common way to reward sales people.
    a. Commission0
    b. Thing
    c. Undefined
    d. Undefined

28. _____ is change in population over time, and can be quantified as the change in the number of individuals in a population per unit time.
    a. Thing
    b. Population growth0
    c. Undefined
    d. Undefined

Chapter 5. Rational Functions and Conics

29. In the scientific method, an _____ (Latin: ex-+-periri, "of (or from) trying"), is a set of actions and observations, performed in the context of solving a particular problem or question, in order to support or falsify a hypothesis or research concerning phenomena.
    a. Experiment0
    b. Thing
    c. Undefined
    d. Undefined

30. _____ is a synonym for information.
    a. Data0
    b. Thing
    c. Undefined
    d. Undefined

31. In geographic information systems, a _____ comprises an entity with a geographic location, typically determined by points, arcs, or polygons. Carriageways and cadastres exemplify _____ data.
    a. Feature0
    b. Thing
    c. Undefined
    d. Undefined

32. In common philosophical language, a proposition or _____, is the content of an assertion, that is, it is true-or-false and defined by the meaning of a particular piece of language.
    a. Concept
    b. Statement0
    c. Undefined
    d. Undefined

33. The _____ of a ring R is defined to be the smallest positive integer n such that $n\,a = 0$, for all a in R.
    a. Characteristic0
    b. Thing
    c. Undefined
    d. Undefined

34. _____ element of an element x with respect to a binary operation * with identity element e is an element y such that x * y = y * x = e. In particular,
    a. Inverse0
    b. Thing
    c. Undefined
    d. Undefined

35. An _____ is a function which does the reverse of a given function.
    a. Thing
    b. Inverse function0
    c. Undefined
    d. Undefined

36. In arithmetic, _____ is a procedure for calculating the division of one integer, called the dividend, by another integer called the divisor, to produce a result called the quotient.
    a. Long division0
    b. Thing
    c. Undefined
    d. Undefined

37. In mathematics, an _____, mean, or central tendency of a data set refers to a measure of the "middle" or "expected" value of the data set.
    a. Concept
    b. Average0
    c. Undefined
    d. Undefined

38. In mathematics, the concept of a _____ tries to capture the intuitive idea of a geometrical one-dimensional and continuous object. A simple example is the circle.

Chapter 5. Rational Functions and Conics

  a. Curve0
  b. Thing
  c. Undefined
  d. Undefined

39. In mathematics, _____ are the intuitive idea of a geometrical one-dimensional and continuous object.
  a. Thing
  b. Curves0
  c. Undefined
  d. Undefined

40. _____ means "constancy", i.e. if something retains a certain feature even after we change a way of looking at it, then it is symmetric.
  a. Thing
  b. Symmetry0
  c. Undefined
  d. Undefined

41. In mathematics, the _____ of a coordinate system is the point where the axes of the system intersect.
  a. Origin0
  b. Thing
  c. Undefined
  d. Undefined

42. Any point where a graph makes contact with an coordinate axis is called an _____ of the graph
  a. Thing
  b. Intercept0
  c. Undefined
  d. Undefined

43. In geometry, an _____ angle is an angle that is not a 90 degree angle, or an angle that is divisible by 90: 180, 270, 360/0
  a. Thing
  b. Oblique0
  c. Undefined
  d. Undefined

44. In mathematics, _____ is the decomposition of an object into a product of other objects, or factors, which when multiplied together give the original.
  a. Factoring0
  b. Thing
  c. Undefined
  d. Undefined

45. In plane geometry, a _____ is a polygon with four equal sides, four right angles, and parallel opposite sides. In algebra, the _____ of a number is that number multiplied by itself.
  a. Square0
  b. Thing
  c. Undefined
  d. Undefined

46. In finance, a _____ is collateral that the holder of a position in securities, options, or futures contracts has to deposit to cover the credit risk of his counterparty.
  a. Thing
  b. Margin0
  c. Undefined
  d. Undefined

47. A _____ is a symbolic representation denoting a quantity or expression. It often represents an "unknown" quantity that has the potential to change.
  a. Variable0
  b. Thing
  c. Undefined
  d. Undefined

48. The deductive-nomological model is a formalized view of scientific _____ in natural language.

Chapter 5. Rational Functions and Conics

a. Explanation0
b. Thing
c. Undefined
d. Undefined

49. A _____ is a negotiable instrument instructing a financial institution to pay a specific amount of a specific currency from a specific demand account held in the maker/depositor's name with that institution. Both the maker and payee may be natural persons or legal entities.
    a. Thing
    b. Check0
    c. Undefined
    d. Undefined

50. Deductive _____ is the kind of _____ in which the conclusion is necessitated by, or reached from, previously known facts (the premises).
    a. Reasoning0
    b. Thing
    c. Undefined
    d. Undefined

51. In mathematics, a _____ is a condition that a solution to an optimization problem must satisfy in order to be acceptable.
    a. Thing
    b. Constraint0
    c. Undefined
    d. Undefined

52. The _____ is the highest point in a certain portion of a graph.
    a. Thing
    b. Relative maximum0
    c. Undefined
    d. Undefined

53. In chemistry, a _____ is substance made by combining two or more different materials in such a way that no chemical reaction occurs.
    a. Thing
    b. Mixture0
    c. Undefined
    d. Undefined

54. _____ is the application of tools and a processing medium to the transformation of raw materials into finished goods for sale.
    a. Manufacturing0
    b. Thing
    c. Undefined
    d. Undefined

55. In mathematics, in the field of group theory, a _____ of a group is a quasisimple subnormal subgroup.
    a. Component0
    b. Concept
    c. Undefined
    d. Undefined

56. The metre (or _____, see spelling differences) is a measure of length. It is the basic unit of length in the metric system and in the International System of Units (SI), used around the world for general and scientific purposes.
    a. Concept
    b. Meter0
    c. Undefined
    d. Undefined

57. The _____ of measurement are a globally standardized and modernized form of the metric system.
    a. Units0
    b. Thing
    c. Undefined
    d. Undefined

Chapter 5. Rational Functions and Conics

58. A _____ is a unit of length, usually used to measure distance, in a number of different systems, including Imperial units, United States customary units and Norwegian/Swedish mil. Its size can vary from system to system, but in each is between 1 and 10 kilometers. In contemporary English contexts _____ refers to either:
   a. Thing
   b. Mile0
   c. Undefined
   d. Undefined

59. _____ is a unit of speed, expressing the number of international miles covered per hour.
   a. Miles per hour0
   b. Thing
   c. Undefined
   d. Undefined

60. An _____ is a combination of numbers, operators, grouping symbols and/or free variables and bound variables arranged in a meaningful way which can be evaluated..
   a. Expression0
   b. Thing
   c. Undefined
   d. Undefined

61. A _____ is a one-dimensional picture in which the integers are shown as specially-marked points evenly spaced on a line.
   a. Number line0
   b. Thing
   c. Undefined
   d. Undefined

62. In mathematics, an _____ is a statement about the relative size or order of two objects.
   a. Thing
   b. Inequality0
   c. Undefined
   d. Undefined

63. In algebra, the _____ decomposition or _____ expansion is used to reduce the degree of either the numerator or the denominator of a rational function.
   a. Thing
   b. Partial fraction0
   c. Undefined
   d. Undefined

64. A _____ fraction is a fraction in which the absolute value of the numerator is less than the denominator--hence, the absolute value of the fraction is less than 1.
   a. Proper0
   b. Thing
   c. Undefined
   d. Undefined

65. _____ refers to the reduction of the body of a formerly living organism into simpler forms of matter.
   a. Thing
   b. Decomposing0
   c. Undefined
   d. Undefined

66. In mathematics, factorization (British English: factorisation) or factoring is the decomposition of an object (for example, a number, a polynomial, or a matrix) into a product of other objects, or _____, which when multiplied together give the original.
   a. Thing
   b. Factors0
   c. Undefined
   d. Undefined

67. A _____ is the part of the dividend that is left over when the dividend is not evenly divisible by the divisor.

Chapter 5. Rational Functions and Conics

a. Remainder0
b. Thing
c. Undefined
d. Undefined

68. In mathematics and the mathematical sciences, a _____ is a fixed, but possibly unspecified, value. This is in contrast to a variable, which is not fixed.
    a. Thing
    b. Constant0
    c. Undefined
    d. Undefined

69. _____ has many meanings, most of which simply .
    a. Power0
    b. Thing
    c. Undefined
    d. Undefined

70. Johann Bernoulli was a Swiss mathematician. He was the brother of Jakob Bernoulli, and the father of Daniel Bernoulli and Nicolaus II Bernoulli. He is also known as Jean or _____. He educated the great mathematician Leonhard Euler in his youth.
    a. Thing
    b. John Bernoulli0
    c. Undefined
    d. Undefined

71. _____ is a mathematical subject that includes the study of limits, derivatives, integrals, and power series and constitutes a major part of modern university curriculum.
    a. Calculus0
    b. Thing
    c. Undefined
    d. Undefined

72. In mathematics, a _____ is a countable collection of open covers of a topological space that satisfies certain separation axioms.
    a. Development0
    b. Thing
    c. Undefined
    d. Undefined

73. Leonhard _____ was a pioneering Swiss mathematician and physicist, who spent most of his life in Russia and Germany.
    a. Euler0
    b. Person
    c. Undefined
    d. Undefined

74. _____ was a pioneering Swiss mathematician and physicist, who spent most of his life in Russia and Germany.
    a. Person
    b. Leonhard Euler0
    c. Undefined
    d. Undefined

75. _____ traditionally refers to the statistical process of determining comparable scores on different forms of an exam
    a. Equating0
    b. Thing
    c. Undefined
    d. Undefined

76. _____ are a set of equations containing multiple variables.
    a. Thing
    b. Systems of equations0
    c. Undefined
    d. Undefined

Chapter 5. Rational Functions and Conics

77. _____ are any documents that aim to streamline particular processes according to a set routine.
   a. Thing
   b. Guidelines0
   c. Undefined
   d. Undefined

78. _____ is a physical property of a system that underlies the common notions of hot and cold; something that is hotter has the greater _____.
   a. Thing
   b. Temperature0
   c. Undefined
   d. Undefined

79. In mathematics, the _____ of a function is the set of all "output" values produced by that function. Given a function $f : A \to B$, the _____ of f, is defined to be the set $\{x \in B : x = f(a) \text{ for some } a \in A\}$.
   a. Thing
   b. Range0
   c. Undefined
   d. Undefined

80. _____ is a temperature scale named after the German physicist Daniel Gabriel _____, who proposed it in 1724.
   a. Fahrenheit0
   b. Thing
   c. Undefined
   d. Undefined

81. _____ is a branch of physics that studies the effects of changes in temperature, pressure, and volume on physical systems at the macroscopic scale by analyzing the collective motion of their particles using statistics.
   a. Thing
   b. Thermodynamics0
   c. Undefined
   d. Undefined

82. In mathematics, the _____ (or modulus) of a real number is its numerical value without regard to its sign.
   a. Thing
   b. Absolute value0
   c. Undefined
   d. Undefined

83. In business, particularly accounting, a _____ is the time intervals that the accounts, statement, payments, or other calculations cover.
   a. Period0
   b. Thing
   c. Undefined
   d. Undefined

84. In mathematics, a _____ is a curve that can be formed by intersecting a cone with a plane.
   a. Thing
   b. Conic section0
   c. Undefined
   d. Undefined

85. In mathematics, a _____ is a two-dimensional manifold or surface that is perfectly flat.
   a. Thing
   b. Plane0
   c. Undefined
   d. Undefined

86. A _____ is a three-dimensional geometric shape formed by straight lines through a fixed point (vertex) to the points of a fixed curve (directrix)
   a. Concept
   b. Cone0
   c. Undefined
   d. Undefined

Chapter 5. Rational Functions and Conics

87. In mathematics, the _____ of two sets A and B is the set that contains all elements of A that also belong to B (or equivalently, all elements of B that also belong to A), but no other elements.
    a. Thing
    b. Intersection0
    c. Undefined
    d. Undefined

88. In geometry, a _____ is a special kind of point, usually a corner of a polygon, polyhedron, or higher dimensional polytope. In the geometry of curves a _____ is a point of where the first derivative of curvature is zero. In graph theory, a _____ is the fundamental unit out of which graphs are formed
    a. Thing
    b. Vertex0
    c. Undefined
    d. Undefined

89. In mathematics, a class _____ is a structure used to organize the various Galois groups and modules that appear in class field theory. They were invented by Emil Artin and John Tate.
    a. Thing
    b. Formation0
    c. Undefined
    d. Undefined

90. In geometry, _____ lines are two lines that share one or more common points.
    a. Thing
    b. Intersecting0
    c. Undefined
    d. Undefined

91. In mathematics, the _____ is a conic section generated by the intersection of a right circular conical surface and a plane parallel to a generating straight line of that surface. It can also be defined as locus of points in a plane which are equidistant from a given point.
    a. Thing
    b. Parabola0
    c. Undefined
    d. Undefined

92. _____ is the middle point of a line segment.
    a. Thing
    b. Midpoint0
    c. Undefined
    d. Undefined

93. An _____ is a straight line around which a geometric figure can be rotated.
    a. Thing
    b. Axis0
    c. Undefined
    d. Undefined

94. _____ is a notation for writing numbers that is often used by scientists and mathematicians to make it easier to write large and small numbers.
    a. Scientific notation0
    b. Thing
    c. Undefined
    d. Undefined

95. In geometry, the _____ of an object is a point in some sense in the middle of the object.
    a. Thing
    b. Center0
    c. Undefined
    d. Undefined

96. In mathematics, an _____ .

Chapter 5. Rational Functions and Conics

a. Ellipse0
b. Thing
c. Undefined
d. Undefined

97. In geometry, the _____ are a pair of special points used in describing conic sections. The four types of conic sections are the circle, parabola, ellipse, and hyperbola.
    a. Thing
    b. Foci0
    c. Undefined
    d. Undefined

98. In geometry, two lines or planes if one falls on the other in such a way as to create congruent adjacent angles. The term may be used as a noun or adjective. Thus, referring to Figure 1, the line AB is the _____ to CD through the point B.
    a. Thing
    b. Perpendicular0
    c. Undefined
    d. Undefined

99. In linear algebra, a _____ of a matrix A is the determinant of some smaller square matrix, cut down from A.
    a. Minor0
    b. Thing
    c. Undefined
    d. Undefined

100. In geometry, an _____ is a point at which a line segment or ray terminates.
    a. Endpoint0
    b. Thing
    c. Undefined
    d. Undefined

101. A _____ is the result of the addition of a set of numbers. The numbers may be natural numbers, complex numbers, matrices, or still more complicated objects. An infinite _____ is a subtle procedure known as a series.
    a. Thing
    b. Sum0
    c. Undefined
    d. Undefined

102. In geometry, a line _____ is a part of a line that is bounded by two end points, and contains every point on the line between its end points.
    a. Segment0
    b. Concept
    c. Undefined
    d. Undefined

103. A _____ is a part of a line that is bounded by two end points, and contains every point on the line between its end points.
    a. Thing
    b. Line segment0
    c. Undefined
    d. Undefined

104. In algebra, a _____ is a binomial formed by taking the opposite of the second term of a binomial.
    a. Thing
    b. Conjugate0
    c. Undefined
    d. Undefined

105. A _____ is a set of numbers that designate location in a given reference system, such as x,y in a planar _____ system or an x,y,z in a three-dimensional _____ system.
    a. Thing
    b. Coordinate0
    c. Undefined
    d. Undefined

Chapter 5. Rational Functions and Conics

106. In geometry, a _____ is the intersection of a body in 2-dimensional space with a line, or of a body in 3-dimensional space with a plane
   a. Cross section0
   b. Thing
   c. Undefined
   d. Undefined

107. A _____, known as a parabolic dish or a parabolic mirror, is a reflective device, commonly formed in the shape of a paraboloid of revolution.
   a. Thing
   b. Parabolic reflector0
   c. Undefined
   d. Undefined

108. _____ is electromagnetic radiation with a wavelength that is visible to the eye (visible _____) or, in a technical or scientific context, electromagnetic radiation of any wavelength.
   a. Light0
   b. Thing
   c. Undefined
   d. Undefined

109. The Yakovlev Yak-25, NATO designation _____-A / Mandrake, was a swept wing, turbojet-powered interceptor aircraft and reconnaissance aircraft used by the Soviet Union.
   a. Thing
   b. Flashlight0
   c. Undefined
   d. Undefined

110. A _____ is a type of bridge that has been created since ancient times as early as 100 AD.
   a. Thing
   b. Suspension bridge0
   c. Undefined
   d. Undefined

111. In mathematics and its applications, a _____ is a system for assigning an n-tuple of numbers or scalars to each point in an n-dimensional space.
   a. Coordinate system0
   b. Concept
   c. Undefined
   d. Undefined

112. _____ is the art and science of designing buildings and structures.
   a. Thing
   b. Architecture0
   c. Undefined
   d. Undefined

113. In a conic section, the _____ is the chord parallel to the directrix through the focus, with the symbol 2l.
   a. Thing
   b. Latus rectum0
   c. Undefined
   d. Undefined

114. A _____ given two distinct points A and B on the _____, is the set of points C on the line containing points A and B such that A is not strictly between C and B.
   a. Ray0
   b. Thing
   c. Undefined
   d. Undefined

115. _____ is the process of planning, recording, and controlling the movement of a craft or vehicle from one place to another.

Chapter 5. Rational Functions and Conics

    a. Navigation0
    c. Undefined
    b. Thing
    d. Undefined

116. In Euclidean geometry, a _____ is the set of all points in a plane at a fixed distance, called the radius, from a given point, the center.
    a. Circle0
    c. Undefined
    b. Thing
    d. Undefined

117. In mathematics, a _____ is a mathematical statement which appears likely to be true, but has not been formally proven to be true under the rules of mathematical logic.
    a. Concept
    c. Undefined
    b. Conjecture0
    d. Undefined

118. In mathematics, a _____ case is a limiting case in which a class of object changes its nature so as to belong to another, usually simpler, class.
    a. Thing
    c. Undefined
    b. Degenerate0
    d. Undefined

119. In mathematics, a conic section is a curve that can be formed by interesting a cone with a plane. _____ is when a plane passes through the apex of a cone.
    a. Degenerate conic0
    c. Undefined
    b. Thing
    d. Undefined

120. In mathematics, an _____ on a real vector space is a choice of which ordered bases are "positively" oriented, or right-handed, and which are "negatively" oriented, or left-handed.
    a. Orientation0
    c. Undefined
    b. Thing
    d. Undefined

121. A _____ is a polynomial function of the form $f(x) = ax^2 + bx + c$, where a, b, c are real numbers and a , 0.
    a. Event
    c. Undefined
    b. Quadratic function0
    d. Undefined

122. Acid _____ ratio measures the ability of a company to use its near cash or quick assets to immediately extinguish its current liabilities.
    a. Thing
    c. Undefined
    b. Test0
    d. Undefined

123. In Euclidean geometry, a _____ is moving every point a constant distance in a specified direction.
    a. Concept
    c. Undefined
    b. Translation0
    d. Undefined

124. In geometry, _____, or general position for a set of points, or other configuration, means the general case situation, as opposed to some more special or coincidental cases that are possible.
    a. Thing
    c. Undefined
    b. Standard position0
    d. Undefined

Chapter 5. Rational Functions and Conics 105

125. In classical geometry, a _____ of a circle or sphere is any line segment from its center to its boundary. By extension, the _____ of a circle or sphere is the length of any such segment. The _____ is half the diameter. In science and engineering the term _____ of curvature is commonly used as a synonym for _____.
   a. Thing
   b. Radius0
   c. Undefined
   d. Undefined

126. In geometry, a _____ is defined as a quadrilateral where all four of its angles are right angles.
   a. Rectangle0
   b. Thing
   c. Undefined
   d. Undefined

127. In physics, an _____ is the path that an object makes around another object while under the influence of a source of centripetal force, such as gravity.
   a. Orbit0
   b. Thing
   c. Undefined
   d. Undefined

128. _____ is a business term for the amount of money that a company receives from its activities in a given period, mostly from sales of products and/or services to customers
   a. Thing
   b. Revenue0
   c. Undefined
   d. Undefined

129. In linear algebra, the _____ of an n-by-n square matrix A is defined to be the sum of the elements on the main diagonal of A,
   a. Trace0
   b. Thing
   c. Undefined
   d. Undefined

130. _____ of an object is its speed in a particular direction.
   a. Velocity0
   b. Thing
   c. Undefined
   d. Undefined

131. For a given gravitational field and a given position, the _____ is the minimum speed an object without propulsion needs to have to move away indefinitely from the source of the field, as opposed to falling back or staying in an orbit within a bounded distance from the source.
   a. Thing
   b. Escape velocity0
   c. Undefined
   d. Undefined

132. A _____ is any object propelled through space by the applicationp of a force.
   a. Projectile0
   b. Thing
   c. Undefined
   d. Undefined

133. _____ is the path a moving object follows through space.
   a. Thing
   b. Projectile motion0
   c. Undefined
   d. Undefined

134. _____ is a parameter associated with every conic section.

Chapter 5. Rational Functions and Conics

a. Thing
b. Eccentricity0
c. Undefined
d. Undefined

135. A _____ is a function that assigns a number to subsets of a given set.
a. Thing
b. Measure0
c. Undefined
d. Undefined

136. _____ is the point in a planet's orbit where it is closest to the sun
a. Thing
b. Perihelion0
c. Undefined
d. Undefined

137. _____ is the point of greatest or least distance of the elliptical orbit of an astronomical object from its center of attraction, which is generally the center of mass of the system.
a. Thing
b. Aphelion0
c. Undefined
d. Undefined

138. _____ is a branch of mathematics concerning the study of structure, relation and quantity.
a. Concept
b. Algebra0
c. Undefined
d. Undefined

139. A _____ is a simplified and structured visual representation of concepts, ideas, constructions, relations, statistical data, anatomy etc used in all aspects of human activities to visualize and clarify the topic.
a. Thing
b. Diagram0
c. Undefined
d. Undefined

140. _____ Any process by which a specified characteristic usually amplitude of the output of a device is prevented from exceeding a predetermined value.
a. Limiting0
b. Thing
c. Undefined
d. Undefined

141. _____ generally, is the synthesis of triose phospates and ultimately starch, glucose and other products from sunlight, carbon dioxide and water.
a. Thing
b. Photosynthesis0
c. Undefined
d. Undefined

142. A _____ is an arch whose intrados is half an ellipse; typically, it is defined as a three or five-centered arch.
a. Thing
b. Semielliptical archway0
c. Undefined
d. Undefined

143. In Euclidean geometry, an _____ is a closed segment of a differentiable curve in the two-dimensional plane; for example, a circular _____ is a segment of a circle.
a. Concept
b. Arc0
c. Undefined
d. Undefined

144. A _____, or stained glass window refers either to the material of colored glass or to the art and craft of working with it.

Chapter 5. Rational Functions and Conics

a. Thing
c. Undefined
b. Church window0
d. Undefined

145. In mathematical analysis and related areas of mathematics, a set is called _____, if it is, in a certain sense, of finite size.
   a. Bounded0
   c. Undefined
   b. Thing
   d. Undefined

146. A _____ is a unit of length in the metric system, equal to one thousand metres, the current SI base unit of length
   a. Thing
   c. Undefined
   b. Kilometer0
   d. Undefined

147. A _____, as defined by the International Astronomical Union, is a celestial body orbiting a star or stellar remnant that is massive enough to be rounded by its own gravity, not massive enough to cause thermonuclear fusion in its core, and has cleared its neighboring region of planetesimals.
   a. Thing
   c. Undefined
   b. Planet0
   d. Undefined

148. A _____ is one of the basic shapes of geometry: a polygon with three vertices and three sides which are straight line segments.
   a. Triangle0
   c. Undefined
   b. Thing
   d. Undefined

149. An _____ is when two lines intersect somewhere on a plane creating a right angle at intersection
   a. Axes0
   c. Undefined
   b. Thing
   d. Undefined

150. In mathematics, a _____ is a demonstration that, assuming certain axioms, some statement is necessarily true.
   a. Thing
   c. Undefined
   b. Proof0
   d. Undefined

151. Mathematical _____ are demonstrations that, assuming certain axioms, some statement is necessarily true.
   a. Proofs0
   c. Undefined
   b. Thing
   d. Undefined

152. The National _____ is an area in the United States Capitol devoted to statues of people and symbols important in American history.
   a. Statuary Hall0
   c. Undefined
   b. Thing
   d. Undefined

153. A _____ is a gallery beneath a dome or vault or enclosed in a circular or elliptical area in which whispers can be heard clearly in other parts of the building.
   a. Thing
   c. Undefined
   b. Whispering gallery0
   d. Undefined

154. _____ is the transport of people on a trip/journey or the process or time involved in a person or object moving from one location to another.
   a. Thing
   b. Travel0
   c. Undefined
   d. Undefined

Chapter 6. Exponential and Logarithmic Functions

1. In mathematics, _____ growth occurs when the growth rate of a function is always proportional to the function's current size.
   - a. Exponential0
   - b. Thing
   - c. Undefined
   - d. Undefined

2. _____ is one of the most important functions in mathematics. A function commonly used to study growth and decay
   - a. Thing
   - b. Exponential function0
   - c. Undefined
   - d. Undefined

3. The mathematical concept of a _____ expresses the intuitive idea of deterministic dependence between two quantities, one of which is viewed as primary and the other as secondary. A _____ then is a way to associate a unique output for each input of a specified type, for example, a real number or an element of a given set.
   - a. Thing
   - b. Function0
   - c. Undefined
   - d. Undefined

4. In mathematics, a _____ may be described informally as a number that can be given by an infinite decimal representation.
   - a. Thing
   - b. Real number0
   - c. Undefined
   - d. Undefined

5. In mathematics and the mathematical sciences, a _____ is a fixed, but possibly unspecified, value. This is in contrast to a variable, which is not fixed.
   - a. Thing
   - b. Constant0
   - c. Undefined
   - d. Undefined

6. _____ is a function whose values do not vary and thus are constant.
   - a. Constant function0
   - b. Thing
   - c. Undefined
   - d. Undefined

7. A _____ is a set of numbers that designate location in a given reference system, such as x,y in a planar _____ system or an x,y,z in a three-dimensional _____ system.
   - a. Coordinate0
   - b. Thing
   - c. Undefined
   - d. Undefined

8. _____ are the basic objects of study in graph theory. Informally speaking, a graph is a set of objects called points, nodes, or vertices connected by links called lines or edges.
   - a. Graphs0
   - b. Thing
   - c. Undefined
   - d. Undefined

9. In mathematics, a _____ is a two-dimensional manifold or surface that is perfectly flat.
   - a. Plane0
   - b. Thing
   - c. Undefined
   - d. Undefined

10. _____ is a mathematical operation, written a^n, involving two numbers, the base a and the exponent n.

Chapter 6. Exponential and Logarithmic Functions

    a. Exponentiating0
    c. Undefined
    b. Thing
    d. Undefined

11. _____ is a mathematical operation, written a^n, involving two numbers, the base a and the exponent n.
    a. Thing
    c. Undefined
    b. Exponentiation0
    d. Undefined

12. In mathematics, the _____ of a function is the set of all "output" values produced by that function. Given a function $f : A \rightarrow B$, the _____ of f, is defined to be the set $\{x \in B : x = f(a) \text{ for some } a \in A\}$.
    a. Thing
    c. Undefined
    b. Range0
    d. Undefined

13. The _____, the average in everyday English, which is also called the arithmetic _____ (and is distinguished from the geometric _____ or harmonic _____). The average is also called the sample _____. The expected value of a random variable, which is also called the population _____.
    a. Mean0
    c. Undefined
    b. Thing
    d. Undefined

14. In mathematics, an _____ number is any real number that is not a rational number- that is, it is a number which cannot be expressed as a fraction m/n, where m and n are integers.
    a. Irrational0
    c. Undefined
    b. Thing
    d. Undefined

15. A _____ is a symbolic representation denoting a quantity or expression. It often represents an "unknown" quantity that has the potential to change.
    a. Thing
    c. Undefined
    b. Variable0
    d. Undefined

16. A _____ function is a function for which, intuitively, small changes in the input result in small changes in the output.
    a. Continuous0
    c. Undefined
    b. Event
    d. Undefined

17. _____ is a kind of property which exists as magnitude or multitude. It is among the basic classes of things along with quality, substance, change, and relation.
    a. Amount0
    c. Undefined
    b. Thing
    d. Undefined

18. _____ is the fee paid on borrowed money.
    a. Interest0
    c. Undefined
    b. Thing
    d. Undefined

19. In banking and accountancy, the outstanding _____ is the amount of money owned, or due, that remains in a deposit account or a loan account at a given date, after all past remittances, payments and withdrawal have been accounted for.

Chapter 6. Exponential and Logarithmic Functions

    a. Balance0
    c. Undefined
    b. Thing
    d. Undefined

20. A _____ is a special kind of ratio, indicating a relationship between two measurements with different units, such as miles to gallons or cents to pounds.
    a. Rate0
    b. Thing
    c. Undefined
    d. Undefined

21. _____ interest refers to the fact that whenever interest is calculated, it is based not only on the original principal, but also on any unpaid interest that has been added to the principal.
    a. Thing
    b. Compound0
    c. Undefined
    d. Undefined

22. _____ refers to the fact that whenever interest is calculated, it is based not only on the original principal, but also on any unpaid interest that has been added to the principal. The more frequently interest is compounded, the faster the balance grows.
    a. Concept
    b. Compound interest0
    c. Undefined
    d. Undefined

23. An _____ is the fee paid on borrow money.
    a. Interest rate0
    b. Concept
    c. Undefined
    d. Undefined

24. In set theory and other branches of mathematics, the _____ of a collection of sets is the set that contains everything that belongs to any of the sets, but nothing else.
    a. Union0
    b. Thing
    c. Undefined
    d. Undefined

25. In plane geometry, a _____ is a polygon with four equal sides, four right angles, and parallel opposite sides. In algebra, the _____ of a number is that number multiplied by itself.
    a. Thing
    b. Square0
    c. Undefined
    d. Undefined

26. A _____ is a unit of length, usually used to measure distance, in a number of different systems, including Imperial units, United States customary units and Norwegian/Swedish mil. Its size can vary from system to system, but in each is between 1 and 10 kilometers. In contemporary English contexts _____ refers to either:
    a. Mile0
    b. Thing
    c. Undefined
    d. Undefined

27. Initial objects are also called _____, and terminal objects are also called final.
    a. Coterminal0
    b. Thing
    c. Undefined
    d. Undefined

28. In mathematics, a _____ in elementary terms is any of a variety of different functions from geometry, such as rotations, reflections and translations.

112 *Chapter 6. Exponential and Logarithmic Functions*

    a. Thing
    b. Transformation0
    c. Undefined
    d. Undefined

29. In mathematics, an _____, mean, or central tendency of a data set refers to a measure of the "middle" or "expected" value of the data set.
    a. Average0
    b. Concept
    c. Undefined
    d. Undefined

30. In mainstream economics, the word _____ refers to a general rise in prices measured against a standard level of purchasing power.
    a. Thing
    b. Inflation0
    c. Undefined
    d. Undefined

31. In mathematics, a _____ is the result of multiplying, or an expression that identifies factors to be multiplied.
    a. Product0
    b. Thing
    c. Undefined
    d. Undefined

32. The _____ of measurement are a globally standardized and modernized form of the metric system.
    a. Units0
    b. Thing
    c. Undefined
    d. Undefined

33. In economics, supply and _____ describe market relations between prospective sellers and buyers of a good.
    a. Demand0
    b. Thing
    c. Undefined
    d. Undefined

34. In sociology and biology a _____ is the collection of people or organisms of a particular species living in a given geographic area or space, usually measured by a census.
    a. Thing
    b. Population0
    c. Undefined
    d. Undefined

35. _____ is change in population over time, and can be quantified as the change in the number of individuals in a population per unit time.
    a. Thing
    b. Population growth0
    c. Undefined
    d. Undefined

36. _____ is the process in which an unstable atomic nucleus loses energy by emitting radiation in the form of particles or electromagnetic waves.
    a. Radioactive decay0
    b. Thing
    c. Undefined
    d. Undefined

37. _____ is the property of a physical object that quantifies the amount of matter and energy it is equivalent to.
    a. Mass0
    b. Thing
    c. Undefined
    d. Undefined

38. In elementary algebra, an _____ is a set that contains every real number between two indicated numbers and may contain the two numbers themselves.

Chapter 6. Exponential and Logarithmic Functions

a. Thing
b. Interval0
c. Undefined
d. Undefined

39. In Euclidean geometry, a _____ is the set of all points in a plane at a fixed distance, called the radius, from a given point, the center.
   a. Circle0
   b. Thing
   c. Undefined
   d. Undefined

40. In classical geometry, a _____ of a circle or sphere is any line segment from its center to its boundary. By extension, the _____ of a circle or sphere is the length of any such segment. The _____ is half the diameter. In science and engineering the term _____ of curvature is commonly used as a synonym for _____.
   a. Radius0
   b. Thing
   c. Undefined
   d. Undefined

41. _____ is a synonym for information.
   a. Thing
   b. Data0
   c. Undefined
   d. Undefined

42. _____ is the act of transforming data with the aim of extracting useful information and facilitating conclusions.
   a. Data analysis0
   b. Concept
   c. Undefined
   d. Undefined

43. _____ is a way of expressing a number as a fraction of 100 per cent meaning "per hundred".
   a. Thing
   b. Percent0
   c. Undefined
   d. Undefined

44. A _____ is a function that assigns a number to subsets of a given set.
   a. Thing
   b. Measure0
   c. Undefined
   d. Undefined

45. An _____ is a straight line or curve A to which another curve B approaches closer and closer as one moves along it. As one moves along B, the space between it and the _____ A becomes smaller and smaller, and can in fact be made as small as one could wish by going far enough along. A curve may or may not touch or cross its _____. In fact, the curve may intersect the _____ an infinite number of times.
   a. Thing
   b. Asymptote0
   c. Undefined
   d. Undefined

46. Blaise _____ was a French mathematician, physicist, and religious philosopher.
   a. Pascal0
   b. Person
   c. Undefined
   d. Undefined

47. In geometry, an _____ of a triangle is a straight line through a vertex and perpendicular to (i.e. forming a right angle with) the opposite side or an extension of the opposite side.
   a. Altitude0
   b. Concept
   c. Undefined
   d. Undefined

Chapter 6. Exponential and Logarithmic Functions

48. The _____ is the highest point in a certain portion of a graph.
    a. Relative maximum0
    b. Thing
    c. Undefined
    d. Undefined

49. An _____ is when two lines intersect somewhere on a plane creating a right angle at intersection
    a. Thing
    b. Axes0
    c. Undefined
    d. Undefined

50. A _____, scatter diagram or scatter graph is a chart that uses Cartesian coordinates to display values for two variables.
    a. Scatter plot0
    b. Thing
    c. Undefined
    d. Undefined

51. A _____ is a unit of length in the metric system, equal to one thousand metres, the current SI base unit of length
    a. Thing
    b. Kilometer0
    c. Undefined
    d. Undefined

52. In common philosophical language, a proposition or _____, is the content of an assertion, that is, it is true-or-false and defined by the meaning of a particular piece of language.
    a. Statement0
    b. Concept
    c. Undefined
    d. Undefined

53. In mathematics, a _____ is a mathematical statement which appears likely to be true, but has not been formally proven to be true under the rules of mathematical logic.
    a. Conjecture0
    b. Concept
    c. Undefined
    d. Undefined

54. In mathematics, an inequality is a statement about the relative size or order of two objects. For example 14 > 10, or 14 is _____ 10.
    a. Greater than0
    b. Thing
    c. Undefined
    d. Undefined

55. In mathematics, a _____ number is a number which can be expressed as a ratio of two integers. Non-integer _____ numbers (commonly called fractions) are usually written as the vulgar fraction a / b, where b is not zero.
    a. Thing
    b. Rational0
    c. Undefined
    d. Undefined

56. In mathematics, a _____ is any function which can be written as the ratio of two polynomial functions.
    a. Rational function0
    b. Thing
    c. Undefined
    d. Undefined

57. In mathematics, an _____ is a statement about the relative size or order of two objects.
    a. Thing
    b. Inequality0
    c. Undefined
    d. Undefined

58. In mathematics, a _____ section is a curve that can be formed by intersecting a cone with a plane.

Chapter 6. Exponential and Logarithmic Functions

a. Conic0
b. Thing
c. Undefined
d. Undefined

59. _____ element of an element x with respect to a binary operation * with identity element e is an element y such that x * y = y * x = e. In particular,
    a. Inverse0
    b. Thing
    c. Undefined
    d. Undefined

60. An _____ is a function which does the reverse of a given function.
    a. Inverse function0
    b. Thing
    c. Undefined
    d. Undefined

61. In astronomy, geography, geometry and related sciences and contexts, a plane is said to be _____ at a given point if it is locally perpendicular to the gradient of the gravity field, i.e., with the direction of the gravitational force at that point.
    a. Thing
    b. Horizontal0
    c. Undefined
    d. Undefined

62. _____ is a test used to determine if a function is injective, surjective or bijective.
    a. Thing
    b. Horizontal line test0
    c. Undefined
    d. Undefined

63. Acid _____ ratio measures the ability of a company to use its near cash or quick assets to immediately extinguish its current liabilities.
    a. Test0
    b. Thing
    c. Undefined
    d. Undefined

64. Equivalence is the condition of being _____ or essentially equal.
    a. Equivalent0
    b. Thing
    c. Undefined
    d. Undefined

65. In mathematics, a _____ of a number x is the exponent y of the power by such that $x = b^y$. The value used for the base b must be neither 0 nor 1, nor a root of 1 in the case of the extension to complex numbers, and is typically 10, e, or 2.
    a. Logarithm0
    b. Thing
    c. Undefined
    d. Undefined

66. In mathematics, the _____ is the logarithm with base 10.
    a. Common logarithm0
    b. Thing
    c. Undefined
    d. Undefined

67. In mathematics, the concept of a _____ tries to capture the intuitive idea of a geometrical one-dimensional and continuous object. A simple example is the circle.
    a. Thing
    b. Curve0
    c. Undefined
    d. Undefined

68. A _____ is a number that is less than zero.

Chapter 6. Exponential and Logarithmic Functions

a. Negative number0
b. Thing
c. Undefined
d. Undefined

69. _____ is a straight line or curve A to which another curve B the one being studied approaches closer and closer as one moves along it.
   a. Thing
   b. Vertical asymptote0
   c. Undefined
   d. Undefined

70. In mathematics, a _____ (also spelled reflexion) is a map that transforms an object into its mirror image.
   a. Reflection0
   b. Concept
   c. Undefined
   d. Undefined

71. In mathematics, a _____ of a k-place relation $L \subseteq X_1 \times ... \times X_k$ is one of the sets X_j, $1 \leq j \leq k$. In the special case where k = 2 and $L \subseteq X_1 \times X_2$ is a function $L : X_1 \to X_2$, it is conventional to refer to X_1 as the _____ of the function and to refer to X_2 as the codomain of the function.
   a. Thing
   b. Domain0
   c. Undefined
   d. Undefined

72. _____ is the logarithm to the base e, where e is an irrational constant approximately equal to 2.718281828459.
   a. Natural logarithm0
   b. Thing
   c. Undefined
   d. Undefined

73. An _____ is a combination of numbers, operators, grouping symbols and/or free variables and bound variables arranged in a meaningful way which can be evaluated..
   a. Expression0
   b. Thing
   c. Undefined
   d. Undefined

74. In the scientific method, an _____ (Latin: ex-+-periri, "of (or from) trying"), is a set of actions and observations, performed in the context of solving a particular problem or question, in order to support or falsify a hypothesis or research concerning phenomena.
   a. Experiment0
   b. Thing
   c. Undefined
   d. Undefined

75. A frame of _____ is a particular perspective from which the universe is observed.
   a. Thing
   b. Reference0
   c. Undefined
   d. Undefined

76. The _____ is the total number of human beings alive on the planet Earth at a given time.
   a. World population0
   b. Thing
   c. Undefined
   d. Undefined

77. The _____, i.e., acoustic intensity is defined as the sound power P_{ac} per unit area A.
   a. Sound intensity0
   b. Thing
   c. Undefined
   d. Undefined

78. The _____ relative to a specified or implied reference level.

Chapter 6. Exponential and Logarithmic Functions

a. Thing
b. Decibel0
c. Undefined
d. Undefined

79. The metre (or _____, see spelling differences) is a measure of length. It is the basic unit of length in the metric system and in the International System of Units (SI), used around the world for general and scientific purposes.
a. Meter0
b. Concept
c. Undefined
d. Undefined

80. A _____ of a number is the product of that number with any integer.
a. Multiple0
b. Thing
c. Undefined
d. Undefined

81. John _____ of Merchistoun, nicknamed Marvellous Merchistoun, was a Scottish mathematician, physicist, astronomer/astrologer and 8th Laird of Merchistoun. He is most remembered as the inventor of logarithms and _____'s bones, and for popularizing the use of the decimal point.
a. Napier0
b. Person
c. Undefined
d. Undefined

82. _____ of Nerchistoun, nicknamed Marvellous Merchistoun, was a Scottish mathematician, physicist, astronomer/astrologer and 8th Laird of Merchistoun.
a. John Napier0
b. Person
c. Undefined
d. Undefined

83. A _____ is a deliberate process for transforming one or more inputs into one or more results.
a. Calculation0
b. Thing
c. Undefined
d. Undefined

84. _____ is a branch of mathematics concerning the study of structure, relation and quantity.
a. Concept
b. Algebra0
c. Undefined
d. Undefined

85. Deductive _____ is the kind of _____ in which the conclusion is necessitated by, or reached from, previously known facts (the premises).
a. Reasoning0
b. Thing
c. Undefined
d. Undefined

86. _____ is the symbold used to indicate the nth root of a number
a. Thing
b. Radical0
c. Undefined
d. Undefined

87. _____ systems represent systems whose behavior is not expressible as a sum of the behaviors of its descriptors.
a. Nonlinear0
b. Thing
c. Undefined
d. Undefined

Chapter 6. Exponential and Logarithmic Functions

88. _____ the expected value of a random variable displays the average or central value of the variable. It is a summary value of the distribution of the variable.
    a. Determining0
    b. Thing
    c. Undefined
    d. Undefined

89. A _____ is a quantity that denotes the proportional amount or magnitude of one quantity relative to another.
    a. Thing
    b. Ratio0
    c. Undefined
    d. Undefined

90. The _____ is a unit of length nearly equal to the semi-major axis of Earth's orbit around the Sun. The currently accepted value of the AU is 149 597 870 691 ± 30 metres.
    a. Thing
    b. Astronomical unit0
    c. Undefined
    d. Undefined

91. A _____, as defined by the International Astronomical Union, is a celestial body orbiting a star or stellar remnant that is massive enough to be rounded by its own gravity, not massive enough to cause thermonuclear fusion in its core, and has cleared its neighboring region of planetesimals.
    a. Thing
    b. Planet0
    c. Undefined
    d. Undefined

92. A _____ is the result of the addition of a set of numbers. The numbers may be natural numbers, complex numbers, matrices, or still more complicated objects. An infinite _____ is a subtle procedure known as a series.
    a. Thing
    b. Sum0
    c. Undefined
    d. Undefined

93. In mathematics, a _____ is a demonstration that, assuming certain axioms, some statement is necessarily true.
    a. Proof0
    b. Thing
    c. Undefined
    d. Undefined

94. A _____ is a negotiable instrument instructing a financial institution to pay a specific amount of a specific currency from a specific demand account held in the maker/depositor's name with that institution. Both the maker and payee may be natural persons or legal entities.
    a. Thing
    b. Check0
    c. Undefined
    d. Undefined

95. In geographic information systems, a _____ comprises an entity with a geographic location, typically determined by points, arcs, or polygons. Carriageways and cadastres exemplify _____ data.
    a. Feature0
    b. Thing
    c. Undefined
    d. Undefined

96. In mathematics, the _____ of two sets A and B is the set that contains all elements of A that also belong to B (or equivalently, all elements of B that also belong to A), but no other elements.
    a. Intersection0
    b. Thing
    c. Undefined
    d. Undefined

Chapter 6. Exponential and Logarithmic Functions

97. In linear algebra, the _____ of an n-by-n square matrix A is defined to be the sum of the elements on the main diagonal of A,
    a. Trace0
    b. Thing
    c. Undefined
    d. Undefined

98. One of the three formats applicable to a quadratic function is the _____ which is defined as $f = ax^2 + bx + c$.
    a. General form0
    b. Thing
    c. Undefined
    d. Undefined

99. A _____ is a set of possible values that a variable can take on in order to satisfy a given set of conditions, which may include equations and inequalities.
    a. Thing
    b. Solution set0
    c. Undefined
    d. Undefined

100. _____ variables are variables other than the independent variable that may bear any effect on the behavior of the subject being studied.
    a. Extraneous0
    b. Thing
    c. Undefined
    d. Undefined

101. _____ or investing is a term with several closely-related meanings in business management, finance and economics, related to saving or deferring consumption.
    a. Investment0
    b. Thing
    c. Undefined
    d. Undefined

102. In mathematics, a _____ is an n-tuple with n being 3.
    a. Triple0
    b. Thing
    c. Undefined
    d. Undefined

103. In geometry, a _____ (Greek words diairo = divide and metro = measure) of a circle is any straight line segment that passes through the centre and whose endpoints are on the circular boundary, or, in more modern usage, the length of such a line segment. When using the word in the more modern sense, one speaks of the _____ rather than a _____, because all diameters of a circle have the same length. This length is twice the radius. The _____ of a circle is also the longest chord that the circle has.
    a. Diameter0
    b. Thing
    c. Undefined
    d. Undefined

104. In geometry, the _____ of an object is a point in some sense in the middle of the object.
    a. Center0
    b. Thing
    c. Undefined
    d. Undefined

105. _____ is a mathematical science pertaining to the collection, analysis, interpretation or explanation, and presentation of data. It is applicable to a wide variety of academic disciplines, from the physical and social sciences to the humanities.
    a. Statistics0
    b. Thing
    c. Undefined
    d. Undefined

Chapter 6. Exponential and Logarithmic Functions

106. _____ is the level of functional and/or metabolic efficiency of an organism at both the micro level.
   a. Health0
   b. Thing
   c. Undefined
   d. Undefined

107. _____ is defined as the rate of change or derivative with respect to time of velocity.
   a. Acceleration0
   b. Thing
   c. Undefined
   d. Undefined

108. In mathematics, a _____ is the end result of a division problem. It can also be expressed as the number of times the divisor divides into the dividend.
   a. Thing
   b. Quotient0
   c. Undefined
   d. Undefined

109. _____ studies and addresses the ways in which individuals, businesses, and organizations raise, allocate, and use monetary resources over time, taking into account the risks entailed in their projects
   a. Thing
   b. Finance0
   c. Undefined
   d. Undefined

110. _____ are any documents that aim to streamline particular processes according to a set routine.
   a. Guidelines0
   b. Thing
   c. Undefined
   d. Undefined

111. A _____ is an abstract model that uses mathematical language to describe the behavior of a system. Eykhoff defined a _____ as 'a representation of the essential aspects of an existing system which presents knowledge of that system in usable form'.
   a. Thing
   b. Mathematical model0
   c. Undefined
   d. Undefined

112. A _____ is a three-dimensional solid object bounded by six square faces, facets, or sides, with three meeting at each vertex.
   a. Cube0
   b. Thing
   c. Undefined
   d. Undefined

113. In mathematics, two quantities are called _____ if they vary in such a way that one of the quantities is a constant multiple of the other, or equivalently if they have a constant ratio.
   a. Thing
   b. Proportional0
   c. Undefined
   d. Undefined

114. _____ is a decrease that follows an exponential function.
   a. Exponential decay0
   b. Thing
   c. Undefined
   d. Undefined

115. In mathematics, _____ occurs when the growth rate of a function is always proportional to the function's current size.

Chapter 6. Exponential and Logarithmic Functions

a. Exponential growth0
b. Thing
c. Undefined
d. Undefined

116. _____ is essentially exponential growth based on a constant rate of compound interest.
a. Thing
b. Exponential growth model0
c. Undefined
d. Undefined

117. _____, or Drosophila Melanoaster is a two-winged insect that belongs to the Diptera, the order of the flies. The species is commonly known as the fruit fly, and is one of the most commonly used model organisms in biology, including studies in genetics, physiology and life history evolution.
a. Fruit flies0
b. Thing
c. Undefined
d. Undefined

118. _____ is a radiometric dating method that uses the naturally occurring isotope carbon-14 to determine the age of carbonaceous materials up to about 60,000 years.
a. Radiocarbon dating0
b. Thing
c. Undefined
d. Undefined

119. _____ is the eighteenth letter of the Greek alphabet.
a. Sigma0
b. Thing
c. Undefined
d. Undefined

120. _____ of a probability distribution, random variable, or population or multiset of values is a measure of the spread of its values.
a. Standard deviation0
b. Thing
c. Undefined
d. Undefined

121. _____ is a measure of difference for interval and ratio variables between the observed value and the mean.
a. Thing
b. Deviation0
c. Undefined
d. Undefined

122. In mathematics, an _____ is any of the arguments, i.e. "inputs", to a function. Thus if we have a function f(x), then x is a _____.
a. Independent variable0
b. Thing
c. Undefined
d. Undefined

123. The _____, also called Gaussian distribution by scientists, is a continuous probability distribution of great importance in many fields.
a. Thing
b. Normal distribution0
c. Undefined
d. Undefined

124. In mathematical analysis, _____ are objects which generalize functions and probability distributions.
a. Thing
b. Distribution0
c. Undefined
d. Undefined

Chapter 6. Exponential and Logarithmic Functions

125. A _____ models the S-curve of growth of some set P. The initial stage of growth is approximately exponential; then, as saturation begins, the growth slows, and at maturity, growth stops.
   a. Logistic function0
   b. Thing
   c. Undefined
   d. Undefined

126. In set theory and its applications throughout mathematics, _____ are a collection of sets (or sometimes other mathematical objects) that can be unambiguously defined by a property that all its members share.
   a. Thing
   b. Classes0
   c. Undefined
   d. Undefined

127. The _____ of a mathematical object is its size: a property by which it can be larger or smaller than other objects of the same kind; in technical terms, an ordering of the class of objects to which it belongs.
   a. Thing
   b. Magnitude0
   c. Undefined
   d. Undefined

128. In Euclidean geometry, a uniform _____ is a linear transformation that enlargers or diminishes objects, and whose _____ factor is the same in all directions. This is also called homothethy.
   a. Thing
   b. Scale0
   c. Undefined
   d. Undefined

129. An _____ is the result from the sudden release of stored energy in the Earth's crust that creates seismic waves.
   a. Thing
   b. Earthquake0
   c. Undefined
   d. Undefined

130. A _____ are accounts maintained by commercial banks, savings and loan associations, credit unions, and mutual savings banks that pay interest but can not be used directly as money by, for example, writing a cheque.
   a. Savings account0
   b. Thing
   c. Undefined
   d. Undefined

131. In business, particularly accounting, a _____ is the time intervals that the accounts, statement, payments, or other calculations cover.
   a. Period0
   b. Thing
   c. Undefined
   d. Undefined

132. _____ is the process in which two clone daughter cells are produced by the cell division of one bacterium.
   a. Bacteria growth0
   b. Thing
   c. Undefined
   d. Undefined

133. _____ is a term that has several possible meanings all closely related to a firm's financial statements.
   a. Thing
   b. Book value0
   c. Undefined
   d. Undefined

134. _____ is a term used in accounting, economics and finance with reference to the fact that assets with finite lives lose value over time.

Chapter 6. Exponential and Logarithmic Functions

    a. Depreciation0   b. Thing
    c. Undefined   d. Undefined

135. _____ is often used to describe the measurement of the steepness, incline, gradient, or grade of a straight line. The _____ is defined as the ratio of the "rise" divided by the "run" between two points on a line, or in other words, the ratio of the altitude change to the horizontal distance between any two points on the line.
    a. Thing   b. Slope0
    c. Undefined   d. Undefined

136. _____, from Latin meaning "to make progress", is defined in two different ways. Pure economic _____ is the increase in wealth that an investor has from making an investment, taking into consideration all costs associated with that investment including the opportunity cost of capital.
    a. Thing   b. Profit0
    c. Undefined   d. Undefined

137. The _____ refers to a relationship between the duration of learning or experience and the resulting progress
    a. Thing   b. Learning curve0
    c. Undefined   d. Undefined

138. A _____ is a large group of animals. The term is usually applied to mammals, particularly ungulates. Other terms are used for similar phenomena in other types of animal.
    a. Thing   b. Herd0
    c. Undefined   d. Undefined

139. _____ is the ability to hold, receive or absorb, or a measure thereof, similar to the concept of volume.
    a. Concept   b. Capacity0
    c. Undefined   d. Undefined

140. _____ usually refers to the biological _____ of a population level that can be supported for an organism, given the quantity of food, habitat, water and other life infrastructure present.
    a. Carrying capacity0   b. Thing
    c. Undefined   d. Undefined

141. _____ is a measure of the acidity or alkalinity of a solution.
    a. PH level0   b. Thing
    c. Undefined   d. Undefined

142. A _____ is a method of using property as security for the payment of a debt.
    a. Mortgage0   b. Thing
    c. Undefined   d. Undefined

143. _____ is a physical property of a system that underlies the common notions of hot and cold; something that is hotter has the greater _____.
    a. Thing   b. Temperature0
    c. Undefined   d. Undefined

Chapter 6. Exponential and Logarithmic Functions

144. _____ is a temperature scale named after the German physicist Daniel Gabriel _____ , who proposed it in 1724.
   a. Fahrenheit0
   b. Thing
   c. Undefined
   d. Undefined

145. In mathematics, there are several meanings of _____ depending on the subject.
   a. Thing
   b. Degree0
   c. Undefined
   d. Undefined

146. A _____ is the part of the dividend that is left over when the dividend is not evenly divisible by the divisor.
   a. Remainder0
   b. Thing
   c. Undefined
   d. Undefined

147. In mathematics, _____ refers to the rewriting of an expression into a simpler form.
   a. Thing
   b. Reduction0
   c. Undefined
   d. Undefined

148. The word _____ comes from the Latin word linearis, which means created by lines.
   a. Linear0
   b. Thing
   c. Undefined
   d. Undefined

149. In mathematics, the _____ (or modulus) of a real number is its numerical value without regard to its sign.
   a. Thing
   b. Absolute value0
   c. Undefined
   d. Undefined

150. In mathematics, a _____ is an expression that is constructed from one or more variables and constants, using only the operations of addition, subtraction, multiplication, and constant positive whole number exponents. is a _____. Note in particular that division by an expression containing a variable is not in general allowed in polynomials. [1]
   a. Polynomial0
   b. Thing
   c. Undefined
   d. Undefined

151. In mathematics, _____ allows the rapid division of any polynomial by a binomial of the form x − r. It was described by Paolo Ruffini in 1809. _____ is a special case of long division when the divisor is a linear factor.
   a. Thing
   b. Ruffini's rule0
   c. Undefined
   d. Undefined

152. _____ is the chance that something is likely to happen or be the case.
   a. Thing
   b. Probability0
   c. Undefined
   d. Undefined

153. _____ are a measure of time.
   a. Minutes0
   b. Thing
   c. Undefined
   d. Undefined

154. A _____ is a polynomial function of the form $f(x) = ax^2 + bx + c$, where a, b, c are real numbers and a , 0.

Chapter 6. Exponential and Logarithmic Functions

a. Quadratic function0   b. Event
c. Undefined   d. Undefined

155. In geometry, a _____ is a special kind of point, usually a corner of a polygon, polyhedron, or higher dimensional polytope. In the geometry of curves a _____ is a point of where the first derivative of curvature is zero. In graph theory, a _____ is the fundamental unit out of which graphs are formed
   a. Vertex0   b. Thing
   c. Undefined   d. Undefined

156. In mathematics, a _____ is a constant multiplicative factor of a certain object. The object can be such things as a variable, a vector, a function, etc. For example, the _____ of $9x^2$ is 9.
   a. Thing   b. Coefficient0
   c. Undefined   d. Undefined

157. Any point where a graph makes contact with an coordinate axis is called an _____ of the graph
   a. Thing   b. Intercept0
   c. Undefined   d. Undefined

158. _____ refers to the reduction of the body of a formerly living organism into simpler forms of matter.
   a. Thing   b. Decomposing0
   c. Undefined   d. Undefined

159. In algebra, the _____ decomposition or _____ expansion is used to reduce the degree of either the numerator or the denominator of a rational function.
   a. Thing   b. Partial fraction0
   c. Undefined   d. Undefined

160. In mathematics, the _____ is a conic section generated by the intersection of a right circular conical surface and a plane parallel to a generating straight line of that surface. It can also be defined as locus of points in a plane which are equidistant from a given point.
   a. Thing   b. Parabola0
   c. Undefined   d. Undefined

161. In mathematics, a _____ is a type of conic section defined as the intersection between a right circular conical surface and a plane which cuts through both halves of the cone.
   a. Thing   b. Hyperbola0
   c. Undefined   d. Undefined

162. In geometry, the _____ are a pair of special points used in describing conic sections. The four types of conic sections are the circle, parabola, ellipse, and hyperbola.
   a. Foci0   b. Thing
   c. Undefined   d. Undefined

163. The _____ rule, also known as a slipstick, is a mechanical analog computer, consisting of at least two finely divided scales, most often a fixed outer pair and a movable inner one, with a sliding window called the cursor.

Chapter 6. Exponential and Logarithmic Functions

a. Thing
b. Slide0
c. Undefined
d. Undefined

164. In mathematics, the _____ functions are functions of an angle; they are important when studying triangles and modeling periodic phenomena, among many other applications.
  a. Trigonometric0
  b. Thing
  c. Undefined
  d. Undefined

165. The _____ are functions of an angle; they are important when studying triangles and modeling periodic phenomena, among many other applications.
  a. Thing
  b. Trigonometric functions0
  c. Undefined
  d. Undefined

166. In mathematics, a _____ of a complex-valued function f is a member x of the domain of f such that f(x) vanishes at x, that is, x : f (x) = 0.
  a. Root0
  b. Thing
  c. Undefined
  d. Undefined

167. In mathematics, a _____ can mean either an element of the set {1, 2, 3, ...} (i.e the positive integers or the counting numbers) or an element of the set {0, 1, 2, 3, ...} (i.e. the non-negative integers).
  a. Thing
  b. Natural number0
  c. Undefined
  d. Undefined

168. In financial mathematics, the _____ volatility of an option contract is the volatility _____ by the market price of the option based on an option pricing model.
  a. Thing
  b. Implied0
  c. Undefined
  d. Undefined

169. _____ is a subset of a population.
  a. Thing
  b. Sample0
  c. Undefined
  d. Undefined

170. _____ is a set, with some particular properties and usually some additional structure, such as the operations of addition or multiplication, for instance.
  a. Thing
  b. Space0
  c. Undefined
  d. Undefined

Chapter 7. Systems of Equations and Inequalities

1. A _____ is a symbolic representation denoting a quantity or expression. It often represents an "unknown" quantity that has the potential to change.
   - a. Variable0
   - b. Thing
   - c. Undefined
   - d. Undefined

2. The mathematical concept of a _____ expresses the intuitive idea of deterministic dependence between two quantities, one of which is viewed as primary and the other as secondary. A _____ then is a way to associate a unique output for each input of a specified type, for example, a real number or an element of a given set.
   - a. Thing
   - b. Function0
   - c. Undefined
   - d. Undefined

3. An _____ is a collection of two not necessarily distinct objects, one of which is distinguished as the first coordinate and the other as the second coordinate.
   - a. Thing
   - b. Ordered pair0
   - c. Undefined
   - d. Undefined

4. A _____ is a negotiable instrument instructing a financial institution to pay a specific amount of a specific currency from a specific demand account held in the maker/depositor's name with that institution. Both the maker and payee may be natural persons or legal entities.
   - a. Check0
   - b. Thing
   - c. Undefined
   - d. Undefined

5. _____ systems represent systems whose behavior is not expressible as a sum of the behaviors of its descriptors.
   - a. Nonlinear0
   - b. Thing
   - c. Undefined
   - d. Undefined

6. An _____ is a combination of numbers, operators, grouping symbols and/or free variables and bound variables arranged in a meaningful way which can be evaluated..
   - a. Expression0
   - b. Thing
   - c. Undefined
   - d. Undefined

7. _____ are the basic objects of study in graph theory. Informally speaking, a graph is a set of objects called points, nodes, or vertices connected by links called lines or edges.
   - a. Graphs0
   - b. Thing
   - c. Undefined
   - d. Undefined

8. _____ are a set of equations containing multiple variables.
   - a. Thing
   - b. Systems of equations0
   - c. Undefined
   - d. Undefined

9. In linear algebra, the _____ of an n-by-n square matrix A is defined to be the sum of the elements on the main diagonal of A,
   - a. Thing
   - b. Trace0
   - c. Undefined
   - d. Undefined

10. A _____ is a set of numbers that designate location in a given reference system, such as x,y in a planar _____ system or an x,y,z in a three-dimensional _____ system.

a. Coordinate0
b. Thing
c. Undefined
d. Undefined

11. In geographic information systems, a _____ comprises an entity with a geographic location, typically determined by points, arcs, or polygons. Carriageways and cadastres exemplify _____ data.
   a. Feature0
   b. Thing
   c. Undefined
   d. Undefined

12. In mathematics, the _____ of two sets A and B is the set that contains all elements of A that also belong to B (or equivalently, all elements of B that also belong to A), but no other elements.
   a. Intersection0
   b. Thing
   c. Undefined
   d. Undefined

13. _____ or arithmetics is the oldest and most elementary branch of mathematics, used by almost everyone, for tasks ranging from simple daily counting to advanced science and business calculations.
   a. Arithmetic0
   b. Thing
   c. Undefined
   d. Undefined

14. In mathematics, an _____ is a statement about the relative size or order of two objects.
   a. Thing
   b. Inequality0
   c. Undefined
   d. Undefined

15. _____ is the fee paid on borrowed money.
   a. Thing
   b. Interest0
   c. Undefined
   d. Undefined

16. _____ is a kind of property which exists as magnitude or multitude. It is among the basic classes of things along with quality, substance, change, and relation.
   a. Amount0
   b. Thing
   c. Undefined
   d. Undefined

17. _____ or investing is a term with several closely-related meanings in business management, finance and economics, related to saving or deferring consumption.
   a. Investment0
   b. Thing
   c. Undefined
   d. Undefined

18. In the scientific method, an _____ (Latin: ex-+-periri, "of (or from) trying"), is a set of actions and observations, performed in the context of solving a particular problem or question, in order to support or falsify a hypothesis or research concerning phenomena.
   a. Thing
   b. Experiment0
   c. Undefined
   d. Undefined

19. A quadratic equation with real solutions, called roots, which may be real or complex, is given by the _____: $x = \frac{-b \pm \sqrt{b^2 - 4ac}}{2a}$

Chapter 7. Systems of Equations and Inequalities

a. Quadratic formula0
b. Thing
c. Undefined
d. Undefined

20. _____ of a polynomial with real or complex coefficients is a certain expression in the coefficients of the polynomial which is equal to zero if and only if the polynomial has a multiple root i.e. a root with multiplicity greater than one in the complex numbers.
a. Thing
b. Discriminant0
c. Undefined
d. Undefined

21. In mathematics, a _____ is a two-dimensional manifold or surface that is perfectly flat.
a. Plane0
b. Thing
c. Undefined
d. Undefined

22. The _____ is used to discard one of the variables in an equation, only to replace it with the actual value when solving multiple equations.
a. Thing
b. Substitution method0
c. Undefined
d. Undefined

23. In mathematics, a _____ is the result of multiplying, or an expression that identifies factors to be multiplied.
a. Thing
b. Product0
c. Undefined
d. Undefined

24. The _____ of measurement are a globally standardized and modernized form of the metric system.
a. Thing
b. Units0
c. Undefined
d. Undefined

25. Initial objects are also called _____, and terminal objects are also called final.
a. Thing
b. Coterminal0
c. Undefined
d. Undefined

26. In mathematics, in the field of group theory, a _____ of a group is a quasisimple subnormal subgroup.
a. Component0
b. Concept
c. Undefined
d. Undefined

27. _____ is a business term for the amount of money that a company receives from its activities in a given period, mostly from sales of products and/or services to customers
a. Revenue0
b. Thing
c. Undefined
d. Undefined

28. _____, from Latin meaning "to make progress", is defined in two different ways. Pure economic _____ is the increase in wealth that an investor has from making an investment, taking into consideration all costs associated with that investment including the opportunity cost of capital.
a. Profit0
b. Thing
c. Undefined
d. Undefined

Chapter 7. Systems of Equations and Inequalities

29. In mathematics, an inequality is a statement about the relative size or order of two objects. For example 14 > 10, or 14 is _____ 10.
    a. Thing
    b. Greater than0
    c. Undefined
    d. Undefined

30. A _____ is a special kind of ratio, indicating a relationship between two measurements with different units, such as miles to gallons or cents to pounds.
    a. Rate0
    b. Thing
    c. Undefined
    d. Undefined

31. In sociology and biology a _____ is the collection of people or organisms of a particular species living in a given geographic area or space, usually measured by a census.
    a. Population0
    b. Thing
    c. Undefined
    d. Undefined

32. A _____ is a unit of length, usually used to measure distance, in a number of different systems, including Imperial units, United States customary units and Norwegian/Swedish mil. Its size can vary from system to system, but in each is between 1 and 10 kilometers. In contemporary English contexts _____ refers to either:
    a. Thing
    b. Mile0
    c. Undefined
    d. Undefined

33. In mathematics, the conjugate _____ or adjoint matrix of an m-by-n matrix A with complex entries is the n-by-m matrix A* obtained from A by taking the transpose and then taking the complex conjugate of each entry.
    a. Pairs0
    b. Thing
    c. Undefined
    d. Undefined

34. In economics, _____ describe market relations between prospective sellers and buyers of a good.
    a. Thing
    b. Supply and demand0
    c. Undefined
    d. Undefined

35. In mathematics, the concept of a _____ tries to capture the intuitive idea of a geometrical one-dimensional and continuous object. A simple example is the circle.
    a. Thing
    b. Curve0
    c. Undefined
    d. Undefined

36. In mathematics, _____ are the intuitive idea of a geometrical one-dimensional and continuous object.
    a. Curves0
    b. Thing
    c. Undefined
    d. Undefined

37. The payment of _____ as remuneration for services rendered or products sold is a common way to reward sales people.
    a. Commission0
    b. Thing
    c. Undefined
    d. Undefined

38. _____ is a form of periodic payment from an employer to an employee, which is specified in an employment contract.

a. Thing
b. Gross pay0
c. Undefined
d. Undefined

39. A _____ is a form of periodic payment from an employer to an employee, which is specified in an employment contract.
   a. Thing
   b. Salary0
   c. Undefined
   d. Undefined

40. The _____ of a solid object is the three-dimensional concept of how much space it occupies, often quantified numerically.
   a. Volume0
   b. Thing
   c. Undefined
   d. Undefined

41. The act of _____ is the calculated approximation of a result which is usable even if input data may be incomplete, uncertain, or noisy.
   a. Thing
   b. Estimating0
   c. Undefined
   d. Undefined

42. In economics, economic _____ is simply a state of the world where economic forces are balanced and in the absence of external influences the values of economic variables will not change.
   a. Thing
   b. Equilibrium0
   c. Undefined
   d. Undefined

43. In economics, economic equilibrium is simply a state of the world where economic forces are balanced and in the absence of external influences the values of economic variables will not change. _____, for example, refers to a condition where a market price is established through competition such that the amount of goods or services sought by buyers is equal to the amount of goods or services produced by sellers
   a. Market equilibrium0
   b. Thing
   c. Undefined
   d. Undefined

44. _____ is a synonym for information.
   a. Data0
   b. Thing
   c. Undefined
   d. Undefined

45. In common philosophical language, a proposition or _____, is the content of an assertion, that is, it is true-or-false and defined by the meaning of a particular piece of language.
   a. Statement0
   b. Concept
   c. Undefined
   d. Undefined

46. The word _____ comes from the Latin word linearis, which means created by lines.
   a. Thing
   b. Linear0
   c. Undefined
   d. Undefined

47. In geometry, a _____ is defined as a quadrilateral where all four of its angles are right angles.

Chapter 7. Systems of Equations and Inequalities

    a. Thing
    c. Undefined
    b. Rectangle0
    d. Undefined

48. _____ is the distance around a given two-dimensional object. As a general rule, the _____ of a polygon can always be calculated by adding all the length of the sides together. So, the formula for triangles is P = a + b + c, where a, b and c stand for each side of it. For quadrilaterals the equation is P = a + b + c + d. For equilateral polygons, P = na, where n is the number of sides and a is the side length.
    a. Thing
    c. Undefined
    b. Perimeter0
    d. Undefined

49. The metre (or _____, see spelling differences) is a measure of length. It is the basic unit of length in the metric system and in the International System of Units (SI), used around the world for general and scientific purposes.
    a. Concept
    c. Undefined
    b. Meter0
    d. Undefined

50. In Euclidean geometry, a _____ is the set of all points in a plane at a fixed distance, called the radius, from a given point, the center.
    a. Thing
    c. Undefined
    b. Circle0
    d. Undefined

51. In mathematics, the _____ is a conic section generated by the intersection of a right circular conical surface and a plane parallel to a generating straight line of that surface. It can also be defined as locus of points in a plane which are equidistant from a given point.
    a. Parabola0
    c. Undefined
    b. Thing
    d. Undefined

52. In mathematics, a _____ is a mathematical statement which appears likely to be true, but has not been formally proven to be true under the rules of mathematical logic.
    a. Concept
    c. Undefined
    b. Conjecture0
    d. Undefined

53. One of the three formats applicable to a quadratic function is the _____ which is defined as $f = ax^2 + bx + c$.
    a. General form0
    c. Undefined
    b. Thing
    d. Undefined

54. _____ is a straight line or curve A to which another curve B the one being studied approaches closer and closer as one moves along it.
    a. Thing
    c. Undefined
    b. Vertical asymptote0
    d. Undefined

55. An _____ is a straight line or curve A to which another curve B approaches closer and closer as one moves along it. As one moves along B, the space between it and the _____ A becomes smaller and smaller, and can in fact be made as small as one could wish by going far enough along. A curve may or may not touch or cross its _____. In fact, the curve may intersect the _____ an infinite number of times.

Chapter 7. Systems of Equations and Inequalities

a. Thing
b. Asymptote0
c. Undefined
d. Undefined

56. In astronomy, geography, geometry and related sciences and contexts, a plane is said to be _____ at a given point if it is locally perpendicular to the gradient of the gravity field, i.e., with the direction of the gravitational force at that point.
a. Thing
b. Horizontal0
c. Undefined
d. Undefined

57. In mathematics, a _____ of a k-place relation $L \subseteq X_1 \times ... \times X_k$ is one of the sets X_j, $1 \leq j \leq k$. In the special case where k = 2 and $L \subseteq X_1 \times X_2$ is a function $L : X_1 \to X_2$, it is conventional to refer to X_1 as the _____ of the function and to refer to X_2 as the codomain of the function.
a. Thing
b. Domain0
c. Undefined
d. Undefined

58. A _____ is an equation in which each term is either a constant or the product of a constant times the first power of a variable.
a. Linear equation0
b. Thing
c. Undefined
d. Undefined

59. In mathematics, a _____ is a constant multiplicative factor of a certain object. The object can be such things as a variable, a vector, a function, etc. For example, the _____ of $9x^2$ is 9.
a. Thing
b. Coefficient0
c. Undefined
d. Undefined

60. A _____ is a set of possible values that a variable can take on in order to satisfy a given set of conditions, which may include equations and inequalities.
a. Thing
b. Solution set0
c. Undefined
d. Undefined

61. Equivalence is the condition of being _____ or essentially equal.
a. Equivalent0
b. Thing
c. Undefined
d. Undefined

62. A _____ of a number is the product of that number with any integer.
a. Multiple0
b. Thing
c. Undefined
d. Undefined

63. In mathematics and the mathematical sciences, a _____ is a fixed, but possibly unspecified, value. This is in contrast to a variable, which is not fixed.
a. Constant0
b. Thing
c. Undefined
d. Undefined

64. _____ is often used to describe the measurement of the steepness, incline, gradient, or grade of a straight line. The _____ is defined as the ratio of the "rise" divided by the "run" between two points on a line, or in other words, the ratio of the altitude change to the horizontal distance between any two points on the line.

Chapter 7. Systems of Equations and Inequalities

    a. Thing
    b. Slope0
    c. Undefined
    d. Undefined

65. _____ is the state of being greater than any finite real or natural number, however large.
    a. Infinite0
    b. Thing
    c. Undefined
    d. Undefined

66. The existence and properties of _____ are the basis of Euclid's parallel postulate. _____ are two lines on the same plane that do not intersect even assuming that lines extend to infinity in either direction.
    a. Thing
    b. Parallel lines0
    c. Undefined
    d. Undefined

67. A _____ is 360° or 2δ radians.
    a. Turn0
    b. Thing
    c. Undefined
    d. Undefined

68. A _____ is an abstract model that uses mathematical language to describe the behavior of a system. Eykhoff defined a _____ as 'a representation of the essential aspects of an existing system which presents knowledge of that system in usable form'.
    a. Thing
    b. Mathematical model0
    c. Undefined
    d. Undefined

69. _____ is the transport of people on a trip/journey or the process or time involved in a person or object moving from one location to another.
    a. Thing
    b. Travel0
    c. Undefined
    d. Undefined

70. _____ are a measure of time.
    a. Minutes0
    b. Thing
    c. Undefined
    d. Undefined

71. A _____ is an individual or household that purchases and uses goods and services generated within the economy.
    a. Thing
    b. Consumer0
    c. Undefined
    d. Undefined

72. In mathematics, the additive inverse, or _____ of a number n is the number that, when added to n, yields zero. The additive inverse of n is denoted −n. For example, 7 is −7, because 7 + (−7) = 0, and the additive inverse of −0.3 is 0.3, because −0.3 + 0.3 = 0.
    a. Opposite0
    b. Thing
    c. Undefined
    d. Undefined

73. In mathematics, _____ are two-dimensional manifolds or surfaces that are perfectly flat.
    a. Planes0
    b. Thing
    c. Undefined
    d. Undefined

Chapter 7. Systems of Equations and Inequalities

74. In mathematics, the _____ of a number n is the number that, when added to n, yields zero. The _____ of n is denoted −n. For example, 7 is −7, because 7 + (−7) = 0, and the _____ of −0.3 is 0.3, because −0.3 + 0.3 = 0.
    a. Thing
    b. Additive inverse0
    c. Undefined
    d. Undefined

75. In chemistry, a _____ is substance made by combining two or more different materials in such a way that no chemical reaction occurs.
    a. Thing
    b. Mixture0
    c. Undefined
    d. Undefined

76. _____ is a way of expressing a number as a fraction of 100 per cent meaning "per hundred".
    a. Percent0
    b. Thing
    c. Undefined
    d. Undefined

77. U.S. liquid _____ is legally defined as 231 cubic inches, and is equal to 3.785411784 litres or abotu 0.13368 cubic feet. This is the most common definition of a _____. The U.S. fluid ounce is defined as 1/128 of a U.S. _____.
    a. Thing
    b. Gallon0
    c. Undefined
    d. Undefined

78. _____ finance, in finance, a debt security, issued by Issuer
    a. Bond0
    b. Thing
    c. Undefined
    d. Undefined

79. _____ consists of the knowledge of various products to protect the public from fraudulent or unforseeable circumstances.
    a. Consumer awareness0
    b. Thing
    c. Undefined
    d. Undefined

80. In plane geometry, a _____ is a polygon with four equal sides, four right angles, and parallel opposite sides. In algebra, the _____ of a number is that number multiplied by itself.
    a. Square0
    b. Thing
    c. Undefined
    d. Undefined

81. In regression analysis, _____, also known as ordinary _____ analysis is a method for linear regression that determines the values of unknown quantities in a statistical model by minimizing the sum of the residuals difference between the predicted and observed values squared.
    a. Thing
    b. Least squares0
    c. Undefined
    d. Undefined

82. _____ is the act of transforming data with the aim of extracting useful information and facilitating conclusions.
    a. Concept
    b. Data analysis0
    c. Undefined
    d. Undefined

83. In mathematics, an _____, mean, or central tendency of a data set refers to a measure of the "middle" or "expected" value of the data set.

Chapter 7. Systems of Equations and Inequalities

  a. Average0
  c. Undefined
  b. Concept
  d. Undefined

84. Acid _____ ratio measures the ability of a company to use its near cash or quick assets to immediately extinguish its current liabilities.
  a. Test0
  c. Undefined
  b. Thing
  d. Undefined

85. A _____ is a one-dimensional picture in which the integers are shown as specially-marked points evenly spaced on a line.
  a. Thing
  c. Undefined
  b. Number line0
  d. Undefined

86. In mathematics, a _____ may be described informally as a number that can be given by an infinite decimal representation.
  a. Thing
  c. Undefined
  b. Real number0
  d. Undefined

87. In mathematics, a _____ number is a number which can be expressed as a ratio of two integers. Non-integer _____ numbers (commonly called fractions) are usually written as the vulgar fraction a / b, where b is not zero.
  a. Rational0
  c. Undefined
  b. Thing
  d. Undefined

88. _____ refers to the reduction of the body of a formerly living organism into simpler forms of matter.
  a. Thing
  c. Undefined
  b. Decomposing0
  d. Undefined

89. In algebra, the _____ decomposition or _____ expansion is used to reduce the degree of either the numerator or the denominator of a rational function.
  a. Thing
  c. Undefined
  b. Partial fraction0
  d. Undefined

90. In mathematics, a _____ of a number x is the exponent y of the power by such that $x = b^y$. The value used for the base b must be neither 0 nor 1, nor a root of 1 in the case of the extension to complex numbers, and is typically 10, e, or 2.
  a. Thing
  c. Undefined
  b. Logarithm0
  d. Undefined

91. In mathematics, a _____ is an n-tuple with n being 3.
  a. Thing
  c. Undefined
  b. Triple0
  d. Undefined

92. _____ is an algorithm which can be used to determine the solutions of a system of linear equations, to find the rank of a matrix, and to calculate the inverse of an invertible square matrix.
  a. Thing
  c. Undefined
  b. Gaussian elimination0
  d. Undefined

Chapter 7. Systems of Equations and Inequalities

93. In mathematics, a matrix can be thought of as each row or _____ being a vector. Hence, a space formed by row vectors or _____ vectors are said to be a row space or a _____ space.
   a. Column0
   b. Concept
   c. Undefined
   d. Undefined

94. In mathematics, a _____ is a rectangular table of numbers or, more generally, a table consisting of abstract quantities that can be added and multiplied.
   a. Thing
   b. Matrix0
   c. Undefined
   d. Undefined

95. In geometry, _____ lines are two lines that share one or more common points.
   a. Thing
   b. Intersecting0
   c. Undefined
   d. Undefined

96. _____ is a set, with some particular properties and usually some additional structure, such as the operations of addition or multiplication, for instance.
   a. Thing
   b. Space0
   c. Undefined
   d. Undefined

97. In set theory, an _____ is a set that is not a finite set. Infinite sets may be countable or uncountable.
   a. Thing
   b. Infinite set0
   c. Undefined
   d. Undefined

98. The _____, the average in everyday English, which is also called the arithmetic _____ (and is distinguished from the geometric _____ or harmonic _____). The average is also called the sample _____. The expected value of a random variable, which is also called the population _____.
   a. Mean0
   b. Thing
   c. Undefined
   d. Undefined

99. In mathematics, and in particular in abstract algebra, the _____ is a property of binary operations that generalises the distributive law from elementary algebra.
   a. Distributive property0
   b. Thing
   c. Undefined
   d. Undefined

100. _____ of an object is its speed in a particular direction.
   a. Thing
   b. Velocity0
   c. Undefined
   d. Undefined

101. _____ is defined as the rate of change or derivative with respect to time of velocity.
   a. Thing
   b. Acceleration0
   c. Undefined
   d. Undefined

102. A _____ is a form of collective investment that pools money from many investors and invests their money in stocks, bonds, short-term money market instruments, and/or other securities.

138　　　　　　　　　　*Chapter 7. Systems of Equations and Inequalities*

    a. Mutual fund0　　　　　　　　　　　　　　b. Thing
    c. Undefined　　　　　　　　　　　　　　　d. Undefined

103. _____ are activities that are governed by a set of rules or customs and often engaged in competitively.
    a. Sports0　　　　　　　　　　　　　　　　b. Thing
    c. Undefined　　　　　　　　　　　　　　　d. Undefined

104. In combinatorial mathematics, a _____ is an un-ordered collection of unique elements.
    a. Concept　　　　　　　　　　　　　　　　b. Combination0
    c. Undefined　　　　　　　　　　　　　　　d. Undefined

105. _____ studies and addresses the ways in which individuals, businesses, and organizations raise, allocate, and use monetary resources over time, taking into account the risks entailed in their projects
    a. Finance0　　　　　　　　　　　　　　　　b. Thing
    c. Undefined　　　　　　　　　　　　　　　d. Undefined

106. In business, particularly accounting, a _____ is the time intervals that the accounts, statement, payments, or other calculations cover.
    a. Period0　　　　　　　　　　　　　　　　b. Thing
    c. Undefined　　　　　　　　　　　　　　　d. Undefined

107. _____ is the production of food, feed, fiber, fuel and other goods by the systematic raizing of plants and animals.
    a. Agriculture0　　　　　　　　　　　　　　b. Thing
    c. Undefined　　　　　　　　　　　　　　　d. Undefined

108. In Graph theory, a _____ is a digraph with weighted edges.
    a. Concept　　　　　　　　　　　　　　　　b. Network0
    c. Undefined　　　　　　　　　　　　　　　d. Undefined

109. _____ is a reaction force applied by a stretched string on the objects which stretch it.
    a. Tension0　　　　　　　　　　　　　　　　b. Thing
    c. Undefined　　　　　　　　　　　　　　　d. Undefined

110. _____ refers to all non-domesticated plants, animals, and other organisms.
    a. Wildlife0　　　　　　　　　　　　　　　　b. Thing
    c. Undefined　　　　　　　　　　　　　　　d. Undefined

111. An _____ is when two lines intersect somewhere on a plane creating a right angle at intersection
    a. Thing　　　　　　　　　　　　　　　　　b. Axes0
    c. Undefined　　　　　　　　　　　　　　　d. Undefined

112. _____ is a unit of speed, expressing the number of international miles covered per hour.
    a. Thing　　　　　　　　　　　　　　　　　b. Miles per hour0
    c. Undefined　　　　　　　　　　　　　　　d. Undefined

Chapter 7. Systems of Equations and Inequalities

113. _____ is a notation for writing numbers that is often used by scientists and mathematicians to make it easier to write large and small numbers.
   a. Scientific notation0
   b. Thing
   c. Undefined
   d. Undefined

114. In mathematics, _____ geometry was the traditional name for the geometry of three-dimensional Euclidean space — for practical purposes the kind of space we live in.
   a. Solid0
   b. Thing
   c. Undefined
   d. Undefined

115. In mathematics and its applications, a _____ is a system for assigning an n-tuple of numbers or scalars to each point in an n-dimensional space.
   a. Concept
   b. Coordinate system0
   c. Undefined
   d. Undefined

116. In geometry, a _____ is a special kind of point, usually a corner of a polygon, polyhedron, or higher dimensional polytope. In the geometry of curves a _____ is a point of where the first derivative of curvature is zero. In graph theory, a _____ is the fundamental unit out of which graphs are formed
   a. Vertex0
   b. Thing
   c. Undefined
   d. Undefined

117. _____ is used in economics for several related quantities
   a. Thing
   b. Producer surplus0
   c. Undefined
   d. Undefined

118. A _____ is a function that assigns a number to subsets of a given set.
   a. Measure0
   b. Thing
   c. Undefined
   d. Undefined

119. A _____ is one of the basic shapes of geometry: a polygon with three vertices and three sides which are straight line segments.
   a. Thing
   b. Triangle0
   c. Undefined
   d. Undefined

120. A _____ is a polygon with four sides and four vertices.
   a. Quadrilateral0
   b. Thing
   c. Undefined
   d. Undefined

121. A _____ is a four-sided plane figure that has two sets of opposite parallel sides.
   a. Concept
   b. Parallelogram0
   c. Undefined
   d. Undefined

122. In geometry, the _____ of an object is a point in some sense in the middle of the object.
   a. Center0
   b. Thing
   c. Undefined
   d. Undefined

Chapter 7. Systems of Equations and Inequalities

123. _____ is a list of goods and materials, or those goods and materials themselves, held available in stock by a business
   a. Thing
   b. Inventory0
   c. Undefined
   d. Undefined

124. _____ is the ability to hold, receive or absorb, or a measure thereof, similar to the concept of volume.
   a. Capacity0
   b. Concept
   c. Undefined
   d. Undefined

125. A _____ is a quadrilateral, which is defined as a shape with four sides, which has a pair of parallel sides.
   a. Thing
   b. Trapezoid0
   c. Undefined
   d. Undefined

126. In mathematical analysis and related areas of mathematics, a set is called _____, if it is, in a certain sense, of finite size.
   a. Thing
   b. Bounded0
   c. Undefined
   d. Undefined

127. In classical geometry, a _____ of a circle or sphere is any line segment from its center to its boundary. By extension, the _____ of a circle or sphere is the length of any such segment. The _____ is half the diameter. In science and engineering the term _____ of curvature is commonly used as a synonym for _____.
   a. Thing
   b. Radius0
   c. Undefined
   d. Undefined

128. Deductive _____ is the kind of _____ in which the conclusion is necessitated by, or reached from, previously known facts (the premises).
   a. Reasoning0
   b. Thing
   c. Undefined
   d. Undefined

129. _____ interest refers to the fact that whenever interest is calculated, it is based not only on the original principal, but also on any unpaid interest that has been added to the principal.
   a. Thing
   b. Compound0
   c. Undefined
   d. Undefined

130. _____ refers to the fact that whenever interest is calculated, it is based not only on the original principal, but also on any unpaid interest that has been added to the principal. The more frequently interest is compounded, the faster the balance grows.
   a. Compound interest0
   b. Concept
   c. Undefined
   d. Undefined

131. In mathematics, _____ problems involve the optimization of a linear objective function, subject to linear equality and inequality constraints.
   a. Thing
   b. Linear programming0
   c. Undefined
   d. Undefined

Chapter 7. Systems of Equations and Inequalities

132. In mathematics, a _____ is a condition that a solution to an optimization problem must satisfy in order to be acceptable.
   a. Constraint0
   b. Thing
   c. Undefined
   d. Undefined

133. In geometry, a line _____ is a part of a line that is bounded by two end points, and contains every point on the line between its end points.
   a. Concept
   b. Segment0
   c. Undefined
   d. Undefined

134. A _____ is a part of a line that is bounded by two end points, and contains every point on the line between its end points.
   a. Thing
   b. Line segment0
   c. Undefined
   d. Undefined

135. In mathematics, a subset of Euclidean space R^n is called _____ if it is closed and bounded.
   a. Thing
   b. Compact0
   c. Undefined
   d. Undefined

136. An _____ or member of a set is an object that when collected together make up the set.
   a. Thing
   b. Element0
   c. Undefined
   d. Undefined

137. The _____ of a ring R is defined to be the smallest positive integer n such that $n\,a = 0$, for all a in R.
   a. Thing
   b. Characteristic0
   c. Undefined
   d. Undefined

138. In mathematics, _____ are essentially word problems that are designed to use mathematical critical thinking in everyday situations.
   a. Thing
   b. Application problems0
   c. Undefined
   d. Undefined

139. An _____ is the fee paid on borrow money.
   a. Interest rate0
   b. Concept
   c. Undefined
   d. Undefined

140. In mathematical analysis, _____ are objects which generalize functions and probability distributions.
   a. Thing
   b. Distribution0
   c. Undefined
   d. Undefined

141. In mathematics, the _____ , or members of a set or more generally a class are all those objects which when collected together make up the set or class.
   a. Elements0
   b. Thing
   c. Undefined
   d. Undefined

142. An _____ triange is a triangle with at least two sides of equal length.

142 *Chapter 7. Systems of Equations and Inequalities*

a. Thing
b. Isosceles0
c. Undefined
d. Undefined

143. An _____ (isosceles trapezium in British English) is a quadrilateral with a line of symmetry bisecting one pair of opposite sides, making it automatically a trapezoid. Also, an _____ 's base angles are congruent.
 a. Isosceles trapezoid0
 b. Concept
 c. Undefined
 d. Undefined

144. In mathematics, a _____ is a demonstration that, assuming certain axioms, some statement is necessarily true.
 a. Proof0
 b. Thing
 c. Undefined
 d. Undefined

145. Mathematical _____ are demonstrations that, assuming certain axioms, some statement is necessarily true.
 a. Thing
 b. Proofs0
 c. Undefined
 d. Undefined

146. In logic, Modus tollens (or Modus ponendo tollens) means to affirm by denying. It is the formal name for _____ proof or proof by contrapositive (contrapositive inference), often abbreviated to MT.
 a. Thing
 b. Indirect0
 c. Undefined
 d. Undefined

147. The material _____, also known as the material implication or truth functional _____, expresses a property of certain conditionals in logic.
 a. Conditional0
 b. Thing
 c. Undefined
 d. Undefined

148. _____ is a type of logical argument where one assumes a claim for the sake of argument, derives an absurd or ridiculous outcome, and then concludes that the original assumption must have been wrong as it led to an absurd result. It makes use of the law of non-contradiction - a statement cannot be both true and false. In some cases it may also make use of the law of excluded middle - a statement must be either true or false. The phrase is traceable back to the Greek ç åéò Üôïðïí áðáãùãÞ , meaning "reduction to the impossible", often used by Aristotle.
 a. Reductio ad absurdum0
 b. Thing
 c. Undefined
 d. Undefined

149. In mathematics, a _____ of an integer n, also called a factor of n, is an integer which evenly divides n without leaving a remainder.
 a. Divisor0
 b. Thing
 c. Undefined
 d. Undefined

150. In mathematics, an _____ number is any real number that is not a rational number- that is, it is a number which cannot be expressed as a fraction m/n, where m and n are integers.
 a. Irrational0
 b. Thing
 c. Undefined
 d. Undefined

Chapter 7. Systems of Equations and Inequalities

151. In mathematics, an _____ is any real number that is not a rational number ¡ª that is, it is a number which cannot be expressed as m/n, where m and n are integers.
    a. Thing
    b. Irrational number0
    c. Undefined
    d. Undefined

152. In mathematics, a _____ is a statement that can be proved on the basis of explicitly stated or previously agreed assumptions.
    a. Thing
    b. Theorem0
    c. Undefined
    d. Undefined

153. In mathematics, a set is called _____ if there is a bijection between the set and some set of the form {1, 2, ..., n} where n is a natural number.
    a. Finite0
    b. Thing
    c. Undefined
    d. Undefined

154. The _____ ma is the mass of an atom at rest, most often expressed in unified _____ units.
    a. Atomic mass0
    b. Thing
    c. Undefined
    d. Undefined

155. _____ is the property of a physical object that quantifies the amount of matter and energy it is equivalent to.
    a. Mass0
    b. Thing
    c. Undefined
    d. Undefined

156. In botany, _____ are above-ground plant organs specialized for photosynthesis. Their characteristics are typically analyzed by using Fiobonacci's sequences.
    a. Thing
    b. Leaves0
    c. Undefined
    d. Undefined

157. The _____ or kilogramme is the SI base unit of mass. It is defined as being equal to the mass of the international prototype of the _____.
    a. Kilogram0
    b. Thing
    c. Undefined
    d. Undefined

158. _____ are any documents that aim to streamline particular processes according to a set routine.
    a. Thing
    b. Guidelines0
    c. Undefined
    d. Undefined

159. _____ is the level of functional and/or metabolic efficiency of an organism at both the micro level.
    a. Health0
    b. Thing
    c. Undefined
    d. Undefined

160. A _____ is a quantity that denotes the proportional amount or magnitude of one quantity relative to another.
    a. Thing
    b. Ratio0
    c. Undefined
    d. Undefined

Chapter 7. Systems of Equations and Inequalities

161. In mathematics, _____ is an elementary arithmetic operation. When one of the numbers is a whole number, _____ is the repeated sum of the other number.
   a. Multiplication0
   b. Thing
   c. Undefined
   d. Undefined

162. In mathematics, particularly linear algebra, a _____ is a matrix with all its entries being zero.
   a. Thing
   b. Zero matrix0
   c. Undefined
   d. Undefined

163. In linear algebra, the _____ refers to a matrix consisting of the coefficients of the variables in a set of linear equations.
   a. Coefficient matrix0
   b. Thing
   c. Undefined
   d. Undefined

164. In linear algebra, the _____ of a matrix is obtained by combining two matrices in such a way that a matrix of coefficients to which has been added a column of constants corresponds to the right hand side of the equations.
   a. Thing
   b. Augmented matrix0
   c. Undefined
   d. Undefined

165. An _____ is an equality that remains true regardless of the values of any variables that appear within it, to distinguish it from an equality which is true under more particular conditions.
   a. Identity0
   b. Thing
   c. Undefined
   d. Undefined

166. In linear algebra, the _____ of a square matrix is the diagonal which runs from the top left corner to the bottom right corner.
   a. Thing
   b. Main diagonal0
   c. Undefined
   d. Undefined

167. In linear algebra, real numbers are called scalars and relate to vectors in a vector space through the operation of _____ multiplication, in which a vector can be multiplied by a number to produce another vector.
   a. Thing
   b. Scalar0
   c. Undefined
   d. Undefined

168. In algebra, a _____ is a function depending on n that associates a scalar, det(A), to every $n \times n$ square matrix A.
   a. Thing
   b. Determinant0
   c. Undefined
   d. Undefined

169. A _____ can refer to a line joining two nonadjacent vertices of a polygon or polyhedron, or in some contexts any upward or downward sloping line. .
   a. Diagonal0
   b. Thing
   c. Undefined
   d. Undefined

170. _____ element of an element x with respect to a binary operation * with identity element e is an element y such that x * y = y * x = e. In particular,

a. Thing
b. Inverse0
c. Undefined
d. Undefined

Chapter 8. Matrices and Determinants

1. A _____ is a symbolic representation denoting a quantity or expression. It often represents an "unknown" quantity that has the potential to change.
   a. Thing
   b. Variable0
   c. Undefined
   d. Undefined

2. _____ are elementary linear transformations on a matrix which preserve matrix equivalence.
   a. Thing
   b. Elementary row operations0
   c. Undefined
   d. Undefined

3. The word _____ comes from the Latin word linearis, which means created by lines.
   a. Linear0
   b. Thing
   c. Undefined
   d. Undefined

4. A _____ is an equation in which each term is either a constant or the product of a constant times the first power of a variable.
   a. Linear equation0
   b. Thing
   c. Undefined
   d. Undefined

5. In mathematics, a _____ is a rectangular table of numbers or, more generally, a table consisting of abstract quantities that can be added and multiplied.
   a. Thing
   b. Matrix0
   c. Undefined
   d. Undefined

6. Elementary _____ are simple transformations which can be applied to a matrix without changing the linear system of equations that it represents.
   a. Thing
   b. Row operations0
   c. Undefined
   d. Undefined

7. In algebra, a _____ is a function depending on n that associates a scalar, det(A), to every $n \times n$ square matrix A.
   a. Determinant0
   b. Thing
   c. Undefined
   d. Undefined

8. _____ is an algorithm which can be used to determine the solutions of a system of linear equations, to find the rank of a matrix, and to calculate the inverse of an invertible square matrix.
   a. Gaussian elimination0
   b. Thing
   c. Undefined
   d. Undefined

9. In mathematics, a matrix can be thought of as each row or _____ being a vector. Hence, a space formed by row vectors or _____ vectors are said to be a row space or a _____ space.
   a. Concept
   b. Column0
   c. Undefined
   d. Undefined

10. In computer science an _____ is a data structure that consists of a group of elements having a single name that are accessed by indexing. In most programming languages each element has the same data type and the _____ occupies a continuous area of storage.

Chapter 8. Matrices and Determinants 147

   a. Thing
   c. Undefined
   b. Array0
   d. Undefined

11. The _____ are the only integral domain whose positive elements are well-ordered, and in which order is preserved by addition. Like the natural numbers, the _____ form a countably infinite set. The set of all _____ is usually denoted in mathematics by a boldface Z .
   a. Thing
   b. Integers0
   c. Undefined
   d. Undefined

12. Mathematical _____ is used to represent ideas.
   a. Thing
   b. Notation0
   c. Undefined
   d. Undefined

13. A _____ is a number, figure, or indicator that appears below the normal line of type, typically used in a formula, mathematical expression, or description of a chemical compound.
   a. Subscript0
   b. Thing
   c. Undefined
   d. Undefined

14. _____ is notation used to indicate some variable between two points each point being represented by one of the subscripts.
   a. Thing
   b. Double subscript notation0
   c. Undefined
   d. Undefined

15. In linear algebra, the _____ of a matrix is obtained by combining two matrices in such a way that a matrix of coefficients to which has been added a column of constants corresponds to the right hand side of the equations.
   a. Augmented matrix0
   b. Thing
   c. Undefined
   d. Undefined

16. _____ is a notation for writing numbers that is often used by scientists and mathematicians to make it easier to write large and small numbers.
   a. Thing
   b. Scientific notation0
   c. Undefined
   d. Undefined

17. In mathematics and the mathematical sciences, a _____ is a fixed, but possibly unspecified, value. This is in contrast to a variable, which is not fixed.
   a. Thing
   b. Constant0
   c. Undefined
   d. Undefined

18. _____ is a fixed, but possibly unspecified, value. This is in contrast to a variable, which is not fixed.
   a. Thing
   b. Constant term0
   c. Undefined
   d. Undefined

19. In mathematics, a _____ is a constant multiplicative factor of a certain object. The object can be such things as a variable, a vector, a function, etc. For example, the _____ of $9x^2$ is 9.

Chapter 8. Matrices and Determinants

    a. Coefficient0
    b. Thing
    c. Undefined
    d. Undefined

20. In linear algebra, the _____ refers to a matrix consisting of the coefficients of the variables in a set of linear equations.
    a. Coefficient matrix0
    b. Thing
    c. Undefined
    d. Undefined

21. A _____ of a number is the product of that number with any integer.
    a. Thing
    b. Multiple0
    c. Undefined
    d. Undefined

22. _____ is the study of terms and their use — of words and compound words that are used in specific contexts.
    a. Terminology0
    b. Thing
    c. Undefined
    d. Undefined

23. Equivalence is the condition of being _____ or essentially equal.
    a. Thing
    b. Equivalent0
    c. Undefined
    d. Undefined

24. In mathematics, a _____ is an ordered list of objects. Like a set, it contains members, also called elements or terms, and the number of terms is called the length of the _____. Unlike a set, order matters, and the exact same elements can appear multiple times at different positions in the _____.
    a. Sequence0
    b. Thing
    c. Undefined
    d. Undefined

25. _____ or arithmetics is the oldest and most elementary branch of mathematics, used by almost everyone, for tasks ranging from simple daily counting to advanced science and business calculations.
    a. Arithmetic0
    b. Thing
    c. Undefined
    d. Undefined

26. A _____ is a negotiable instrument instructing a financial institution to pay a specific amount of a specific currency from a specific demand account held in the maker/depositor's name with that institution. Both the maker and payee may be natural persons or legal entities.
    a. Thing
    b. Check0
    c. Undefined
    d. Undefined

27. An _____ or member of a set is an object that when collected together make up the set.
    a. Thing
    b. Element0
    c. Undefined
    d. Undefined

28. In mathematics, the _____, or members of a set or more generally a class are all those objects which when collected together make up the set or class.
    a. Elements0
    b. Thing
    c. Undefined
    d. Undefined

Chapter 8. Matrices and Determinants

29. In mathematics, _____ refers to the rewriting of an expression into a simpler form.
    a. Thing
    b. Reduction0
    c. Undefined
    d. Undefined

30. Johann _____ was a German mathematician and scientist of profound genius who contributed significantly to many fields, including number theory, analysis, differential geometry, geodesy, magnetism, astronomy, and optics. He completed Disquisitiones Arithmeticae, his magnum opus, at the age of twenty-one.
    a. Person
    b. Carl Friedrich Gauss0
    c. Undefined
    d. Undefined

31. _____ is the state of being greater than any finite real or natural number, however large.
    a. Thing
    b. Infinite0
    c. Undefined
    d. Undefined

32. In mathematics, a _____ may be described informally as a number that can be given by an infinite decimal representation.
    a. Thing
    b. Real number0
    c. Undefined
    d. Undefined

33. A _____ is a set of possible values that a variable can take on in order to satisfy a given set of conditions, which may include equations and inequalities.
    a. Thing
    b. Solution set0
    c. Undefined
    d. Undefined

34. In Graph theory, a _____ is a digraph with weighted edges.
    a. Concept
    b. Network0
    c. Undefined
    d. Undefined

35. The _____, in practice often shortened to amp, is a unit of electric current, or amount of electric charge per second.
    a. Thing
    b. Amperes0
    c. Undefined
    d. Undefined

36. In mathematics, a _____ number is a number which can be expressed as a ratio of two integers. Non-integer _____ numbers (commonly called fractions) are usually written as the vulgar fraction a / b, where b is not zero.
    a. Rational0
    b. Thing
    c. Undefined
    d. Undefined

37. _____ refers to the reduction of the body of a formerly living organism into simpler forms of matter.
    a. Thing
    b. Decomposing0
    c. Undefined
    d. Undefined

38. An _____ is a combination of numbers, operators, grouping symbols and/or free variables and bound variables arranged in a meaningful way which can be evaluated..

Chapter 8. Matrices and Determinants

    a. Expression0
    b. Thing
    c. Undefined
    d. Undefined

39. In algebra, the _____ decomposition or _____ expansion is used to reduce the degree of either the numerator or the denominator of a rational function.
    a. Thing
    b. Partial fraction0
    c. Undefined
    d. Undefined

40. _____ studies and addresses the ways in which individuals, businesses, and organizations raise, allocate, and use monetary resources over time, taking into account the risks entailed in their projects
    a. Finance0
    b. Thing
    c. Undefined
    d. Undefined

41. A _____ is a special kind of ratio, indicating a relationship between two measurements with different units, such as miles to gallons or cents to pounds.
    a. Rate0
    b. Thing
    c. Undefined
    d. Undefined

42. _____ is a kind of property which exists as magnitude or multitude. It is among the basic classes of things along with quality, substance, change, and relation.
    a. Amount0
    b. Thing
    c. Undefined
    d. Undefined

43. _____ is the fee paid on borrowed money.
    a. Interest0
    b. Thing
    c. Undefined
    d. Undefined

44. In mathematics, the _____ is a conic section generated by the intersection of a right circular conical surface and a plane parallel to a generating straight line of that surface. It can also be defined as locus of points in a plane which are equidistant from a given point.
    a. Parabola0
    b. Thing
    c. Undefined
    d. Undefined

45. _____ is the analysis of networks through network theory or more generally graph theory.
    a. Network analysis0
    b. Thing
    c. Undefined
    d. Undefined

46. The metre (or _____, see spelling differences) is a measure of length. It is the basic unit of length in the metric system and in the International System of Units (SI), used around the world for general and scientific purposes.
    a. Concept
    b. Meter0
    c. Undefined
    d. Undefined

47. In common philosophical language, a proposition or _____, is the content of an assertion, that is, it is true-or-false and defined by the meaning of a particular piece of language.

Chapter 8. Matrices and Determinants

a. Statement0
b. Concept
c. Undefined
d. Undefined

48. In Euclidean geometry, a _____ is the set of all points in a plane at a fixed distance, called the radius, from a given point, the center.
    a. Circle0
    b. Thing
    c. Undefined
    d. Undefined

49. In mathematics, an _____ .
    a. Ellipse0
    b. Thing
    c. Undefined
    d. Undefined

50. In mathematics, a _____ is a type of conic section defined as the intersection between a right circular conical surface and a plane which cuts through both halves of the cone.
    a. Hyperbola0
    b. Thing
    c. Undefined
    d. Undefined

51. The mathematical concept of a _____ expresses the intuitive idea of deterministic dependence between two quantities, one of which is viewed as primary and the other as secondary. A _____ then is a way to associate a unique output for each input of a specified type, for example, a real number or an element of a given set.
    a. Function0
    b. Thing
    c. Undefined
    d. Undefined

52. Two mathematical objects are equal if and only if they are precisely the same in every way. This defines a binary relation, _____, denoted by the sign of _____ "=" in such a way that the statement "x = y" means that x and y are equal.
    a. Thing
    b. Equality0
    c. Undefined
    d. Undefined

53. A _____ is the result of the addition of a set of numbers. The numbers may be natural numbers, complex numbers, matrices, or still more complicated objects. An infinite _____ is a subtle procedure known as a series.
    a. Thing
    b. Sum0
    c. Undefined
    d. Undefined

54. In mathematics, defined and _____ are used to explain whether or not expressions have meaningful, sensible, and unambiguous values.
    a. Undefined0
    b. Thing
    c. Undefined
    d. Undefined

55. In linear algebra, real numbers are called scalars and relate to vectors in a vector space through the operation of _____ multiplication, in which a vector can be multiplied by a number to produce another vector.
    a. Thing
    b. Scalar0
    c. Undefined
    d. Undefined

56. In mathematics, _____ is an elementary arithmetic operation. When one of the numbers is a whole number, _____ is the repeated sum of the other number.

a. Multiplication0 b. Thing
c. Undefined d. Undefined

57. _____ is one of the basic operations defining a vector space in linear algebra.
a. Scalar multiplication0 b. Thing
c. Undefined d. Undefined

58. _____ was a British mathematician. He helped found the modern British school of pure mathematics.
a. Person b. Arthur Cayley0
c. Undefined d. Undefined

59. In mathematics, a _____ in elementary terms is any of a variety of different functions from geometry, such as rotations, reflections and translations.
a. Thing b. Transformation0
c. Undefined d. Undefined

60. In mathematics, a _____ is a countable collection of open covers of a topological space that satisfies certain separation axioms.
a. Development0 b. Thing
c. Undefined d. Undefined

61. _____ is a branch of mathematics concerning the study of structure, relation and quantity.
a. Algebra0 b. Concept
c. Undefined d. Undefined

62. In arithmetic and algebra, when a number or expression is both preceded and followed by a binary operation, an _____ is required for which operation should be applied first.
a. Thing b. Order of operations0
c. Undefined d. Undefined

63. In mathematics, _____ is the decomposition of an object into a product of other objects, or factors, which when multiplied together give the original.
a. Factoring0 b. Thing
c. Undefined d. Undefined

64. In logic and mathematics, _____ is an operation on logical values, for example, the logical value of a proposition, that sends true to false and false to true.
a. Person b. Negation0
c. Undefined d. Undefined

65. In mathematics, _____ is a property that a binary operation can have. Within an expression containing two or more of the same associative operators in a row, the order of operations does not matter as long as the sequence of the operands is not changed.
a. Thing b. Associativity0
c. Undefined d. Undefined

Chapter 8. Matrices and Determinants

66. An _____ is an equality that remains true regardless of the values of any variables that appear within it, to distinguish it from an equality which is true under more particular conditions.
    a. Identity0
    b. Thing
    c. Undefined
    d. Undefined

67. In mathematics, and in particular in abstract algebra, the _____ is a property of binary operations that generalises the distributive law from elementary algebra.
    a. Distributive property0
    b. Thing
    c. Undefined
    d. Undefined

68. In mathematics, the _____ inverse, or opposite, of a number n is the number that, when added to n, yields zero. The _____ inverse of n is denoted −n.
    a. Thing
    b. Additive0
    c. Undefined
    d. Undefined

69. In mathematics the _____ of a set which is equipped with the operation of addition is an element which, when added to any other element x in the set, yields x.
    a. Concept
    b. Additive identity0
    c. Undefined
    d. Undefined

70. In mathematics, a _____ is the result of multiplying, or an expression that identifies factors to be multiplied.
    a. Product0
    b. Thing
    c. Undefined
    d. Undefined

71. In plane geometry, a _____ is a polygon with four equal sides, four right angles, and parallel opposite sides. In algebra, the _____ of a number is that number multiplied by itself.
    a. Square0
    b. Thing
    c. Undefined
    d. Undefined

72. In linear algebra, the _____ of a square matrix is the diagonal which runs from the top left corner to the bottom right corner.
    a. Thing
    b. Main diagonal0
    c. Undefined
    d. Undefined

73. A _____ can refer to a line joining two nonadjacent vertices of a polygon or polyhedron, or in some contexts any upward or downward sloping line. .
    a. Diagonal0
    b. Thing
    c. Undefined
    d. Undefined

74. In mathematics, a matrix is in row _____ if is satisfies the following requirements: • All nonzero rows are above any rows of all zeroes.   • The leading coefficient of a row is always strictly to the right of the leading coefficient of the row above it.
    a. Thing
    b. Echelon form0
    c. Undefined
    d. Undefined

Chapter 8. Matrices and Determinants

75. _____ is the application of tools and a processing medium to the transformation of raw materials into finished goods for sale.
    a. Thing
    b. Manufacturing0
    c. Undefined
    d. Undefined

76. The _____ of measurement are a globally standardized and modernized form of the metric system.
    a. Units0
    b. Thing
    c. Undefined
    d. Undefined

77. _____ is the production of food, feed, fiber, fuel and other goods by the systematic raizing of plants and animals.
    a. Thing
    b. Agriculture0
    c. Undefined
    d. Undefined

78. _____, from Latin meaning "to make progress", is defined in two different ways. Pure economic _____ is the increase in wealth that an investor has from making an investment, taking into consideration all costs associated with that investment including the opportunity cost of capital.
    a. Profit0
    b. Thing
    c. Undefined
    d. Undefined

79. _____ is a business term for the amount of money that a company receives from its activities in a given period, mostly from sales of products and/or services to customers
    a. Revenue0
    b. Thing
    c. Undefined
    d. Undefined

80. _____ is a list of goods and materials, or those goods and materials themselves, held available in stock by a business
    a. Inventory0
    b. Thing
    c. Undefined
    d. Undefined

81. According to the United Nations Statistics Division, _____ is the resale sale without transformation of new and used goods to retailers, to industrial, commercial, institutional or professional users, or to other wholesalers, or involves acting as an agent or broker in buying merchandise for, or selling merchandise, to such persons or companies.
    a. Thing
    b. Wholesale0
    c. Undefined
    d. Undefined

82. _____, from the Greek "stochos" or "aim, guess", means of, relating to, or characterized by conjecture and randomness. A _____ process is one whose behavior is non-deterministic in that a state does not fully determine its next state.
    a. Thing
    b. Stochastic0
    c. Undefined
    d. Undefined

83. In mathematics, a _____ describes the transitions of a Markov chain. It has found use in probability theory, statistics and linear algebra, as well as computer science.
    a. Stochastic matrix0
    b. Thing
    c. Undefined
    d. Undefined

Chapter 8. Matrices and Determinants

84. _____ is a special mathematical relationship between two quantities. Two quantities are called proportional if they vary in such a way that one of the quantities is a constant multiple of the other, or equivalently if they have a constant ratio.
  a. Proportionality0
  b. Thing
  c. Undefined
  d. Undefined

85. In sociology and biology a _____ is the collection of people or organisms of a particular species living in a given geographic area or space, usually measured by a census.
  a. Thing
  b. Population0
  c. Undefined
  d. Undefined

86. A _____ is a compensation which workers receive in exchange for their labor.
  a. Wage0
  b. Thing
  c. Undefined
  d. Undefined

87. A _____ fraction is a fraction in which the absolute value of the numerator is less than the denominator--hence, the absolute value of the fraction is less than 1.
  a. Proper0
  b. Thing
  c. Undefined
  d. Undefined

88. In mathematics, the conjugate _____ or adjoint matrix of an m-by-n matrix A with complex entries is the n-by-m matrix A* obtained from A by taking the transpose and then taking the complex conjugate of each entry.
  a. Pairs0
  b. Thing
  c. Undefined
  d. Undefined

89. In mathematics, a _____ is a mathematical statement which appears likely to be true, but has not been formally proven to be true under the rules of mathematical logic.
  a. Conjecture0
  b. Concept
  c. Undefined
  d. Undefined

90. In mathematics, the _____ inverse of a number x, denoted 1/x or x^{-1}, is the number which, when multiplied by x, yields 1. The _____ inverse of x is also called the reciprocal of x.
  a. Multiplicative0
  b. Thing
  c. Undefined
  d. Undefined

91. _____ element of an element x with respect to a binary operation * with identity element e is an element y such that x * y = y * x = e. In particular,
  a. Thing
  b. Inverse0
  c. Undefined
  d. Undefined

92. _____ traditionally refers to the statistical process of determining comparable scores on different forms of an exam
  a. Equating0
  b. Thing
  c. Undefined
  d. Undefined

Chapter 8. Matrices and Determinants

93. In mathematics, computing, linguistics, and related disciplines, an _____ is a finite list of well-defined instructions for accomplishing some task which, given an initial state, will terminate in a defined end-state.
   a. Algorithm0
   b. Concept
   c. Undefined
   d. Undefined

94. In mathematics, the idea of _____ generalises the concepts of negation, in relation to addition, and reciprocal, in relation to multiplication.
   a. Thing
   b. Inverse element0
   c. Undefined
   d. Undefined

95. In mathematics, an _____, mean, or central tendency of a data set refers to a measure of the "middle" or "expected" value of the data set.
   a. Average0
   b. Concept
   c. Undefined
   d. Undefined

96. _____ finance, in finance, a debt security, issued by Issuer
   a. Bond0
   b. Thing
   c. Undefined
   d. Undefined

97. An _____ is a square matrix which has an inverse.
   a. Invertible matrix0
   b. Thing
   c. Undefined
   d. Undefined

98. _____ is the difference of electrical potential between two points of an electrical or electronic circuit, expressed in volts
   a. Thing
   b. Voltage0
   c. Undefined
   d. Undefined

99. In regression analysis, _____, also known as ordinary _____ analysis is a method for linear regression that determines the values of unknown quantities in a statistical model by minimizing the sum of the residuals difference between the predicted and observed values squared.
   a. Least squares0
   b. Thing
   c. Undefined
   d. Undefined

100. A _____ is a one-dimensional picture in which the integers are shown as specially-marked points evenly spaced on a line.
   a. Thing
   b. Number line0
   c. Undefined
   d. Undefined

101. In mathematics, an _____ is a statement about the relative size or order of two objects.
   a. Inequality0
   b. Thing
   c. Undefined
   d. Undefined

102. In linear algebra, a _____ or minor of a matrix A is the determinant of some smaller square matrix, cut down from A.

Chapter 8. Matrices and Determinants

a. Cofactor0
b. Thing
c. Undefined
d. Undefined

103. In linear algebra, a _____ of a matrix A is the determinant of some smaller square matrix, cut down from A.
a. Thing
b. Minor0
c. Undefined
d. Undefined

104. In mathematics, for a statement to be mathematically _____, such a statement must be true of all natural numbers.
a. Thing
b. Inductive0
c. Undefined
d. Undefined

105. An _____ of a product of sums expresses it as a sum of products by using the fact that multiplication distributes over addition.
a. Thing
b. Expansion0
c. Undefined
d. Undefined

106. _____ is a mathematical subject that includes the study of limits, derivatives, integrals, and power series and constitutes a major part of modern university curriculum.
a. Thing
b. Calculus0
c. Undefined
d. Undefined

107. In mathematics, a _____ section is a curve that can be formed by intersecting a cone with a plane.
a. Conic0
b. Thing
c. Undefined
d. Undefined

108. In geometry, a _____ is a special kind of point, usually a corner of a polygon, polyhedron, or higher dimensional polytope. In the geometry of curves a _____ is a point of where the first derivative of curvature is zero. In graph theory, a _____ is the fundamental unit out of which graphs are formed
a. Thing
b. Vertex0
c. Undefined
d. Undefined

109. In geometry, the _____ are a pair of special points used in describing conic sections. The four types of conic sections are the circle, parabola, ellipse, and hyperbola.
a. Thing
b. Foci0
c. Undefined
d. Undefined

110. A _____ is a numeral used to indicate a count. The most common use of the word today is to name the part of a fraction that tells the number or count of equal parts.
a. Thing
b. Numerator0
c. Undefined
d. Undefined

111. A _____ is the part of a fraction that tells how many equal parts make up a whole, and which is used in the name of the fraction: "halves", "thirds", "fourths" or "quarters", "fifths" and so on.

Chapter 8. Matrices and Determinants

  a. Concept
  b. Denominator0
  c. Undefined
  d. Undefined

112. A _____ is one of the basic shapes of geometry: a polygon with three vertices and three sides which are straight line segments.
  a. Triangle0
  b. Thing
  c. Undefined
  d. Undefined

113. In mathematical logic, a Gödel numbering (or Gödel _____) is a function that assigns to each symbol and well-formed formula of some formal language a unique natural number called its Gödel number.
  a. Thing
  b. Code0
  c. Undefined
  d. Undefined

114. Three or more points that lie on the same line are called _____.
  a. Collinear0
  b. Thing
  c. Undefined
  d. Undefined

115. In three or more dimensions, lines may also be skew, meaning they don't meet, but also don't define a plane. Two distinct planes intersect in at most one line. Three or more points that lie on the same line are called _____.
  a. Collinear points0
  b. Concept
  c. Undefined
  d. Undefined

116. Acid _____ ratio measures the ability of a company to use its near cash or quick assets to immediately extinguish its current liabilities.
  a. Thing
  b. Test0
  c. Undefined
  d. Undefined

117. In mathematics, a _____ is the end result of a division problem. It can also be expressed as the number of times the divisor divides into the dividend.
  a. Quotient0
  b. Thing
  c. Undefined
  d. Undefined

118. A _____ is a set of numbers that designate location in a given reference system, such as x,y in a planar _____ system or an x,y,z in a three-dimensional _____ system.
  a. Coordinate0
  b. Thing
  c. Undefined
  d. Undefined

119. In mathematics, a _____ is a two-dimensional manifold or surface that is perfectly flat.
  a. Plane0
  b. Thing
  c. Undefined
  d. Undefined

120. _____ is a set, with some particular properties and usually some additional structure, such as the operations of addition or multiplication, for instance.
  a. Space0
  b. Thing
  c. Undefined
  d. Undefined

Chapter 8. Matrices and Determinants

121. A _____ is a unit of length, usually used to measure distance, in a number of different systems, including Imperial units, United States customary units and Norwegian/Swedish mil. Its size can vary from system to system, but in each is between 1 and 10 kilometers. In contemporary English contexts _____ refers to either:
 a. Mile0
 b. Thing
 c. Undefined
 d. Undefined

122. In mathematics, a _____ is a condition that a solution to an optimization problem must satisfy in order to be acceptable.
 a. Thing
 b. Constraint0
 c. Undefined
 d. Undefined

123. _____ has many meanings, most of which simply .
 a. Thing
 b. Power0
 c. Undefined
 d. Undefined

124. In mathematics, a _____ is a demonstration that, assuming certain axioms, some statement is necessarily true.
 a. Thing
 b. Proof0
 c. Undefined
 d. Undefined

125. Mathematical _____ are demonstrations that, assuming certain axioms, some statement is necessarily true.
 a. Thing
 b. Proofs0
 c. Undefined
 d. Undefined

126. In mathematics, a _____ is a statement that can be proved on the basis of explicitly stated or previously agreed assumptions.
 a. Thing
 b. Theorem0
 c. Undefined
 d. Undefined

127. A _____ is a simplified and structured visual representation of concepts, ideas, constructions, relations, statistical data, anatomy etc used in all aspects of human activities to visualize and clarify the topic.
 a. Diagram0
 b. Thing
 c. Undefined
 d. Undefined

128. _____ is a way of expressing a number as a fraction of 100 per cent meaning "per hundred".
 a. Thing
 b. Percent0
 c. Undefined
 d. Undefined

129. In mathematics and computer science, the concept of _____ arises in a number of places in abstract algebra; in particular, in the theory of projectors, closure operators and functional programming, in which it is connected to the property of referential transparency.
 a. Idempotence0
 b. Thing
 c. Undefined
 d. Undefined

130. The _____ ma is the mass of an atom at rest, most often expressed in unified _____ units.

a. Atomic mass0
b. Thing
c. Undefined
d. Undefined

131. _____ is the property of a physical object that quantifies the amount of matter and energy it is equivalent to.
   a. Thing
   b. Mass0
   c. Undefined
   d. Undefined

132. _____ are a set of equations containing multiple variables.
   a. Systems of equations0
   b. Thing
   c. Undefined
   d. Undefined

133. _____ is electromagnetic radiation with a wavelength that is visible to the eye (visible _____) or, in a technical or scientific context, electromagnetic radiation of any wavelength.
   a. Thing
   b. Light0
   c. Undefined
   d. Undefined

Chapter 9. Sequences, Series, and Probability

1. _____ is the chance that something is likely to happen or be the case.
   a. Thing
   b. Probability0
   c. Undefined
   d. Undefined

2. In mathematics, a _____ is an ordered list of objects. Like a set, it contains members, also called elements or terms, and the number of terms is called the length of the _____. Unlike a set, order matters, and the exact same elements can appear multiple times at different positions in the _____.
   a. Sequence0
   b. Thing
   c. Undefined
   d. Undefined

3. A _____ is the sum of the elements of a sequence.
   a. Series0
   b. Thing
   c. Undefined
   d. Undefined

4. The _____, the average in everyday English, which is also called the arithmetic _____ (and is distinguished from the geometric _____ or harmonic _____). The average is also called the sample _____. The expected value of a random variable, which is also called the population _____.
   a. Mean0
   b. Thing
   c. Undefined
   d. Undefined

5. The _____ are the only integral domain whose positive elements are well-ordered, and in which order is preserved by addition. Like the natural numbers, the _____ form a countably infinite set. The set of all _____ is usually denoted in mathematics by a boldface Z .
   a. Integers0
   b. Thing
   c. Undefined
   d. Undefined

6. In mathematics, a _____ of a k-place relation $L \subseteq X_1 \times ... \times X_k$ is one of the sets X_j, $1 \leq j \leq k$. In the special case where k = 2 and $L \subseteq X_1 \times X_2$ is a function $L : X_1 \rightarrow X_2$, it is conventional to refer to X_1 as the _____ of the function and to refer to X_2 as the codomain of the function.
   a. Thing
   b. Domain0
   c. Undefined
   d. Undefined

7. _____ is the state of being greater than any finite real or natural number, however large.
   a. Infinite0
   b. Thing
   c. Undefined
   d. Undefined

8. The mathematical concept of a _____ expresses the intuitive idea of deterministic dependence between two quantities, one of which is viewed as primary and the other as secondary. A _____ then is a way to associate a unique output for each input of a specified type, for example, a real number or an element of a given set.
   a. Function0
   b. Thing
   c. Undefined
   d. Undefined

9. In mathematics, a set is called _____ if there is a bijection between the set and some set of the form {1, 2, ..., n} where n is a natural number.
   a. Thing
   b. Finite0
   c. Undefined
   d. Undefined

10. An _____ is a combination of numbers, operators, grouping symbols and/or free variables and bound variables arranged in a meaningful way which can be evaluated..
   a. Thing
   b. Expression0
   c. Undefined
   d. Undefined

11. In statistics, _____ means the most frequent value assumed by a random variable, or occurring in a sampling of a random variable.
   a. Concept
   b. Mode0
   c. Undefined
   d. Undefined

12. Leonardo of Pisa (1170s or 1180s – 1250), also known as Leonardo Pisano, Leonardo Bonacci, Leonardo _____, or, most commonly, simply _____, was an Italian mathematician, considered by some "the most talented mathematician of the Middle Ages."
   a. Fibonacci0
   b. Person
   c. Undefined
   d. Undefined

13. In mathematics, when a method of defining functions is utilized, in which the function being defined is applied within its own definition, that pertaining function is called _____.
   a. Recursive0
   b. Thing
   c. Undefined
   d. Undefined

14. _____ is a method of defining functions in which the function being defined is applied within its own definition. The term is also used more generally to describe a process of repeating objects in a self-similar way.
   a. Recursion0
   b. Thing
   c. Undefined
   d. Undefined

15. In mathematics, a _____ is the result of multiplying, or an expression that identifies factors to be multiplied.
   a. Thing
   b. Product0
   c. Undefined
   d. Undefined

16. _____ of a non-negative integer n is the product of all positive integers less than or equal to n.
   a. Factorial0
   b. Thing
   c. Undefined
   d. Undefined

17. A _____ is a symbolic representation denoting a quantity or expression. It often represents an "unknown" quantity that has the potential to change.
   a. Thing
   b. Variable0
   c. Undefined
   d. Undefined

18. A _____ is a number, figure, or indicator that appears below the normal line of type, typically used in a formula, mathematical expression, or description of a chemical compound.
   a. Subscript0
   b. Thing
   c. Undefined
   d. Undefined

19. In arithmetic and algebra, when a number or expression is both preceded and followed by a binary operation, an _____ is required for which operation should be applied first.

Chapter 9. Sequences, Series, and Probability 163

   a. Order of operations0   b. Thing
   c. Undefined   d. Undefined

20. _____ is a mathematical operation, written a^n, involving two numbers, the base a and the exponent n.
   a. Exponentiating0   b. Thing
   c. Undefined   d. Undefined

21. _____ is a mathematical operation, written a^n, involving two numbers, the base a and the exponent n.
   a. Thing   b. Exponentiation0
   c. Undefined   d. Undefined

22. A _____ is a set of numbers that designate location in a given reference system, such as x,y in a planar _____ system or an x,y,z in a three-dimensional _____ system.
   a. Thing   b. Coordinate0
   c. Undefined   d. Undefined

23. An _____ is when two lines intersect somewhere on a plane creating a right angle at intersection
   a. Thing   b. Axes0
   c. Undefined   d. Undefined

24. Mathematical _____ is used to represent ideas.
   a. Thing   b. Notation0
   c. Undefined   d. Undefined

25. A _____ is the result of the addition of a set of numbers. The numbers may be natural numbers, complex numbers, matrices, or still more complicated objects. An infinite _____ is a subtle procedure known as a series.
   a. Sum0   b. Thing
   c. Undefined   d. Undefined

26. _____ is the addition of a set of numbers; the result is their sum. The "numbers" to be summed may be natural numbers, complex numbers, matrices, or still more complicated objects. An infinite sum is a subtle procedure known as a series.
   a. Summation0   b. Thing
   c. Undefined   d. Undefined

27. _____ is the eighteenth letter of the Greek alphabet.
   a. Sigma0   b. Thing
   c. Undefined   d. Undefined

28. _____ is used as the symbol for summation. Summation is the addition of a set of numbers; the result is their sum. The "numbers" to be summed may be natural numbers, complex numbers, matrices, or still more complicated objects. An infinite sum is a subtle procedure known as a series.
   a. Thing   b. Sigma notation0
   c. Undefined   d. Undefined

29. The word _____ is used in a variety of ways in mathematics.

a. Thing
b. Index0
c. Undefined
d. Undefined

30. A _____ is a negotiable instrument instructing a financial institution to pay a specific amount of a specific currency from a specific demand account held in the maker/depositor's name with that institution. Both the maker and payee may be natural persons or legal entities.
    a. Thing
    b. Check0
    c. Undefined
    d. Undefined

31. In geographic information systems, a _____ comprises an entity with a geographic location, typically determined by points, arcs, or polygons. Carriageways and cadastres exemplify _____ data.
    a. Thing
    b. Feature0
    c. Undefined
    d. Undefined

32. In mathematics and the mathematical sciences, a _____ is a fixed, but possibly unspecified, value. This is in contrast to a variable, which is not fixed.
    a. Thing
    b. Constant0
    c. Undefined
    d. Undefined

33. In sociology and biology a _____ is the collection of people or organisms of a particular species living in a given geographic area or space, usually measured by a census.
    a. Population0
    b. Thing
    c. Undefined
    d. Undefined

34. In business, particularly accounting, a _____ is the time intervals that the accounts, statement, payments, or other calculations cover.
    a. Thing
    b. Period0
    c. Undefined
    d. Undefined

35. The _____ (symbol _____) and the millibar (symbol mbar, also mb) are units of pressure.
    a. Thing
    b. Bar0
    c. Undefined
    d. Undefined

36. A bar chart, also known as a _____, is a chart with rectangular bars of lengths usually proportional to the magnitudes or frequencies of what they represent.
    a. Bar graph0
    b. Thing
    c. Undefined
    d. Undefined

37. _____ is the fee paid on borrowed money.
    a. Thing
    b. Interest0
    c. Undefined
    d. Undefined

38. _____ interest refers to the fact that whenever interest is calculated, it is based not only on the original principal, but also on any unpaid interest that has been added to the principal.

Chapter 9. Sequences, Series, and Probability

    a. Thing   b. Compound0
    c. Undefined   d. Undefined

39. _____ refers to the fact that whenever interest is calculated, it is based not only on the original principal, but also on any unpaid interest that has been added to the principal. The more frequently interest is compounded, the faster the balance grows.
    a. Compound interest0   b. Concept
    c. Undefined   d. Undefined

40. In banking and accountancy, the outstanding _____ is the amount of money owned, or due, that remains in a deposit account or a loan account at a given date, after all past remittances, payments and withdrawal have been accounted for.
    a. Balance0   b. Thing
    c. Undefined   d. Undefined

41. In geometry, the _____ of an object is a point in some sense in the middle of the object.
    a. Thing   b. Center0
    c. Undefined   d. Undefined

42. In mathematics, a _____ or rhodonea curve is a sinusoid plotted in polar coordinates.
    a. Rose0   b. Thing
    c. Undefined   d. Undefined

43. In topology and related areas of mathematics a _____ or Moore-Smith sequence is a generalization of a sequence, intended to unify the various notions of limit and generalize them to arbitrary topological spaces.
    a. Net0   b. Thing
    c. Undefined   d. Undefined

44. _____ is an accounting term which is commonly used in business.
    a. Net profit0   b. Thing
    c. Undefined   d. Undefined

45. _____, from Latin meaning "to make progress", is defined in two different ways. Pure economic _____ is the increase in wealth that an investor has from making an investment, taking into consideration all costs associated with that investment including the opportunity cost of capital.
    a. Profit0   b. Thing
    c. Undefined   d. Undefined

46. _____ is a synonym for information.
    a. Thing   b. Data0
    c. Undefined   d. Undefined

47. The word _____ comes from the Latin word linearis, which means created by lines.
    a. Linear0   b. Thing
    c. Undefined   d. Undefined

Chapter 9. Sequences, Series, and Probability

48. _____ is a Fortune 200 company, and the third largest consumer electronics retailer in the United States with over $11 billion USD in sales, behind Best Buy and Wal-Mart.
   a. Thing
   b. Circuit City0
   c. Undefined
   d. Undefined

49. In common philosophical language, a proposition or _____, is the content of an assertion, that is, it is true-or-false and defined by the meaning of a particular piece of language.
   a. Statement0
   b. Concept
   c. Undefined
   d. Undefined

50. _____ or arithmetics is the oldest and most elementary branch of mathematics, used by almost everyone, for tasks ranging from simple daily counting to advanced science and business calculations.
   a. Arithmetic0
   b. Thing
   c. Undefined
   d. Undefined

51. _____ of a list of numbers is the sum of all the members of the list divided by the number of items in the list.
   a. Thing
   b. Arithmetic mean0
   c. Undefined
   d. Undefined

52. In mathematics, a _____ is a demonstration that, assuming certain axioms, some statement is necessarily true.
   a. Thing
   b. Proof0
   c. Undefined
   d. Undefined

53. _____ element of an element x with respect to a binary operation * with identity element e is an element y such that x * y = y * x = e. In particular,
   a. Thing
   b. Inverse0
   c. Undefined
   d. Undefined

54. An _____ is a function which does the reverse of a given function.
   a. Thing
   b. Inverse function0
   c. Undefined
   d. Undefined

55. In mathematics, a _____ is a rectangular table of numbers or, more generally, a table consisting of abstract quantities that can be added and multiplied.
   a. Matrix0
   b. Thing
   c. Undefined
   d. Undefined

56. In algebra, a _____ is a function depending on n that associates a scalar, $\det(A)$, to every $n \times n$ square matrix A.
   a. Determinant0
   b. Thing
   c. Undefined
   d. Undefined

57. _____ is a sequence of numbers such that the difference of any two successive members of the sequence is a constant.
   a. Thing
   b. Arithmetic sequence0
   c. Undefined
   d. Undefined

Chapter 9. Sequences, Series, and Probability

58. _____ means in succession or back-to-back
 a. Thing
 b. Consecutive0
 c. Undefined
 d. Undefined

59. In mathematics, a _____ can mean either an element of the set {1, 2, 3, ...} (i.e the positive integers or the counting numbers) or an element of the set {0, 1, 2, 3, ...} (i.e. the non-negative integers).
 a. Thing
 b. Natural number0
 c. Undefined
 d. Undefined

60. A _____ is a first degree polynomial mathematical function of the form: f(x) = mx + b where m and b are real constants and x is a real variable.
 a. Thing
 b. Linear function0
 c. Undefined
 d. Undefined

61. Johann _____ was a German mathematician and scientist of profound genius who contributed significantly to many fields, including number theory, analysis, differential geometry, geodesy, magnetism, astronomy, and optics. He completed Disquisitiones Arithmeticae, his magnum opus, at the age of twenty-one.
 a. Person
 b. Carl Friedrich Gauss0
 c. Undefined
 d. Undefined

62. _____ is a form of periodic payment from an employer to an employee, which is specified in an employment contract.
 a. Thing
 b. Gross pay0
 c. Undefined
 d. Undefined

63. A _____ is a form of periodic payment from an employer to an employee, which is specified in an employment contract.
 a. Thing
 b. Salary0
 c. Undefined
 d. Undefined

64. In mathematics, a matrix can be thought of as each row or _____ being a vector. Hence, a space formed by row vectors or _____ vectors are said to be a row space or a _____ space.
 a. Concept
 b. Column0
 c. Undefined
 d. Undefined

65. In mathematics, a _____ is a two-dimensional manifold or surface that is perfectly flat.
 a. Plane0
 b. Thing
 c. Undefined
 d. Undefined

66. In mathematics, a _____ is a mathematical statement which appears likely to be true, but has not been formally proven to be true under the rules of mathematical logic.
 a. Concept
 b. Conjecture0
 c. Undefined
 d. Undefined

168 *Chapter 9. Sequences, Series, and Probability*

67. _____ is often used to describe the measurement of the steepness, incline, gradient, or grade of a straight line. The _____ is defined as the ratio of the "rise" divided by the "run" between two points on a line, or in other words, the ratio of the altitude change to the horizontal distance between any two points on the line.
   a. Thing
   b. Slope0
   c. Undefined
   d. Undefined

68. A _____ is a sequence of numbers where each term after the first is found by multiplying the previous one by a fixed non-zero number called the common ratio.
   a. Thing
   b. Geometric sequence0
   c. Undefined
   d. Undefined

69. A _____ is a quantity that denotes the proportional amount or magnitude of one quantity relative to another.
   a. Thing
   b. Ratio0
   c. Undefined
   d. Undefined

70. In mathematics, _____ growth occurs when the growth rate of a function is always proportional to the function's current size.
   a. Thing
   b. Exponential0
   c. Undefined
   d. Undefined

71. _____ is one of the most important functions in mathematics. A function commonly used to study growth and decay
   a. Thing
   b. Exponential function0
   c. Undefined
   d. Undefined

72. In mathematics, a _____ of a complex-valued function f is a member x of the domain of f such that f(x) vanishes at x, that is, x : f (x) = 0.
   a. Root0
   b. Thing
   c. Undefined
   d. Undefined

73. _____ is the income from capital investment paid in a series of regular payments.
   a. Annuity0
   b. Thing
   c. Undefined
   d. Undefined

74. A _____ are accounts maintained by commercial banks, savings and loan associations, credit unions, and mutual savings banks that pay interest but can not be used directly as money by, for example, writing a cheque.
   a. Thing
   b. Savings account0
   c. Undefined
   d. Undefined

75. In the scientific method, an _____ (Latin: ex-+-periri, "of (or from) trying"), is a set of actions and observations, performed in the context of solving a particular problem or question, in order to support or falsify a hypothesis or research concerning phenomena.
   a. Experiment0
   b. Thing
   c. Undefined
   d. Undefined

76. A _____ is a function that assigns a number to subsets of a given set.

Chapter 9. Sequences, Series, and Probability

   a. Thing
   c. Undefined
   b. Measure0
   d. Undefined

77. In mathematics, a _____ number is a number which can be expressed as a ratio of two integers. Non-integer _____ numbers (commonly called fractions) are usually written as the vulgar fraction a / b, where b is not zero.
   a. Rational0
   c. Undefined
   b. Thing
   d. Undefined

78. A _____ decimal is a number whose decimal representation eventually becomes periodic (i.e. the same number sequence _____ indefinitely).
   a. Repeating0
   c. Undefined
   b. Thing
   d. Undefined

79. A _____ is a special kind of ratio, indicating a relationship between two measurements with different units, such as miles to gallons or cents to pounds.
   a. Rate0
   c. Undefined
   b. Thing
   d. Undefined

80. _____ is a term used in accounting, economics and finance with reference to the fact that assets with finite lives lose value over time.
   a. Depreciation0
   c. Undefined
   b. Thing
   d. Undefined

81. An _____ is the fee paid on borrow money.
   a. Interest rate0
   c. Undefined
   b. Concept
   d. Undefined

82. Initial objects are also called _____, and terminal objects are also called final.
   a. Coterminal0
   c. Undefined
   b. Thing
   d. Undefined

83. _____ is a kind of property which exists as magnitude or multitude. It is among the basic classes of things along with quality, substance, change, and relation.
   a. Amount0
   c. Undefined
   b. Thing
   d. Undefined

84. In plane geometry, a _____ is a polygon with four equal sides, four right angles, and parallel opposite sides. In algebra, the _____ of a number is that number multiplied by itself.
   a. Square0
   c. Undefined
   b. Thing
   d. Undefined

85. A _____ is one of the basic shapes of geometry: a polygon with three vertices and three sides which are straight line segments.
   a. Thing
   c. Undefined
   b. Triangle0
   d. Undefined

Chapter 9. Sequences, Series, and Probability

86. _____ is the middle point of a line segment.
   a. Thing
   b. Midpoint0
   c. Undefined
   d. Undefined

87. _____ or investing is a term with several closely-related meanings in business management, finance and economics, related to saving or deferring consumption.
   a. Investment0
   b. Thing
   c. Undefined
   d. Undefined

88. _____ has many meanings, most of which simply .
   a. Thing
   b. Power0
   c. Undefined
   d. Undefined

89. The _____ of a mathematical object is its size: a property by which it can be larger or smaller than other objects of the same kind; in technical terms, an ordering of the class of objects to which it belongs.
   a. Magnitude0
   b. Thing
   c. Undefined
   d. Undefined

90. In mathematics, a _____ number (or a _____) is a natural number that has exactly two (distinct) natural number divisors, which are 1 and the _____ number itself.
   a. Thing
   b. Prime0
   c. Undefined
   d. Undefined

91. _____ was a French lawyer and a mathematician who is given credit for early developments that led to modern calculus. In particular, he is recognized for his discovery of an original method of finding the greatest and the smallest ordinates of curved lines, which is analogous to that of the then unknown differential calculus.
   a. Pierre de Fermat0
   b. Person
   c. Undefined
   d. Undefined

92. In statistics, a _____ measure is one which is measuring what is supposed to measure.
   a. Thing
   b. Valid0
   c. Undefined
   d. Undefined

93. _____ is a method of mathematical proof typically used to establish that a given statement is true of all natural numbers
   a. Thing
   b. Mathematical induction0
   c. Undefined
   d. Undefined

94. A _____ signifies a point or points of probability on a subject e.g., the _____ of creativity, which allows for the formation of rule or norm or law by interpretation of the phenomena events that can be created.
   a. Principle0
   b. Thing
   c. Undefined
   d. Undefined

95. There are two main approaches to _____ in mathematics. They are the model theory of _____ and the proof theory of _____.

a. Thing
b. Truth0
c. Undefined
d. Undefined

96. A _____ is a three-dimensional solid object bounded by six square faces, facets, or sides, with three meeting at each vertex.
a. Cube0
b. Thing
c. Undefined
d. Undefined

97. _____ are of a number n in its third power-the result of multiplying it by itself three times.
a. Thing
b. Cubes0
c. Undefined
d. Undefined

98. In mathematics, an _____ is a statement about the relative size or order of two objects.
a. Thing
b. Inequality0
c. Undefined
d. Undefined

99. A _____ consists either of a suggested explanation for a phenomenon or of a reasoned proposal suggesting a possible correlation between multiple phenomena.
a. Hypothesis0
b. Thing
c. Undefined
d. Undefined

100. A _____ is an equation in which each term is either a constant or the product of a constant times the first power of a variable.
a. Linear equation0
b. Thing
c. Undefined
d. Undefined

101. In algebra, a _____ is a binomial formed by taking the opposite of the second term of a binomial.
a. Thing
b. Conjugate0
c. Undefined
d. Undefined

102. The _____ relates to the binary operation of multiplication and addition.
a. Thing
b. Distributive law0
c. Undefined
d. Undefined

103. In mathematics, _____ allows the rapid division of any polynomial by a binomial of the form x − r. It was described by Paolo Ruffini in 1809. _____ is a special case of long division when the divisor is a linear factor.
a. Ruffini's rule0
b. Thing
c. Undefined
d. Undefined

104. In mathematics, a _____ is any function which can be written as the ratio of two polynomial functions.
a. Rational function0
b. Thing
c. Undefined
d. Undefined

105. _____ means "constancy", i.e. if something retains a certain feature even after we change a way of looking at it, then it is symmetric.

a. Symmetry0 b. Thing
c. Undefined d. Undefined

106. An _____ is a straight line or curve A to which another curve B approaches closer and closer as one moves along it. As one moves along B, the space between it and the _____ A becomes smaller and smaller, and can in fact be made as small as one could wish by going far enough along. A curve may or may not touch or cross its _____. In fact, the curve may intersect the _____ an infinite number of times.
a. Asymptote0 b. Thing
c. Undefined d. Undefined

107. In astronomy, geography, geometry and related sciences and contexts, a plane is said to be _____ at a given point if it is locally perpendicular to the gradient of the gravity field, i.e., with the direction of the gravitational force at that point.
a. Horizontal0 b. Thing
c. Undefined d. Undefined

108. Any point where a graph makes contact with an coordinate axis is called an _____ of the graph
a. Thing b. Intercept0
c. Undefined d. Undcfincd

109. In mathematics, a _____ is a constant multiplicative factor of a certain object. The object can be such things as a variable, a vector, a function, etc. For example, the _____ of $9x^2$ is 9.
a. Thing b. Coefficient0
c. Undefined d. Undefined

110. In mathematics, a _____ is an expression that is constructed from one or more variables and constants, using only the operations of addition, subtraction, multiplication, and constant positive whole number exponents. is a _____. Note in particular that division by an expression containing a variable is not in general allowed in polynomials. [1]
a. Thing b. Polynomial0
c. Undefined d. Undefined

111. In elementary algebra, a _____ is a polynomial with two terms: the sum of two monomials. It is the simplest kind of polynomial except for a monomial.
a. Thing b. Binomial0
c. Undefined d. Undefined

112. In mathematics, particularly in combinatorics, the _____ of the natural number n and the integer k is the number of combinations that exist.
a. Thing b. Binomial coefficient0
c. Undefined d. Undefined

113. An _____ of a product of sums expresses it as a sum of products by using the fact that multiplication distributes over addition.
a. Expansion0 b. Thing
c. Undefined d. Undefined

114. In mathematics, the _____ is an important formula giving the expansion of powers of sums.

Chapter 9. Sequences, Series, and Probability

a. Binomial Theorem0
b. Thing
c. Undefined
d. Undefined

115. In mathematics, a _____ is a statement that can be proved on the basis of explicitly stated or previously agreed assumptions.
a. Thing
b. Theorem0
c. Undefined
d. Undefined

116. In mathematics, factorization (British English: factorisation) or factoring is the decomposition of an object (for example, a number, a polynomial, or a matrix) into a product of other objects, or _____, which when multiplied together give the original.
a. Thing
b. Factors0
c. Undefined
d. Undefined

117. Blaise _____ was a French mathematician, physicist, and religious philosopher.
a. Pascal0
b. Person
c. Undefined
d. Undefined

118. Deductive _____ is the kind of _____ in which the conclusion is necessitated by, or reached from, previously known facts (the premises).
a. Reasoning0
b. Thing
c. Undefined
d. Undefined

119. _____ is a notation for writing numbers that is often used by scientists and mathematicians to make it easier to write large and small numbers.
a. Thing
b. Scientific notation0
c. Undefined
d. Undefined

120. The _____ of measurement are a globally standardized and modernized form of the metric system.
a. Thing
b. Units0
c. Undefined
d. Undefined

121. _____ or life assurance is a contract between the policy owner and the insurer, where the insurer agrees to pay a sum of money upon the occurrence of the policy owner's death.
a. Thing
b. Life insurance0
c. Undefined
d. Undefined

122. _____, in law and economics, is a form of risk management primarily used to hedge against the risk of a contingent loss.
a. Insurance0
b. Thing
c. Undefined
d. Undefined

123. _____ is the mathematical action of repeatedly adding or subtracting one, usually to find out how many objects there are or to set aside a desired number of objects.

a. Thing
c. Undefined
b. Counting0
d. Undefined

124. In combinatorial mathematics, a _____ is an un-ordered collection of unique elements.
   a. Concept
   b. Combination0
   c. Undefined
   d. Undefined

125. _____ is the rearrangement of objects or symbols into distinguishable sequences.
   a. Thing
   b. Permutation0
   c. Undefined
   d. Undefined

126. The _____ is a method that is used to calculate all of the possibilities of a pertaining number of events.
   a. Fundamental Counting Principle0
   b. Thing
   c. Undefined
   d. Undefined

127. In probability theory, _____ are various sets of outcomes (a subset of the sample space) to which a probability is assigned.
   a. Events0
   b. Thing
   c. Undefined
   d. Undefined

128. In mathematics, the conjugate _____ or adjoint matrix of an m-by-n matrix A with complex entries is the n-by-m matrix A* obtained from A by taking the transpose and then taking the complex conjugate of each entry.
   a. Pairs0
   b. Thing
   c. Undefined
   d. Undefined

129. An _____ or member of a set is an object that when collected together make up the set.
   a. Element0
   b. Thing
   c. Undefined
   d. Undefined

130. In mathematics, the _____ , or members of a set or more generally a class are all those objects which when collected together make up the set or class.
   a. Thing
   b. Elements0
   c. Undefined
   d. Undefined

131. In mathematical logic, a Gödel numbering (or Gödel _____) is a function that assigns to each symbol and well-formed formula of some formal language a unique natural number called its Gödel number.
   a. Code0
   b. Thing
   c. Undefined
   d. Undefined

132. Order theory is a branch of mathematics that studies various kinds of binary relations that capture the intuitive notion of a mathematical _____.
   a. Ordering0
   b. Thing
   c. Undefined
   d. Undefined

133. _____ the expected value of a random variable displays the average or central value of the variable. It is a summary value of the distribution of the variable.

Chapter 9. Sequences, Series, and Probability

a. Thing
c. Undefined
b. Determining0
d. Undefined

134. In mathematics, a _____ is an n-tuple with n being 3.
a. Thing
c. Undefined
b. Triple0
d. Undefined

135. A _____ is a set whose members are members of another set or a set contained within another set.
a. Thing
c. Undefined
b. Subset0
d. Undefined

136. _____ are groups whose members are members of another set or a set contained within another set.
a. Thing
c. Undefined
b. Subsets0
d. Undefined

137. In mathematics, an inequality is a statement about the relative size or order of two objects. For example 14 > 10, or 14 is _____ 10.
a. Thing
c. Undefined
b. Greater than0
d. Undefined

138. In mathematics, a subset of Euclidean space R^n is called _____ if it is closed and bounded.
a. Thing
c. Undefined
b. Compact0
d. Undefined

139. In mathematics, a _____ of an integer n, also called a factor of n, is an integer which evenly divides n without leaving a remainder.
a. Thing
c. Undefined
b. Divisor0
d. Undefined

140. Acid _____ ratio measures the ability of a company to use its near cash or quick assets to immediately extinguish its current liabilities.
a. Test0
c. Undefined
b. Thing
d. Undefined

141. The _____ is a popular form of gambling which involves the drawing of lots for a prize. Some governments forbid it, while others endorse it to the extent of organizign a national _____
a. Lottery0
c. Undefined
b. Thing
d. Undefined

142. _____ is the property of a physical object that quantifies the amount of matter and energy it is equivalent to.
a. Mass0
c. Undefined
b. Thing
d. Undefined

143. _____ usually refers to money in the form of liquid currency, such as banknotes or coins.

Chapter 9. Sequences, Series, and Probability

    a. Thing
    b. Cash0
    c. Undefined
    d. Undefined

144. In mathematics, a _____ is a countable collection of open covers of a topological space that satisfies certain separation axioms.
    a. Thing
    b. Development0
    c. Undefined
    d. Undefined

145. In geometry a _____ is a plane figure that is bounded by a closed path or circuit, composed of a finite number of sequential line segments.
    a. Polygon0
    b. Thing
    c. Undefined
    d. Undefined

146. A _____ can refer to a line joining two nonadjacent vertices of a polygon or polyhedron, or in some contexts any upward or downward sloping line. .
    a. Thing
    b. Diagonal0
    c. Undefined
    d. Undefined

147. In geometry, a _____ is any polygon with ten sides and ten angles, and usually refers to a regular _____, having all sides of equal length and all angles equal to 144¡ã, therefore making each angle of a regular _____ be 144¡ã.
    a. Decagon0
    b. Thing
    c. Undefined
    d. Undefined

148. A _____ is a polygon with six edges and six vertices.
    a. Hexagon0
    b. Thing
    c. Undefined
    d. Undefined

149. An _____ is an equality that remains true regardless of the values of any variables that appear within it, to distinguish it from an equality which is true under more particular conditions.
    a. Thing
    b. Identity0
    c. Undefined
    d. Undefined

150. In mathematics, an _____ is any of the arguments, i.e. "inputs", to a function. Thus if we have a function f(x), then x is a _____.
    a. Independent variable0
    b. Thing
    c. Undefined
    d. Undefined

151. _____ is a set, with some particular properties and usually some additional structure, such as the operations of addition or multiplication, for instance.
    a. Space0
    b. Thing
    c. Undefined
    d. Undefined

152. _____ is a subset of a population.
    a. Sample0
    b. Thing
    c. Undefined
    d. Undefined

Chapter 9. Sequences, Series, and Probability

153. In probability theory, the _____ or universal _____, often denoted S, Ù or U (for "universe"), of an experiment or random trial is the set of all possible outcomes.
   a. Sample space0
   b. Thing
   c. Undefined
   d. Undefined

154. If the probabilities of simple events are all the same, then they are _____. This occurs in a uniform sample space.
   a. Thing
   b. Equally likely0
   c. Undefined
   d. Undefined

155. _____ is a way of expressing a number as a fraction of 100 per cent meaning "per hundred".
   a. Thing
   b. Percent0
   c. Undefined
   d. Undefined

156. In logic, two _____ (or "mutual exclusive" according to some sources) propositions are propositions that logically cannot both be true.
   a. Concept
   b. Mutually exclusive0
   c. Undefined
   d. Undefined

157. _____ is an adjective usually refering to being in the centre.
   a. Central0
   b. Thing
   c. Undefined
   d. Undefined

158. _____ is a mathematical science pertaining to the collection, analysis, interpretation or explanation, and presentation of data. It is applicable to a wide variety of academic disciplines, from the physical and social sciences to the humanities.
   a. Statistics0
   b. Thing
   c. Undefined
   d. Undefined

159. In mathematics and more specifically set theory, the _____ set is the unique set which contains no elements.
   a. Thing
   b. Empty0
   c. Undefined
   d. Undefined

160. _____ is the study of terms and their use — of words and compound words that are used in specific contexts.
   a. Terminology0
   b. Thing
   c. Undefined
   d. Undefined

161. In mathematics, the _____ of two sets A and B is the set that contains all elements of A that also belong to B (or equivalently, all elements of B that also belong to A), but no other elements.
   a. Thing
   b. Intersection0
   c. Undefined
   d. Undefined

162. In set theory and other branches of mathematics, the _____ of a collection of sets is the set that contains everything that belongs to any of the sets, but nothing else.

Chapter 9. Sequences, Series, and Probability

a. Union0
b. Thing
c. Undefined
d. Undefined

163. In set theory and other branches of mathematics, two kinds of complements are defined, the relative _____ and the absolute _____.
   a. Thing
   b. Complement0
   c. Undefined
   d. Undefined

164. In mathematics, an _____, mean, or central tendency of a data set refers to a measure of the "middle" or "expected" value of the data set.
   a. Concept
   b. Average0
   c. Undefined
   d. Undefined

165. _____ is the act of transforming data with the aim of extracting useful information and facilitating conclusions.
   a. Data analysis0
   b. Concept
   c. Undefined
   d. Undefined

166. Transport or _____ is the movement of people and goods from one place to another.
   a. Transportation0
   b. Thing
   c. Undefined
   d. Undefined

167. _____ is the application of tools and a processing medium to the transformation of raw materials into finished goods for sale.
   a. Thing
   b. Manufacturing0
   c. Undefined
   d. Undefined

168. According to the United Nations Statistics Division, _____ is the resale sale without transformation of new and used goods to retailers, to industrial, commercial, institutional or professional users, or to other wholesalers, or involves acting as an agent or broker in buying merchandise for, or selling merchandise, to such persons or companies.
   a. Wholesale0
   b. Thing
   c. Undefined
   d. Undefined

169. _____ studies and addresses the ways in which individuals, businesses, and organizations raise, allocate, and use monetary resources over time, taking into account the risks entailed in their projects
   a. Finance0
   b. Thing
   c. Undefined
   d. Undefined

170. Compass and straightedge or ruler-and-compass _____ is the _____ of lengths or angles using only an idealized ruler and compass.
   a. Construction0
   b. Thing
   c. Undefined
   d. Undefined

171. In a company, _____ is the sum of all financial records of salaries, wages, bonuses, and deductions.
   a. Payroll0
   b. Thing
   c. Undefined
   d. Undefined

Chapter 9. Sequences, Series, and Probability

172. A _____ fraction is a fraction in which the absolute value of the numerator is less than the denominator--hence, the absolute value of the fraction is less than 1.
- a. Thing
- b. Proper0
- c. Undefined
- d. Undefined

173. A _____ is a computational or physical device designed to generate a sequence of numbers or symbols that lack any pattern, i.e. appear random. Computer-based systems for random number generation are widely used, but often fall short of this goal, though they may meet some statistical tests for randomness intended to ensure that they do not have any easily discernible patterns.
- a. Random number generator0
- b. Thing
- c. Undefined
- d. Undefined

174. In economics, supply and _____ describe market relations between prospective sellers and buyers of a good.
- a. Thing
- b. Demand0
- c. Undefined
- d. Undefined

175. In physics, a _____ may refer to the scalar _____ or to the vector _____.
- a. Potential0
- b. Thing
- c. Undefined
- d. Undefined

176. _____ is often represented as the sum of a sequence of terms.
- a. Thing
- b. Infinite series0
- c. Undefined
- d. Undefined

177. A _____ of a number is the product of that number with any integer.
- a. Thing
- b. Multiple0
- c. Undefined
- d. Undefined

178. _____ are a measure of time.
- a. Thing
- b. Minutes0
- c. Undefined
- d. Undefined

179. A _____ is a unit of length, usually used to measure distance, in a number of different systems, including Imperial units, United States customary units and Norwegian/Swedish mil. Its size can vary from system to system, but in each is between 1 and 10 kilometers. In contemporary English contexts _____ refers to either:
- a. Mile0
- b. Thing
- c. Undefined
- d. Undefined

180. _____, in economics and political economy, are the distributions or payments awarded to the various suppliers of the factors of production.
- a. Returns0
- b. Thing
- c. Undefined
- d. Undefined

181. The _____ of a solid object is the three-dimensional concept of how much space it occupies, often quantified numerically.

180 **Chapter 9. Sequences, Series, and Probability**

a. Volume0
b. Thing
c. Undefined
d. Undefined

182. A _____ is a deliberate process for transforming one or more inputs into one or more results.
a. Calculation0
b. Thing
c. Undefined
d. Undefined

183. A _____ is a set of possible values that a variable can take on in order to satisfy a given set of conditions, which may include equations and inequalities.
a. Thing
b. Solution set0
c. Undefined
d. Undefined

184. In mathematics, a _____ is a condition that a solution to an optimization problem must satisfy in order to be acceptable.
a. Constraint0
b. Thing
c. Undefined
d. Undefined

185. In mathematics, the _____ is a conic section generated by the intersection of a right circular conical surface and a plane parallel to a generating straight line of that surface. It can also be defined as locus of points in a plane which are equidistant from a given point.
a. Thing
b. Parabola0
c. Undefined
d. Undefined

186. In linear algebra, the _____ of a matrix is obtained by combining two matrices in such a way that a matrix of coefficients to which has been added a column of constants corresponds to the right hand side of the equations.
a. Thing
b. Augmented matrix0
c. Undefined
d. Undefined

187. In mathematics, and in particular in abstract algebra, the _____ is a property of binary operations that generalises the distributive law from elementary algebra.
a. Thing
b. Distributive property0
c. Undefined
d. Undefined

188. _____ is the state of being greater than any finite number, however large.
a. Infinity0
b. Thing
c. Undefined
d. Undefined

189. In Euclidean geometry, a uniform _____ is a linear transformation that enlargers or diminishes objects, and whose _____ factor is the same in all directions. This is also called homothethy.
a. Scale0
b. Thing
c. Undefined
d. Undefined

190. In colloquial usage, a _____ is "a rough or fragmented geometric shape that can be subdivided in parts, each of which is, at least approximately, a reduced-size copy of the whole."

Chapter 9. Sequences, Series, and Probability

a. Fractal0
b. Concept
c. Undefined
d. Undefined

191. _____ was a Polish mathematician.
a. Sierpinski0
b. Thing
c. Undefined
d. Undefined

192. The _____ is a fractal named after Wacław Sierpiński who described it in 1915. Originally constructed as a curve, this is one of the basic examples of self-similar sets, i.e. it is a mathematically generated pattern that can be reproducible at any magnification or reduction.
a. Sierpinski Triangle0
b. Thing
c. Undefined
d. Undefined

193. In probability theory and statistics the _____ in favour of an event or a proposition are the quantity p / 1 − p , where p is the probability of the event or proposition. In other words, an event with m to n _____ would have probability m/ m + n.
a. Odds0
b. Thing
c. Undefined
d. Undefined

194. In mathematics, the multiplicative inverse of a number x, denoted 1/x or x^{-1}, is the number which, when multiplied by x, yields 1. The multiplicative inverse of x is also called the _____ of x.
a. Thing
b. Reciprocal0
c. Undefined
d. Undefined

195. In mathematics, a _____ may be described informally as a number that can be given by an infinite decimal representation.
a. Thing
b. Real number0
c. Undefined
d. Undefined

196. In mathematics, defined and _____ are used to explain whether or not expressions have meaningful, sensible, and unambiguous values.
a. Thing
b. Undefined0
c. Undefined
d. Undefined

197. In mathematics, _____ is an elementary arithmetic operation. When one of the numbers is a whole number, _____ is the repeated sum of the other number.
a. Thing
b. Multiplication0
c. Undefined
d. Undefined

198. In mathematics, the _____ inverse of a number x, denoted 1/x or x^{-1}, is the number which, when multiplied by x, yields 1. The _____ inverse of x is also called the reciprocal of x.
a. Multiplicative0
b. Thing
c. Undefined
d. Undefined

199. The _____ is a property of multiplication or addition where the product or sum remains the same, regardless of whether or not the order of the addends or factors are changed.

182 **Chapter 9. Sequences, Series, and Probability**

    a. Thing
    b. Commutative property0
    c. Undefined
    d. Undefined

200. _____ is a natural number that has exactly two distinct natural number divisors, which are 1 and the _____ itself.
    a. Prime number0
    b. Thing
    c. Undefined
    d. Undefined

201. In mathematics, there are several meanings of _____ depending on the subject.
    a. Thing
    b. Degree0
    c. Undefined
    d. Undefined

202. The _____ integers are all the integers from zero on upwards.
    a. Thing
    b. Nonnegative0
    c. Undefined
    d. Undefined

203. Equivalence is the condition of being _____ or essentially equal.
    a. Equivalent0
    b. Thing
    c. Undefined
    d. Undefined

204. A _____ is a numeral used to indicate a count. The most common use of the word today is to name the part of a fraction that tells the number or count of equal parts.
    a. Thing
    b. Numerator0
    c. Undefined
    d. Undefined

205. A _____ is the part of a fraction that tells how many equal parts make up a whole, and which is used in the name of the fraction: "halves", "thirds", "fourths" or "quarters", "fifths" and so on.
    a. Denominator0
    b. Concept
    c. Undefined
    d. Undefined

206. The plus and _____ signs are mathematical symbols used to represent the notions of positive and negative as well as the operations of addition and subtraction.
    a. Thing
    b. Minus0
    c. Undefined
    d. Undefined

207. _____ is the largest positive integer that divides both numbers without remainder.
    a. Common Factor0
    b. Thing
    c. Undefined
    d. Undefined

208. In abstract algebra, _____ consists of sets with binary operations that satisfy certain axioms.
    a. Thing
    b. Grouping0
    c. Undefined
    d. Undefined

209. _____ are objects, characters, or other concrete representations of ideas, concepts, or other abstractions.

Chapter 9. Sequences, Series, and Probability

    a. Thing
    b. Symbols0
    c. Undefined
    d. Undefined

210. In mathematics, _____ is the decomposition of an object into a product of other objects, or factors, which when multiplied together give the original.
    a. Thing
    b. Factoring0
    c. Undefined
    d. Undefined

211. A _____ consists of one quarter of the coordinate plane.
    a. Quadrant0
    b. Thing
    c. Undefined
    d. Undefined

212. In mathematics, the _____ of a coordinate system is the point where the axes of the system intersect.
    a. Thing
    b. Origin0
    c. Undefined
    d. Undefined

213. A _____ is a four-sided plane figure that has two sets of opposite parallel sides.
    a. Parallelogram0
    b. Concept
    c. Undefined
    d. Undefined

214. _____ is the symbold used to indicate the nth root of a number
    a. Thing
    b. Radical0
    c. Undefined
    d. Undefined

215. In mathematics, _____ are used to indicate the square root of a number.
    a. Thing
    b. Radicals0
    c. Undefined
    d. Undefined

216. The _____ is the number or expression underneath the radical sign.
    a. Thing
    b. Radicand0
    c. Undefined
    d. Undefined

217. In mathematics, _____ is a property that a binary operation can have. Within an expression containing two or more of the same associative operators in a row, the order of operations does not matter as long as the sequence of the operands is not changed.
    a. Associativity0
    b. Thing
    c. Undefined
    d. Undefined

218. In mathematics, the _____ inverse, or opposite, of a number n is the number that, when added to n, yields zero. The _____ inverse of n is denoted −n.
    a. Thing
    b. Additive0
    c. Undefined
    d. Undefined

219. In mathematics the _____ of a set which is equipped with the operation of addition is an element which, when added to any other element x in the set, yields x.

184 Chapter 9. Sequences, Series, and Probability

a. Additive identity0
b. Concept
c. Undefined
d. Undefined

220. The deductive-nomological model is a formalized view of scientific _____ in natural language.
a. Thing
b. Explanation0
c. Undefined
d. Undefined

221. _____, either of the curved-bracket punctuation marks that together make a set of _____
a. Thing
b. Parentheses0
c. Undefined
d. Undefined

222. _____ forms part of thinking. Considered the most complex of all intellectual functions, _____ has been defined as higher-order cognitive process that requires the modulation and control of more routine or fundamental skills.
a. Problem solving0
b. Thing
c. Undefined
d. Undefined

223. The _____ or kilogramme is the SI base unit of mass. It is defined as being equal to the mass of the international prototype of the _____.
a. Kilogram0
b. Thing
c. Undefined
d. Undefined

224. In classical geometry, a _____ of a circle or sphere is any line segment from its center to its boundary. By extension, the _____ of a circle or sphere is the length of any such segment. The _____ is half the diameter. In science and engineering the term _____ of curvature is commonly used as a synonym for _____.
a. Thing
b. Radius0
c. Undefined
d. Undefined

225. In mathematics, the concept of a _____ tries to capture the intuitive idea of a geometrical one-dimensional and continuous object. A simple example is the circle.
a. Thing
b. Curve0
c. Undefined
d. Undefined

226. The material _____, also known as the material implication or truth functional _____, expresses a property of certain conditionals in logic.
a. Thing
b. Conditional0
c. Undefined
d. Undefined

227. In elementary algebra, an _____ is a set that contains every real number between two indicated numbers and may contain the two numbers themselves.
a. Thing
b. Interval0
c. Undefined
d. Undefined

228. The metre (or _____, see spelling differences) is a measure of length. It is the basic unit of length in the metric system and in the International System of Units (SI), used around the world for general and scientific purposes.

Chapter 9. Sequences, Series, and Probability

185

a. Meter0
b. Concept
c. Undefined
d. Undefined

229. A _____ is a unit of length in the metric system, equal to one thousand metres, the current SI base unit of length
a. Kilometer0
b. Thing
c. Undefined
d. Undefined

230. _____ is a unit of speed, expressing the number of international miles covered per hour.
a. Miles per hour0
b. Thing
c. Undefined
d. Undefined

231. _____ is the transport of people on a trip/journey or the process or time involved in a person or object moving from one location to another.
a. Thing
b. Travel0
c. Undefined
d. Undefined

232. In mathematics, a _____ is a polynomial equation of the second degree. The general form is $ax^2 + bx + c = 0$.
a. Quadratic equation0
b. Thing
c. Undefined
d. Undefined

233. In mathematics, the _____ of a number n is the number that, when added to n, yields zero. The _____ of n is denoted −n. For example, 7 is −7, because 7 + (−7) = 0, and the _____ of −0.3 is 0.3, because −0.3 + 0.3 = 0.
a. Thing
b. Additive inverse0
c. Undefined
d. Undefined

234. In mathematics, a _____ is a number in the form of a + bi where a and b are real numbers, and i is the imaginary unit, with the property i 2 = −1. The real number a is called the real part of the _____, and the real number b is the imaginary part.
a. Thing
b. Complex number0
c. Undefined
d. Undefined

235. In mathematical analysis and related areas of mathematics, a set is called _____, if it is, in a certain sense, of finite size.
a. Thing
b. Bounded0
c. Undefined
d. Undefined

236. _____ variables are variables other than the independent variable that may bear any effect on the behavior of the subject being studied.
a. Thing
b. Extraneous0
c. Undefined
d. Undefined

237. A _____ is a type of debt. All material things can be lent but this article focuses exclusively on monetary loans. Like all debt instruments, a _____ entails the redistribution of financial assets over time, between the lender and the borrower.

a. Thing
b. Loan0
c. Undefined
d. Undefined

238. _____ is the estimation of a physical quantity such as distance, energy, temperature, or time.
a. Thing
b. Measurement0
c. Undefined
d. Undefined

239. _____, or EPS are the earnings returned on the initial investment amount.
a. Thing
b. Earnings per share0
c. Undefined
d. Undefined

240. A _____ is a compensation which workers receive in exchange for their labor.
a. Wage0
b. Thing
c. Undefined
d. Undefined

241. In geometry, two lines or planes if one falls on the other in such a way as to create congruent adjacent angles. The term may be used as a noun or adjective. Thus, referring to Figure 1, the line AB is the _____ to CD through the point B.
a. Thing
b. Perpendicular0
c. Undefined
d. Undefined

242. _____ is a relation in Euclidean geometry among the three sides of a right triangle.
a. Thing
b. Pythagorean Theorem0
c. Undefined
d. Undefined

243. _____ is a business term for the amount of money that a company receives from its activities in a given period, mostly from sales of products and/or services to customers
a. Revenue0
b. Thing
c. Undefined
d. Undefined

244. In mathematics, the _____ of a function is the set of all "output" values produced by that function. Given a function $f : A \to B$, the _____ of f, is defined to be the set $\{x \in B : x = f(a) \text{ for some } a \in A\}$.
a. Range0
b. Thing
c. Undefined
d. Undefined

245. The _____ is the lowest point in a certain portion of a graph.
a. Thing
b. Relative minimum0
c. Undefined
d. Undefined

246. The _____ is the highest point in a certain portion of a graph.
a. Relative maximum0
b. Thing
c. Undefined
d. Undefined

247. In mathematics, a _____ (also spelled reflexion) is a map that transforms an object into its mirror image.
a. Reflection0
b. Concept
c. Undefined
d. Undefined

Chapter 9. Sequences, Series, and Probability

248. _____ are the basic objects of study in graph theory. Informally speaking, a graph is a set of objects called points, nodes, or vertices connected by links called lines or edges.
   a. Thing
   b. Graphs0
   c. Undefined
   d. Undefined

249. _____ is a temperature scale named after the German physicist Daniel Gabriel _____ , who proposed it in 1724.
   a. Thing
   b. Fahrenheit0
   c. Undefined
   d. Undefined

250. In Euclidean geometry, a _____ is moving every point a constant distance in a specified direction.
   a. Concept
   b. Translation0
   c. Undefined
   d. Undefined

251. In geometry, a _____ is a special kind of point, usually a corner of a polygon, polyhedron, or higher dimensional polytope. In the geometry of curves a _____ is a point of where the first derivative of curvature is zero. In graph theory, a _____ is the fundamental unit out of which graphs are formed
   a. Thing
   b. Vertex0
   c. Undefined
   d. Undefined

252. The _____ of a member of a multiset is how many memberships in the multiset it has.
   a. Multiplicity0
   b. Thing
   c. Undefined
   d. Undefined

253. A _____ is the part of the dividend that is left over when the dividend is not evenly divisible by the divisor.
   a. Thing
   b. Remainder0
   c. Undefined
   d. Undefined

254. In mathematics, an _____ number is a complex number whose square is a negative real number. They were defined in 1572 by Rafael Bombelli.
   a. Imaginary0
   b. Thing
   c. Undefined
   d. Undefined

255. In mathematics, two quantities are called _____ if they vary in such a way that one of the quantities is a constant multiple of the other, or equivalently if they have a constant ratio.
   a. Proportional0
   b. Thing
   c. Undefined
   d. Undefined

256. In mathematics, a _____ is the set of all points in three-dimensional space (R^3) which are at distance r from a fixed point of that space, where r is a positive real number called the radius of the _____. The fixed point is called the center or centre, and is not part of the _____ itself.
   a. Sphere0
   b. Thing
   c. Undefined
   d. Undefined

257. _____ of an object is its speed in a particular direction.

Chapter 9. Sequences, Series, and Probability

  a. Thing
  b. Velocity0
  c. Undefined
  d. Undefined

258. _____ is a straight line or curve A to which another curve B the one being studied approaches closer and closer as one moves along it.
  a. Vertical asymptote0
  b. Thing
  c. Undefined
  d. Undefined

259. An _____ is a straight line around which a geometric figure can be rotated.
  a. Thing
  b. Axis0
  c. Undefined
  d. Undefined

260. In mathematics, in the field of group theory, a _____ of a group is a quasisimple subnormal subgroup.
  a. Concept
  b. Component0
  c. Undefined
  d. Undefined

261. _____ refers to the reduction of the body of a formerly living organism into simpler forms of matter.
  a. Thing
  b. Decomposing0
  c. Undefined
  d. Undefined

262. In algebra, the _____ decomposition or _____ expansion is used to reduce the degree of either the numerator or the denominator of a rational function.
  a. Partial fraction0
  b. Thing
  c. Undefined
  d. Undefined

263. In mathematics, a _____ is a type of conic section defined as the intersection between a right circular conical surface and a plane which cuts through both halves of the cone.
  a. Hyperbola0
  b. Thing
  c. Undefined
  d. Undefined

264. In geometry, _____ lines are two lines that share one or more common points.
  a. Thing
  b. Intersecting0
  c. Undefined
  d. Undefined

265. In Euclidean geometry, a _____ is the set of all points in a plane at a fixed distance, called the radius, from a given point, the center.
  a. Circle0
  b. Thing
  c. Undefined
  d. Undefined

266. In mathematics, an _____ .
  a. Ellipse0
  b. Thing
  c. Undefined
  d. Undefined

267. In geometry, the _____ are a pair of special points used in describing conic sections. The four types of conic sections are the circle, parabola, ellipse, and hyperbola.

Chapter 9. Sequences, Series, and Probability

a. Foci0
b. Thing
c. Undefined
d. Undefined

268. The _____ states that - a number and its additive inverse have a sum of zero (0).
   a. Concept
   b. Additive inverse property0
   c. Undefined
   d. Undefined

269. In mathematics, a _____ of a number x is a number r such that $r^2 = x$, or in words, a number r whose square (the result of multiplying the number by itself) is x.
   a. Thing
   b. Square root0
   c. Undefined
   d. Undefined

270. A _____ function is a function for which, intuitively, small changes in the input result in small changes in the output.
   a. Continuous0
   b. Event
   c. Undefined
   d. Undefined

271. The _____ relative to a specified or implied reference level.
   a. Decibel0
   b. Thing
   c. Undefined
   d. Undefined

272. _____ finance, in finance, a debt security, issued by Issuer
   a. Thing
   b. Bond0
   c. Undefined
   d. Undefined

273. In geometry, a line _____ is a part of a line that is bounded by two end points, and contains every point on the line between its end points.
   a. Segment0
   b. Concept
   c. Undefined
   d. Undefined

274. A _____ is a part of a line that is bounded by two end points, and contains every point on the line between its end points.
   a. Line segment0
   b. Thing
   c. Undefined
   d. Undefined

275. In geometry, a _____ is defined as a quadrilateral where all four of its angles are right angles.
   a. Rectangle0
   b. Thing
   c. Undefined
   d. Undefined

276. In mathematics and its applications, a _____ is a system for assigning an n-tuple of numbers or scalars to each point in an n-dimensional space.
   a. Concept
   b. Coordinate system0
   c. Undefined
   d. Undefined

277. A _____ is a one-dimensional picture in which the integers are shown as specially-marked points evenly spaced on a line.

a. Number line0   b. Thing
c. Undefined   d. Undefined

278. _____ is used in economics for several related quantities
    a. Producer surplus0   b. Thing
    c. Undefined   d. Undefined

279. A _____ is an individual or household that purchases and uses goods and services generated within the economy.
    a. Thing   b. Consumer0
    c. Undefined   d. Undefined

280. A _____ is a quadrilateral, which is defined as a shape with four sides, which has a pair of parallel sides.
    a. Trapezoid0   b. Thing
    c. Undefined   d. Undefined

281. An _____ triange is a triangle with at least two sides of equal length.
    a. Isosceles0   b. Thing
    c. Undefined   d. Undefined

282. An _____ (isosceles trapezium in British English) is a quadrilateral with a line of symmetry bisecting one pair of opposite sides, making it automatically a trapezoid. Also, an _____'s base angles are congruent.
    a. Concept   b. Isosceles trapezoid0
    c. Undefined   d. Undefined

283. _____ is an algorithm which can be used to determine the solutions of a system of linear equations, to find the rank of a matrix, and to calculate the inverse of an invertible square matrix.
    a. Thing   b. Gaussian elimination0
    c. Undefined   d. Undefined

284. _____ is a list of goods and materials, or those goods and materials themselves, held available in stock by a business
    a. Inventory0   b. Thing
    c. Undefined   d. Undefined

285. The _____, in practice often shortened to amp, is a unit of electric current, or amount of electric charge per second.
    a. Thing   b. Amperes0
    c. Undefined   d. Undefined

286. In linear algebra, a _____ or minor of a matrix A is the determinant of some smaller square matrix, cut down from A.
    a. Thing   b. Cofactor0
    c. Undefined   d. Undefined

Chapter 9. Sequences, Series, and Probability

287. In computer science an _____ is a data structure that consists of a group of elements having a single name that are accessed by indexing. In most programming languages each element has the same data type and the _____ occupies a continuous area of storage.
   a. Thing
   b. Array0
   c. Undefined
   d. Undefined

288. In linear algebra, the _____ refers to a matrix consisting of the coefficients of the variables in a set of linear equations.
   a. Thing
   b. Coefficient matrix0
   c. Undefined
   d. Undefined

289. Three or more points that lie on the same line are called _____.
   a. Thing
   b. Collinear0
   c. Undefined
   d. Undefined

290. In mathematics, particularly linear algebra, a _____ is a matrix with all its entries being zero.
   a. Thing
   b. Zero matrix0
   c. Undefined
   d. Undefined

291. A _____ is a number which is the cube of an integer.
   a. Perfect cube0
   b. Thing
   c. Undefined
   d. Undefined

Chapter 1

1. b	2. b	3. b	4. b	5. b	6. b	7. a	8. a	9. b	10. b
11. b	12. b	13. b	14. b	15. b	16. a	17. a	18. a	19. b	20. b
21. b	22. a	23. b	24. b	25. b	26. a	27. b	28. a	29. b	30. a
31. a	32. a	33. a	34. b	35. a	36. b	37. b	38. a	39. a	40. a
41. b	42. b	43. b	44. a	45. b	46. a	47. a	48. b	49. a	50. b
51. a	52. b	53. b	54. b	55. a	56. b	57. a	58. a	59. a	60. a
61. a	62. a	63. a	64. a	65. b	66. b	67. a	68. b	69. a	70. a
71. a	72. b	73. a	74. a	75. a	76. a	77. a	78. b	79. a	80. a
81. b	82. a	83. a	84. b	85. b	86. b	87. a	88. b	89. a	90. b
91. a	92. a	93. b	94. b	95. b	96. b	97. b	98. b	99. b	100. a
101. b	102. a	103. a	104. a	105. a	106. b	107. a	108. b	109. a	110. b
111. a	112. a	113. a	114. a	115. a	116. a	117. a	118. b	119. a	120. b
121. b	122. a	123. b	124. a	125. a	126. a	127. b	128. b	129. b	130. a
131. a	132. b	133. b	134. a	135. b	136. b	137. a	138. a	139. a	140. a
141. b	142. b	143. b	144. b	145. b	146. a	147. a	148. a	149. a	150. b
151. b	152. a	153. a	154. b	155. b	156. a	157. a	158. b	159. b	160. a
161. b	162. b	163. b	164. a	165. b	166. a	167. a	168. a	169. b	170. a
171. b	172. b	173. a	174. b	175. b	176. a	177. b	178. a	179. b	180. b
181. b	182. b	183. a	184. a	185. a	186. a	187. a	188. a	189. b	190. a
191. a	192. a	193. b	194. a	195. a	196. b	197. b	198. a	199. a	200. a
201. b	202. b	203. b	204. a	205. b	206. b	207. b	208. a	209. a	210. b
211. b	212. a	213. a	214. a	215. b	216. b	217. b	218. b		

ANSWER KEY

Chapter 2

1. b	2. b	3. b	4. a	5. b	6. b	7. b	8. b	9. a	10. a
11. a	12. a	13. a	14. b	15. b	16. a	17. a	18. b	19. b	20. a
21. b	22. b	23. a	24. b	25. a	26. b	27. b	28. a	29. b	30. b
31. a	32. a	33. a	34. a	35. a	36. a	37. a	38. b	39. b	40. a
41. a	42. b	43. b	44. b	45. a	46. b	47. a	48. b	49. a	50. b
51. a	52. b	53. a	54. a	55. a	56. a	57. b	58. b	59. b	60. a
61. b	62. a	63. b	64. b	65. b	66. b	67. b	68. b	69. a	70. b
71. b	72. b	73. b	74. b	75. a	76. a	77. a	78. a	79. a	80. b
81. a	82. b	83. b	84. a	85. a	86. b	87. b	88. a	89. a	90. b
91. b	92. a	93. a	94. a	95. a	96. b	97. a	98. b	99. b	100. b
101. b	102. a	103. b	104. a	105. b	106. b	107. a	108. a	109. a	110. a
111. a	112. b	113. b	114. a	115. b	116. a	117. b	118. b	119. b	120. b
121. a	122. a	123. a	124. b	125. a	126. b	127. b	128. b	129. b	130. b
131. b	132. b	133. b	134. a	135. b	136. b	137. a	138. b	139. a	140. a
141. b	142. a	143. b	144. b	145. a	146. b	147. b	148. b	149. a	150. a
151. a	152. b	153. a	154. a	155. a	156. b	157. b	158. a	159. a	160. b
161. b	162. b	163. b	164. a	165. b	166. a	167. a	168. a	169. b	170. b
171. b	172. a	173. b	174. a	175. b	176. b	177. a	178. a	179. b	180. a
181. a	182. b	183. b	184. a	185. b	186. b	187. a	188. a	189. a	190. a
191. a	192. b	193. a	194. a	195. b	196. b	197. a	198. b	199. b	200. b
201. a	202. a	203. b	204. b	205. a	206. b	207. a	208. b	209. a	210. a
211. a	212. b	213. b	214. a	215. b	216. b	217. b	218. b	219. b	220. b
221. b	222. a	223. a	224. b	225. b	226. a	227. a			

Chapter 3

1. a	2. a	3. b	4. a	5. b	6. b	7. b	8. b	9. a	10. a
11. a	12. a	13. a	14. b	15. b	16. b	17. a	18. b	19. b	20. a
21. b	22. b	23. b	24. a	25. a	26. b	27. a	28. a	29. a	30. b
31. a	32. a	33. a	34. b	35. a	36. a	37. b	38. b	39. b	40. a
41. a	42. b	43. a	44. a	45. b	46. b	47. b	48. a	49. b	50. b
51. b	52. a	53. b	54. a	55. a	56. b	57. b	58. b	59. b	60. b
61. b	62. a	63. b	64. b	65. a	66. b	67. a	68. a	69. a	70. b
71. b	72. a	73. b	74. b	75. b	76. b	77. a	78. a	79. b	80. a
81. b	82. b	83. a	84. b	85. a	86. b	87. b	88. a	89. b	90. a
91. a	92. a	93. a	94. a	95. b	96. b	97. a	98. a	99. b	100. a
101. b	102. b	103. b	104. a	105. b	106. a	107. a	108. a	109. b	110. b
111. a	112. a	113. a	114. a	115. a	116. a	117. b	118. a	119. b	120. a
121. a	122. a	123. b	124. a	125. a	126. a	127. b	128. b	129. b	130. b
131. a	132. b	133. b	134. a	135. a	136. b	137. b	138. b	139. a	140. b
141. a	142. a	143. b	144. b	145. a	146. b	147. a	148. a	149. b	150. a
151. a	152. b	153. b	154. b	155. a	156. b	157. b	158. b	159. b	160. a
161. b	162. a	163. b	164. a	165. a	166. a	167. b	168. b	169. b	170. a
171. a	172. b	173. b	174. b	175. a	176. b	177. b	178. a	179. a	180. b
181. a	182. a	183. a	184. a	185. a	186. a	187. b	188. b	189. b	190. a
191. b	192. a	193. b	194. b	195. a	196. a	197. b	198. a	199. b	

Chapter 4

1. b	2. a	3. b	4. b	5. b	6. b	7. b	8. b	9. b	10. b
11. b	12. b	13. a	14. a	15. a	16. b	17. a	18. a	19. a	20. b
21. a	22. b	23. a	24. b	25. b	26. a	27. a	28. a	29. a	30. b
31. b	32. a	33. a	34. a	35. b	36. a	37. a	38. a	39. a	40. a
41. a	42. b	43. a	44. a	45. a	46. a	47. b	48. b	49. b	50. b
51. b	52. a	53. b	54. a	55. a	56. b	57. a	58. a	59. b	60. b
61. a	62. b	63. b	64. a	65. a	66. a	67. a	68. b	69. a	70. b
71. a	72. a	73. a	74. b	75. a	76. a	77. a	78. b	79. b	80. b
81. b	82. b	83. a	84. b	85. a	86. a	87. a	88. b	89. a	90. b
91. a	92. a	93. a	94. a	95. b	96. b	97. a	98. b	99. a	100. b
101. b	102. a	103. b	104. b	105. a	106. a	107. b	108. a	109. a	110. a
111. b	112. a	113. b	114. a	115. b	116. b	117. a	118. a	119. b	120. b
121. b	122. a	123. a	124. a	125. b	126. a	127. b	128. b	129. a	130. a
131. b	132. a	133. a	134. b	135. a	136. a	137. a	138. b	139. b	140. b
141. b	142. b	143. b	144. a	145. a	146. b	147. a	148. b	149. b	150. b
151. b	152. a	153. b	154. b	155. b	156. a	157. b	158. b	159. b	160. b
161. b	162. b	163. b	164. b	165. a	166. a	167. b	168. b	169. b	170. a
171. a	172. a	173. b	174. b	175. b	176. a	177. b	178. a	179. a	180. b
181. a	182. b	183. b	184. b	185. a	186. a	187. b	188. b	189. a	190. a
191. b	192. a	193. b	194. b						

ANSWER KEY

Chapter 5

1. b	2. a	3. a	4. a	5. b	6. a	7. a	8. b	9. a	10. b
11. b	12. b	13. a	14. b	15. a	16. b	17. a	18. b	19. a	20. a
21. a	22. b	23. b	24. a	25. b	26. b	27. a	28. b	29. a	30. a
31. a	32. b	33. a	34. a	35. b	36. a	37. b	38. a	39. b	40. b
41. a	42. b	43. b	44. a	45. a	46. b	47. a	48. a	49. b	50. a
51. b	52. b	53. b	54. a	55. a	56. b	57. a	58. b	59. a	60. a
61. a	62. b	63. b	64. a	65. b	66. b	67. a	68. b	69. a	70. b
71. a	72. a	73. a	74. b	75. a	76. b	77. b	78. b	79. b	80. a
81. b	82. b	83. a	84. b	85. b	86. b	87. b	88. b	89. b	90. b
91. b	92. b	93. b	94. a	95. b	96. a	97. b	98. b	99. a	100. a
101. b	102. a	103. b	104. b	105. b	106. a	107. b	108. a	109. b	110. b
111. a	112. b	113. b	114. a	115. a	116. a	117. b	118. b	119. a	120. a
121. b	122. b	123. b	124. b	125. b	126. a	127. a	128. b	129. a	130. a
131. b	132. a	133. b	134. b	135. b	136. b	137. b	138. b	139. b	140. a
141. b	142. b	143. b	144. b	145. a	146. b	147. b	148. a	149. a	150. b
151. a	152. a	153. b	154. b						

Chapter 6

1. a	2. b	3. b	4. b	5. b	6. a	7. a	8. a	9. a	10. a
11. b	12. b	13. a	14. a	15. b	16. a	17. a	18. a	19. a	20. a
21. b	22. b	23. a	24. a	25. b	26. a	27. a	28. b	29. a	30. b
31. a	32. a	33. a	34. b	35. b	36. a	37. a	38. b	39. a	40. a
41. b	42. a	43. b	44. b	45. b	46. a	47. a	48. a	49. b	50. a
51. b	52. a	53. a	54. a	55. b	56. a	57. b	58. a	59. a	60. a
61. b	62. b	63. a	64. a	65. a	66. a	67. b	68. a	69. b	70. a
71. b	72. a	73. a	74. a	75. b	76. a	77. a	78. b	79. a	80. a
81. a	82. a	83. a	84. b	85. a	86. b	87. a	88. a	89. b	90. b
91. b	92. b	93. a	94. b	95. a	96. a	97. a	98. a	99. b	100. a
101. a	102. a	103. a	104. a	105. a	106. a	107. a	108. b	109. b	110. a
111. b	112. a	113. b	114. a	115. a	116. b	117. a	118. a	119. a	120. a
121. b	122. a	123. b	124. b	125. a	126. b	127. b	128. b	129. b	130. a
131. a	132. a	133. b	134. a	135. b	136. b	137. b	138. b	139. b	140. a
141. a	142. a	143. b	144. a	145. b	146. a	147. b	148. a	149. b	150. a
151. b	152. b	153. a	154. a	155. a	156. b	157. b	158. b	159. b	160. b
161. b	162. a	163. b	164. a	165. b	166. a	167. b	168. b	169. b	170. b

Chapter 7

1. a	2. b	3. b	4. a	5. a	6. a	7. a	8. b	9. b	10. a
11. a	12. a	13. a	14. b	15. b	16. a	17. a	18. b	19. a	20. b
21. a	22. b	23. b	24. b	25. b	26. a	27. a	28. a	29. b	30. a
31. a	32. b	33. a	34. b	35. b	36. a	37. a	38. b	39. b	40. a
41. b	42. b	43. a	44. a	45. a	46. b	47. b	48. b	49. b	50. b
51. a	52. b	53. a	54. b	55. b	56. b	57. b	58. a	59. b	60. b
61. a	62. a	63. a	64. b	65. a	66. b	67. a	68. b	69. b	70. a
71. b	72. a	73. a	74. b	75. b	76. a	77. b	78. a	79. a	80. a
81. b	82. b	83. a	84. a	85. b	86. b	87. a	88. b	89. b	90. b
91. b	92. b	93. a	94. b	95. b	96. b	97. b	98. a	99. a	100. b
101. b	102. a	103. a	104. b	105. a	106. a	107. a	108. b	109. a	110. a
111. b	112. b	113. a	114. a	115. b	116. a	117. b	118. a	119. b	120. a
121. b	122. a	123. b	124. a	125. b	126. b	127. b	128. a	129. b	130. a
131. b	132. a	133. b	134. b	135. b	136. b	137. b	138. b	139. a	140. b
141. a	142. b	143. a	144. a	145. b	146. b	147. a	148. a	149. a	150. a
151. b	152. b	153. a	154. a	155. a	156. b	157. a	158. b	159. a	160. a
161. a	162. b	163. a	164. b	165. a	166. b	167. b	168. b	169. a	170. b

Chapter 8

1. b	2. b	3. a	4. a	5. b	6. b	7. a	8. a	9. b	10. b
11. b	12. b	13. a	14. b	15. a	16. b	17. b	18. b	19. a	20. a
21. b	22. a	23. b	24. a	25. a	26. b	27. b	28. a	29. b	30. b
31. b	32. b	33. b	34. b	35. b	36. a	37. b	38. a	39. b	40. a
41. a	42. a	43. a	44. a	45. a	46. b	47. a	48. a	49. a	50. a
51. a	52. b	53. b	54. a	55. b	56. a	57. a	58. b	59. b	60. a
61. a	62. b	63. a	64. b	65. b	66. a	67. a	68. b	69. b	70. a
71. a	72. b	73. a	74. b	75. b	76. a	77. b	78. a	79. a	80. a
81. b	82. b	83. a	84. a	85. b	86. a	87. a	88. a	89. a	90. a
91. b	92. a	93. a	94. b	95. a	96. a	97. a	98. b	99. a	100. b
101. a	102. a	103. b	104. b	105. b	106. b	107. a	108. b	109. b	110. b
111. b	112. a	113. b	114. a	115. a	116. b	117. a	118. a	119. a	120. a
121. a	122. b	123. b	124. b	125. b	126. b	127. a	128. b	129. a	130. a
131. b	132. a	133. b							

ANSWER KEY

Chapter 9

1. b	2. a	3. a	4. a	5. a	6. b	7. a	8. a	9. b	10. b
11. b	12. a	13. a	14. a	15. b	16. a	17. b	18. a	19. a	20. a
21. b	22. b	23. b	24. b	25. a	26. a	27. a	28. b	29. b	30. b
31. b	32. b	33. a	34. b	35. b	36. a	37. b	38. b	39. a	40. a
41. b	42. a	43. a	44. a	45. a	46. b	47. a	48. b	49. a	50. a
51. b	52. b	53. b	54. b	55. a	56. a	57. b	58. b	59. b	60. b
61. b	62. b	63. b	64. b	65. a	66. b	67. b	68. b	69. b	70. b
71. b	72. a	73. a	74. b	75. a	76. b	77. a	78. a	79. a	80. a
81. a	82. a	83. a	84. a	85. b	86. b	87. a	88. b	89. a	90. b
91. a	92. b	93. b	94. a	95. b	96. a	97. b	98. b	99. a	100. a
101. b	102. b	103. a	104. a	105. a	106. a	107. a	108. b	109. b	110. b
111. b	112. b	113. a	114. a	115. b	116. b	117. a	118. a	119. b	120. b
121. b	122. a	123. b	124. b	125. b	126. a	127. a	128. a	129. a	130. b
131. a	132. a	133. b	134. b	135. b	136. b	137. b	138. b	139. b	140. a
141. a	142. a	143. b	144. b	145. a	146. b	147. a	148. a	149. b	150. a
151. a	152. a	153. a	154. b	155. b	156. b	157. a	158. a	159. b	160. a
161. b	162. a	163. b	164. b	165. a	166. a	167. b	168. a	169. a	170. b
171. a	172. b	173. a	174. b	175. a	176. b	177. b	178. b	179. a	180. b
181. a	182. a	183. b	184. a	185. b	186. b	187. b	188. a	189. a	190. b
191. a	192. a	193. a	194. b	195. b	196. b	197. b	198. a	199. b	200. a
201. b	202. b	203. a	204. b	205. a	206. b	207. a	208. b	209. b	210. b
211. a	212. b	213. a	214. b	215. b	216. b	217. a	218. b	219. a	220. b
221. b	222. a	223. a	224. b	225. b	226. b	227. b	228. a	229. a	230. a
231. b	232. a	233. b	234. b	235. b	236. b	237. b	238. b	239. b	240. a
241. b	242. b	243. a	244. a	245. b	246. a	247. a	248. b	249. b	250. b
251. b	252. a	253. b	254. a	255. a	256. a	257. b	258. a	259. b	260. b
261. b	262. a	263. a	264. b	265. a	266. a	267. a	268. b	269. b	270. a
271. a	272. b	273. a	274. a	275. a	276. b	277. a	278. a	279. b	280. a
281. a	282. b	283. b	284. a	285. b	286. b	287. b	288. b	289. b	290. b
291. a